Also by John Money

Hermaphroditism: An Inquiry into the Nature of a Human Paradox, 1952

The Psychologic Study of Man, 1957

A Standardized Road-Map Test of Direction Sense (with D. Alexander and H. T. Walker, Jr.), 1965

Man and Woman, Boy and Girl: The Differentiation and Dimorphism of Gender Identity from Conception to Maturity (with A. A. Ehrhardt), 1972

Sexual Signatures (with Patricia Tucker), 1975

Love and Love Sickness: The Science of Sex, Gender Difference, and Pairbonding, 1980

The Destroying Angel: Sex, Fitness, and Food in the Legacy of Degeneracy Theory, Graham Crackers, Kellogg's Corn Flakes, and American Health History, 1985

Lovemaps: Clinical Concepts of Sexual/Erotic Health and Pathology, Paraphilia, and Gender Transposition in Childhood, Adolescence, and Maturity, 1986

Venuses Penuses: Sexology, Sexosophy, and Exigency Theory, 1986

Gas, Straight, and In-Between: The Sexology of Erotic Orientation, 1988

Vandalized Lovemaps: Paraphilic Outcome of Seven Cases in Pediatric Sexology (with M. Lamacz), 1989

Biographies of Gender and Hermaphroditism in Paired Comparisons: Clinical Supplement to the Handbook of Sexology, 1991

The Breathless Orgasm: A Lovemap Biography of Asphyxiophilia (with G. Wainwright and D. Hingsburger), 1991

The Kaspar Hauser Syndrome of "Psychosocial Dwarfism": Deficient Statural, Intellectual, and Social Growth Induced by Child Abuse, 1992

The Adam Principle: Genes, Genitals, Hormones, and Gender: Selected Readings in Sexology, 1993

The Armed Robbery Orgasm: A Lovemap Autobiography of Masochism (with R. Keyes), 1993

Sex Errors of the Body and Related Syndromes: A Guide to Counseling Children, Adolescents, and their Families, 1994

Edited by John Money

Reading Disability: Progress and Research Needs in Dyxlexia, 1962

Sex Research: New Developments, 1965

The Disabled Reader: Education of the Dyslexic Child, 1966

Transsexualism and Sex Reassignment (with R. Green), 1969

Contemporary Sexual Behavior: Critical Issues in the 1970s (with J. Zubin), 1973

Developmental Human Behavior Genetics (with W. K. Schaie, E. Anderson, and G. McClearn), 1975

Handbook of Sexology, volumes 1–5 (with H. Musaph), 1977

Traumatic Abuse and Neglect of Children at Home (with G. Williams), 1980

Handbook of Human Sexuality (with B. B. Wolman), 1980

Handbook of Sexology, volume 6 (with H. Musaph and J. M. A. Sitsen), 1988

Handbook of Sexology, volume 7 (with H. Musaph and M. Perry), 1990

Handbook of Sexology, volume 8 (with J. Krivacska), 1994

Reinterpreting the Unspeakable

HUMAN SEXUALITY 2000

The Complete Interviewer and
Clinical Biographer, Exigency
Theory, and Sexology for
the Third Millennium

JOHN MONEY

CONTINUUM · NEW YORK

1994
The Continuum Publishing Company
370 Lexington Avenue, New York, NY 10017

Copyright © 1994 by John Money

Printed in the United States of America

Library of Congress Cataloging-in-Publication Data

Money, John, 1921–
  Reinterpreting the unspeakable : human sexuality 2000: the complete interviewer and clini-
cal biographer, exigency theory, and sexology for the third millennium /
John Money.
    p.   cm.
  Includes bibliographical references and index.
  ISBN 0-8264-0651-3 (alk. paper)
  1. Sexual deviance. 2. Psychosexual disorders. 3. Sexual
disorders. 4. Psychology, Pathological. 5. Defense mechanisms
(Psychology) 6. Adjustment (Psychology) 7. Interview technique 8. Sex-
ology I. Title.
RC556.M665   1994
616.85'83—dc 20   93-45465
                                                                    CIP

Contents

Preface

Monster: Latin, monstrum, *any occurrence out of the ordinary course of nature supposed to indicate the will of the gods. From* monere, *to admonish or warn.*

In the early years of the sexual revolution, from the late 1950s onward, Cherry Grove on Fire Island was preponderantly a weekend and summer resort for the gay community of New York City. There were no streets, only boardwalks along which the cottages were identified by name. In the sandy front yard of a small guest house stood a large and weathered architectural ornament, a wooden dragon. Beside it, on a wooden stele, was inscribed a poem. Its title, "The Monster," had become the name by which the house was known. The poem, reflective and of a psychological bent, began with the words, "There is a monster in all our lives."

The monster and I did not have much commerce for well-nigh thirty years. Then it declared itself to be not only a monster, but also an unspeakable monster. In a research report on what happens to children born as hermaphrodites (Money and Norman, 1987, p. 91), I wrote of it as the unspeakable monster of sex, appeased only by sacrificing some victims of birth defects of the sex organs on the altar of stigmatization, which is part of the price of genital defect exacted by our taboo-ridden, antisexual culture. The unspeakable monster exists in the lives not only of hermaphrodites, but of many of the people, juveniles and teenagers as well as their parents and other adults, who have come into my office for consultation and counseling. Being literally unspeakable, an unspeakable monster is not spoken of. Never. It lurks behind a barricade of elective mutism. If remembered, its existence is censored. The premises of its syllogism are disconnected. They are brushed off as irrelevant and of no present consequence. Unspeakable monsters are detected by inference before their disguise is unmasked and they are directly confronted. Their very existence challenged me to formulate the principles of their detection and, in response to the urgings of many people, to write this book.

It is a book of instruction for the training or self-training of the complete interviewer. It is addressed to any interviewer irrespective of specialty focus, whether in the professions, the media, or an informal mutual counseling group. For the professional, it includes instructions on how to write up findings, and how to be a complete clinical biographer. It offers a special service to clinical sexology by illustrating general principles with examples from the still very young science of sexology. The principles themselves have very wide applicability. The theory to which they all belong is exigency theory, or the theory of five universal exigencies of being human, and its three taxa of coping strategies. Unspeakable monsters in individual lives have their locus in at least one of the five exigencies, and their camouflage in a pathological anomaly of at least one of the strategies of coping. Without exigency theory and its three taxa, an interviewer is not complete.

For many months, the working title of this book was "Unspeakable Monsters in All Our Lives." For publication the title was changed to *Reinterpreting the Unspeakable: Human Sexuality 2000* so as to be consistent with the fact that it formulates a paradigm shift for the theory and practice of sexology in the third millennium.

Acknowledgements

Sally A. Hopkins and William P. Wang worked industriously on the manuscript of this book.

The National Institute of Child Health and Human Development, Department of Health and Human Services, United States Public Health Service has supported the author in psychohormonal research for thirty-seven years, currently under Grant number HD00325-37.

It encourages me that my sister, Joyce Hopkins, and her husband, Humphrey, appreciate the principles and applications of this book, and to them it is dedicated.

· 1 ·

Camouflage and Coping

Danger and Camouflage

Inside the fortress of our skins we human beings have remarkable defenses against enemy intrusions, but we are not impregnable. Our immune system, for example, is defenseless against the intrusion of the AIDS virus, HIV. The nutritional system has no defense against total deprivation of various trace elements and vitamins. The brain has no defense against toxins like carbon monoxide, or amanitine, the poisonous mushroom alkaloid, or botulin, the anaerobic bacterial neurotoxin that poisons improperly canned foods. Our existence as a whole being has no defense against being lost in space on a broken-down satellite, or being shipped in a cattle car to interrogation, torture, and the gas chambers of a concentration camp.

Although compatible with survival, there are some dangers, experienced or threatened, that cripple our defenses against them. In the era before penicillin treatment, the spirochetes of syphilis eventually crippled the body's defenses against them in the deterioration of tertiary syphilis. Complete sensory and social isolation and lack of parental stroking and rubbing cripples a baby's defenses against cachexia and developmental retardation. Reprisals for telling about abusive neglect and cruelty in childhood, versus continued abuse for keeping silent, cripples one's defenses against eventually becoming an abusive adult oneself. After testifying to a history of parental incest, having one's father or mother imprisoned and oneself remanded to a sexually abusive foster family cripples one's defenses against long-term pathology of sexual and erotic functioning.

The dangerous agent, as is evident in the foregoing examples, has different guises, different modes of action, and different types of outcome. In each of its guises it has a specific name, but there is no generic, one-word name for dangerous experiences, stigmas, traumas, stresses, abuses, threats, and humiliations that cripple one's defenses. Hence the utility of the generic term, monster or better still monstrum, with its etymological meaning of that which warns or admonishes.

There are different traditions for classifying monsters. According to a long-standing medical tradition they are either innate and constitutional, or acquired. If acquired, the acquisition may be by infection, injury, radiation, toxicity, learning, psychogenesis, or other means. The polarity of organic versus psychogenic is a very popular one, but it does not allow for multivariate determinism, nor for sequential discontinuity versus continuity in the course of development. To illustrate, a person for whom homoerotic attraction constitutes not a variation like left-handedness but an unspeakable monster in his/her life may have been born with a prenatally, neurohormonally programed bipotential for either homoerotic or heteroerotic orientation, whereas the ultimate outcome was contingent on early postnatal socialization experience.

The earliest event in a chain of determinants is not necessarily the most powerful or effective one. Thus an unspeakable monster in a child's life may begin as an error in the genetic code which is expressed as an ugly deformity of the face, which in turn evokes the derision and cruelty of other children, without which there would be no unspeakable monster.

Whatever the multivariate, sequential chain of its derivation, the unspeakable monster at the end of the chain represents a danger or threat of danger, past, present, or anticipated in the future, sufficient to cripple the defenses of one's personal integrity as a whole. The penalty for not speaking about the danger or threat of danger is to be caged like a prisoner in a dark and silent isolation chamber. The penalty for speaking about it is to have the lock turned and the key thrown away by those whose response to what they hear is wrath, retribution, and derision. For the defendant, it's a no-win situation of being damned if you do, damned if you don't—total entrapment in a Catch-22. Therein lies the prodigious power of the unspeakable monster.

A Catch-22 is a dilemma that is subjectively experienced. It is, therefore, defined not as an external occurrence or pressure alone, but as that occurrence or pressure translated into subjective experience. Subjectively, a Catch-22 includes the residuals of past experience, the occurrence of present happenings, or the rehearsal in imagery and ideation of what may happen next.

In the society of Christendom, the sexual taboo is powerful and pervasive, and has many faces. It's no wonder, then, that unspeakable sexual monsters have assumed a preponderance of influence in the theory and practice of twentieth-century psychotherapy.

Failing to conform to a stereotype or standard has a lot to do with aggression and hostility, also a major theme in contemporary psychotherapy. Unspeakable monsters have more to do with failure to meet the required standards of aggression and assertiveness than with exceeding them—failure to be man enough, for example, breaking down under the stress of combat, or being the victim of abuse. But violence may be secretive.

Being brave or heroic when under attack has its counterpart in other situations—as in being courageous and silent in suffering, or in the face of death; and in not going to pieces but holding together as a victim of catastrophe or as a rescue worker.

Guilt of betrayal, guilt of survival and guilt of success all represent a reaction to some sort of elevation of self at the expense of another, which contravenes the stereotype of unselfishness and obedience, especially in childhood. Betrayal of kin and others includes committing crimes against them or murdering them, and then being haunted by the unspeakability of what one has done. Guilt of survival haunts the survivors of a killing catastrophe. Guilt of success haunts those who have achieved at the expense of others.

The younger the organism, the greater the dependency on someone else's support to buffer the foregoing types of Catch-22. When that support is missing, as is all too frequently the case in childhood, it allows the power, pervasiveness, and tenacity of the unspeakable monster's influence to become consolidated and long-lasting. It also provides no brakes to hinder internalization of responsibility for existence of the unspeakable monster, nor to hinder self-blame for what someone else may have done. Childhood vulnerability provides a fertile spawning ground for the proliferation of unspeakable monsters.

The natural history of an unspeakable monster includes the possibility that it will go into a state of dormancy and leave no continuing evidence of itself. The prevalence of this type of outcome can be ascertained only in prospective long-term follow-up studies which, like all outcome studies, are logistically and financially difficult and have not been done.

Another possible outcome is that the monster will become speakable. This may happen either of its own accord, or under the influence of exchange of confidentiality, or in psychotherapy. If the latter, then confirmation from unbiased informants or records is imperative so as to avoid the errors of faulty biographical recall, of not separating fantasy from history in the biography, and of therapeutic indoctrination—all of which are errors of the so-called false memory syndrome.

Another possible outcome, and the one most likely to come to professional attention, is that the unspeakable monster becomes metamorphosed. Disguised and camouflaged, it communicates in a rebus-like code that combines body language and word language. The manifestations of the metamorphosis are not a haphazard conglomerate. On the contrary, they depict the monster in terms of how it copes with the unspeakable happening that brought it into being in the first place.

In colloquial language, the unspeakable monster's coping measures have a threefold distribution: having crazy ideas, suffering ill health, and making trouble. For a very long period of human history extending to the present, coping measures in all three divisions have been attributed to possession by spirits. The spirits responsible for craziness might also be responsible for illness, and some for trouble-making. The latter became mostly the province of law and punishment, and the former of medicine and therapeutics.

Modern therapeutics had its early beginnings partly in the successes of shamans, medicine men, exorcists, and faith-healers in their treatment of people made ill by unspeakable monsters. Such illnesses have been their stock in trade for millennia, for they are illnesses that lend themselves to remission or reversibility in a way that lethal infections and other diseases do not.

Medical theory, like modern therapeutics, also had early origins in the treatment of unspeakable-monster illnesses. In early Chinese Taoist medical theory, the spirits or principles of the yin and yang bring on illness by being out of balance. In the theory of acupuncture, the spirits are replaced by meridians. Correcting them when out of alignment restores health. In the Tantric theory of Buddhism, spiritual balance and good health are restored by meditation and the exercises of yoga. In the traditional Ayurvedic medical theory of India, good health is maintained by conservation of the sukra, the vital spirit which in males is stored predominantly in the semen. For incurable illnesses, there is the Hindu theory of karma, one's spiritual destiny carried over from a past incarnation being cleansed by present suffering. The Hippocratic medicine of Greece began the move away from spiritual to empirical theory. Early Christian teaching brought Old Testament theory of Jehovah's wrath against sin together with Persian-derived Gnostic theory of evil spirits and produced a demon-possession theory of illness which flourished throughout the Middle Ages, and still has not been completely superseded. In nineteenth-century medicine, spirits and demons become replaced by mind or psyche, the specialty of today's medical psychology and psychiatry.

Referring again to the vernacular, psychology and psychiatry have, by and large, relegated the unspeakable monster's masquerade in stirring up trouble to criminology, and kept for themselves its masquerade in crazy ideas and in the suffering of ill health. In the syndromes of ill health, the symptoms may simulate those of another syndrome which is not as outlandish as at first it may appear.

No symptom of illness is the exclusive property of any one disease. Syphilis has long been known as the great pretender or imitator. In its manifold and individually varied symptomatology in the tertiary stage, syphilis is able to simulate other syndromes. One example is that of congenital syphilis, after a juvenile period of dormancy, simulating early adolescent schizophrenia in the absence of any signs of syphilis other than a positive

Wassermann test. Syphilis is like AIDS, and the unspeakable monster is like both of them in being a good mimic.

Post-Traumatic Masquerade of Symptoms

In the example that follows, there was an unspeakable monster that mimicked symptoms of other syndromes and defied diagnosis for eight years between the ages of twenty-two and thirty. This was the second unspeakable monster in the patient's life. The first was manifested as literal unspeakableness when, in late childhood, the patient became electively mute and totally unable to say anything about changing to live as a girl instead of a boy. This dilemma arose from having a history of birth defect of the sex organs, namely, female hermaphroditism, associated with the syndrome of congenital virilizing adrenal hyperplasia (CVAH). The declared sex and early rearing had been as a boy until, at around age nine, a pediatrician, having correctly ascertained the diagnosis, recommended sex reassignment. After an extensive workup during which elective mutism was surmounted by resorting to writing, sex reassignment was carried out, hormonally, surgically, and socially (Money, 1991a, Chapter 9). Despite ups and downs, general health and well being were satisfactory until age twenty-two. Then began an incapacitating series of illnesses of unascertainable etiology that proved resistant to treatment. The most disabling and recurrent symptoms included severe headache, possibly migraine in type; arthritic joint pain in the neck, arms, and hands; dizzy spells or syncope, once with a fall down stairs; right-sided numbness and paresthesia; leg cramps; blurred vision; fatigue and sleeplessness; palpitations, sweating, shakiness, and breathlessness; labile hypertension; swelling of the right face and neck; polydipsia and nocturia with urinary tract infection; nausea, vomiting, and burning sensation in the stomach; vaginal discharge; and right inguinal hernia, surgically repaired. At age twenty-five, the VDRL antigen test for syphilis was weakly positive, and a course of antibiotic treatment was successfully completed. Comprehensive diagnostic workups and specialty-clinic referrals on different occasions failed to reveal a specific etiology for the symptoms, except for those that were infection-derived, those that might have been sequelae of an automobile accident, and those that were surgically treatable—for example, hernia. The origin of other symptoms as being those of a post-traumatic shock syndrome would not be ascertained until the patient was thirty years old. Then, nearly nine years after the event, she was for the first time able to reveal the trauma of a brutal gang rape.

The traumatic incident began when the patient was lured from a neighborhood tavern by a woman who proved to be the accomplice of three sadistically assaultive men who brutally gang-raped her, vaginally and anally, at gunpoint. The post-traumatic stress (shock) disorder that ensued has proved to be permanently incapacitating, with only slight improvement with the passage of time. The event became subject to a return of elective mutism, and was totally unspeakable for nine years, at which time she disclosed it to her trusted psychohormonal counselor, a woman. It was not for another seven years, however, that she could speak about it fluently. Her account was as follows:

"I had my own apartment. I was living on Forest Hill in the 1600 block, and I was working. I had got me a job. I had just got off work. I didn't go straight home. I went to a club where most people that I knew hung out. At the time when me and my boyfriend were together, that's where he had taught me how to shoot pool and everything. That's why I used to go there. There was a lady—there were quite a few people in there—but there was a lady at the bar. She had started talking to me and asked me could she buy me a beer. I told her no because I didn't drink. She offered me a soda, so I sat there and I talked with her. I drank my soda. I had told her that I had to leave because I had some place else to go, and I was going home to change my clothes. I'm trying to get it all coming back to me. I was living at home with my mother, but it was only because me and my boyfriend broke up, and I had went back to my mother. I left the bar that I was in, and I went home and changed clothes, because she had asked me to meet her back at the bar where she was. I told her I would, and I went home, took my bath, and changed from my uniform and stuff and put on street clothes. I went back to the bar, and she was still sitting there. We talked for a few more minutes, and she asked me to go home with her while she changed her clothes."

"This was not somebody who was in with your friends, not anybody that you knew?"

"No, I had just seen her when I went into the bar that evening. We left the bar to go to her house. I don't know if we were on Clinton Avenue or if we were on Heather, because they're kind of close and the houses look the same just about. I don't know what block we were in. We were in the house not even a good half hour, I think, and she was taking a shower. I think she was because I heard the water running, and there was somebody at her door because they kept ringing the bell. I went to the bathroom door to tell her somebody was at the door. She asked me to open it, and I opened it. There was three guys at the door. She took so long in the bathroom, I was getting ready to leave. I hollered through the door, and told her I had to go because she was taking too long. When I tried to leave, they wouldn't let me."

"The men? (Pause: 17 seconds.) And then what happened?" (Pause: 35 seconds.)

"Excuse me." (Pause: 13 seconds.) "All the guys, they raped me, and they kind of beat me up real bad. I didn't fight very much because one of them had a gun."

"I remember you telling me before when you told me about this, that they had raped you vaginally and anally."

"Yes."

"Where was she when all this was going on?"

"She was there in the room."

"Watching?"

"Yes. I can't remember how I got home. I didn't go to my mother's. I wasn't at my mother's when I came to myself. I was at the apartment where I used to live with my boyfriend. I don't know how I got there. I guess I must have went there because it was closer, being in the 1600 block of Forest Hill Avenue. Somehow I had gotten into my ex-boyfriend's apartment. I don't know how long I stayed there."

"Was anybody there?"

"No. I still had the key, but he very seldom was there.

"I think I waited a couple of days. I don't quite remember. I know I went and had myself checked out by a doctor. I didn't go to a regular hospital. I went to the health clinic. I didn't tell them anything about what had happened. I just told them that I thought there might be something wrong with me, and that I wanted to be treated, for venereal disease or anything like that."

"And you didn't tell them you had been raped?"

"No."

"After you went to the clinic, you went back to your boyfriend's apartment?"

"Yes, I still had a few things there. I got everything that was mine together, and then I went to my mother's. I remember the clinic, the health clinic—I went there, and I can't remember if I was waiting for the doctor to see me or he had already seen me and I was in the waiting room or whatever, but I know I passed out for like fifteen seconds. I was just out."

"Was this the next day after the rape?"

"No, I think it was like a couple of days. I'm not sure. I can't really remember. After I left the clinic, I know I got the rest of my things from the apartment, and then I went to my mother's. That's where I've been ever since. I was getting myself together to explain to her why I was going through all the changes I was going through."

"Okay, what kind of changes were you going through?"

"I was afraid to even be in the house by myself without her being there. One time she was the only person that I would go out with, anywhere, for a very long time."

"Was there any time during this period when you couldn't go out, even with her?"

"It was a while before I—when I first went home, I spent all of my time in my bedroom."

"I remember you said you spent all your time in your room, but you had to know that somebody else was in the house with you."

"Yes. She had to work and everything, but my sisters were there, my brothers. As long as they were in the house, the changes that I was going through when she would be out of the house, she would make them stay home with me, even though she didn't know what was wrong with me. She would make somebody always be in the house. I don't even think I went nowhere. The first time I came out with my mother, I think, she had made me come over here."

"To the hospital?"

"Yes, she made me come here. After that first visit over here, and I had talked to you all about what was wrong with me, it got a little bit easier but not much. I wouldn't go any place with anyone but my mother. Now if she's unable to go, I will go with my father. He'll go places with me, if I have to go somewhere."

"But it always has to be somebody older, I mean a grown-up, an adult?"

"An adult, yes. Somebody that I feel like I trust. If I feel like I can't trust them, I won't go anywhere with them. It's only just those people, my mother and my father, and I have a niece—well, she's more like a sister to me. She's thirty years old now. If I have someplace to go, she'll go with me, if can't nobody else go."

In the aftermath of the gang rape, the patient's relapse into elective mutism for everything concerning it made it impossible for her to explain to her mother why she had returned to live at home, and why she was phobically housebound. After she had been at home for four months, she experienced the trauma of losing one of her brothers with whom she was quite close. Under circumstances that could not be explained, he was killed on the street by one of his companions. Seventeen months later there was another blow. Her favorite cousin, with whom she had shared the closest attachment since infancy, was killed as a consequence of an interracial love affair. His white girlfriend's brother fired a gun at his genitalia and killed him. The patient had foreseen this possibility, and had warned her cousin, but to no avail.

Following this tragedy, the mother observed that the patient became increasingly quiet and reclusive, and that she would act like a young child, playing with children and talking with them, but not with adults. For long periods she would sit and suck her finger. Her mother's patience and tolerance gave out when she discovered that the patient had not been menstruating for two years during which time she had been secretive about not having replenished her supply of medication (prednisone) and about having been too phobic to keep clinic appointments. A month after the cousin's death, the mother herself took time off from work and accompanied her daughter to the clinic. The patient would undergo another seven years of undiagnosable mental and physical disablements, however, before her first words regarding the gang rape would be uttered, and the unspeakable monster exposed. Only then would the multiplicity of symptoms begin to fall into place as all belonging to one syndrome, namely, that of post-traumatic stress (shock) disorder. Only then would she begin the tediously slow process of recovering which still has not been sufficient to allow her to lead a normal adult life socially and occupationally.

Diagnosis and the Unspeakable Monster

The diagnostic challenge of the unspeakable monster which, by definition, is not spoken about, is very well illustrated in the Kaspar Hauser syndrome of dwarfism, conventionally known also as psychosocial dwarfism (Money, 1992b). The most conspicuous symptom, and the one for which a child is usually referred for a diagnostic workup, is variously characterized descriptively as retarded growth, failure to thrive, or dwarfism.

The diagnostician familiar with the Kaspar Hauser syndrome knows that the findings from the initial laboratory tests will not differentiate this syndrome from the syndrome of dwarfism with irreversible pituitary impairment. It is the reversibility of the findings that establishes the difference between the two syndromes. The test to demonstrate reversibility and confirm the diagnosis of the Kaspar Hauser syndrome is the real-life test of a change of domicile. If in the new domicile catch-up growth commences, and the pituitary gland resumes secreting its growth hormone, then the likelihood of a history of traumatic abuse and neglect at home is very strong. The evidence of abuse and neglect must be substantiated painstakingly. It is impossible to ascertain by direct inquiry alone. Abuse and neglect constitute an unspeakable monster in the lives of the parents and of the child. Each one of the three colludes with the other two in keeping it unspoken.

Having discovered a history of child abuse and neglect when first presented with a case of dwarfism, the diagnostician cannot legitimately bypass a complete clinical and laboratory workup and simply assume a diagnosis of Kaspar Hauser syndrome. One must not discount the possibility of a false positive. In any case of dwarfism, regardless of etiology and diagnosis, a child may have a history of parental abuse and neglect.

Unspeakable-monster symptoms may coexist with those of another syndrome. Then the manifest complex of symptoms may be very difficult to sort out etiologically, just as they were in the CVAH case of the preceding section. The symptoms that actually belong to an unspeakable-monster syndrome may be misattributed. In the Kaspar Hauser syndrome, for example, intellectual retardation and low IQ, and retarded development of speech and of social maturation may be misdiagnosed. Together with statural retardation they are correctly diagnosed as symptoms of the over-all reversible retardation that constitutes the Kaspar Hauser syndrome.

Decoding the Monster

The unspeakable monster's manifest clues serve simultaneously to camouflage its existence and to cope with its unspeakability. In this latter respect they qualify as strategies for coping with the unspeakable. In the first section of this chapter, coping strategies were classified into three taxa under the colloquialisms of having crazy ideas, suffering ill health, and making trouble. The formal names for each of these three taxa are: programatics (mapping and programing), scissilics (deconnecting and dissociating), and praxics (doing and taking action).

Programatics (Greek *pro-*, before + *graphein* to write) pertains to the organism's processes of recognizing, storing, and discarding data, comparing them for constancy, and systematizing them into complex mindbrain maps or programs.

Scissilics (Latin, *scissilis* from *scissam*, past participle of *scindere*, to cut or split) pertains to the organism's processes of failing to register connections and associations, of separating them, or of closing them down.

Praxics (Greek, *praxis*, from *prassein*, to do) pertains to the organism's processes of commencing and maintaining performances, actions, and the doing of something.

Each one of these three taxons has its own set of strategies for camouflaging and coping with an unspeakable monster, and each strategy encompasses a subset of lesser strategies variable in their degree of idiosyncrasy.

A strategy is classified according to which taxon is in the ascendant, but ascendancy does not signify total exclusion from one or both of the other taxa. In the case of the Kaspar Hauser syndrome, for example, parental cruelty and abuse of the child is praxic, but the parents' fixed idea or delusion of its justification is programatic, and their failure to recognize a connection between acting abusively now, and having been formerly the recipient of unspeakable abuse oneself, is scissilic.

A strategy is not, in and of itself alone, either pathological or nonpathological. Both attributes are culturally ascribed and are transculturally variable. Shamanism, for instance, in a tribal culture may have the power and prestige of spiritual leadership and healing, whereas in a nontribal culture it may be derided as charlatanism or delusion. Cultural relativity is not without limits, however, so that a strategy is liable to be rated as pathological, transculturally, if it meets the criteria of being immutably fixated, intense, reiterative, and overinclusive.

Strategies for coping pertain to five universal exigencies of being human. These exigencies are named: pairbondance, troopbondance, abidance, ycleptance, and foredoomance. One's very existence is dependent on the degree to which one's strategies for encountering the five universal exigencies is sufficient, even though imperfect.

The theory of universal exigencies of being human is an alternative to theories of motivational determinism, and to theories of behavioristic determinism. In addition to being an alternative to these older theories, exigency theory is also an alternative to deterministic theories of any type. It is, first and foremost, a phenomenological theory with no a priori dogma of determinism. Instead, it is a theory that provides a classificatory system within which to locate determinants of any and all types as they are experimentally and observationally substantiated, and eventually, in the far future, to fit all of them together into a cohesive explanation of causality. In the application of exigency theory, there is no a priori recourse to motivation, feeling, or emotion as a cause of anything.

The full-length version of the five universal exigencies is in Chapter 2. There is also an abridged version that often suffices for rapid screening under conditions of clinical urgency, when a patient is in crisis and his/her strategies of coping are faltering. In the abridged version, sex and death are foremost (Chapter 7). If death, then suicide or homicide, actual or potential. If sex, then inanimate or animate in practice. If inanimate, then mineral or vegetable. If animate, then animal or human. If human, alone or partnered. If partnered, then male or female, adult or child (Chapter 7).

In an alternative abridged version, sex is paired not with death but with autonomy and financial independence—aphoristically, when coping strategies falter and crisis takes hold, sex and the checkbook are the two issues to be distinguished. The problems presented in marriage counseling and sex therapy are with great frequency, in the ultimate analysis, reducible to sex or the checkbook; and likewise the problems of divorce and child custody. Achieving autonomy and independence in earning and spending money is one of the two great challenges of adolescence. The other is love and establishing a sex life. When parents and their adolescent sons or daughters collide, these are the two uppermost issues, as they are also when adolescents meet on a collision course with community and societal organization.

· 2 ·

Five Universal Exigencies
of Being Human

Pairbondance

Pairbondance, from the verb "to pairbond," signifies the reciprocal attachment of two individuals, each to the other. The attachment is one of mutual interdependency. Positive pairbondance is reciprocally cooperative and consensual. Negative pairbondance (or pairbondage) is reciprocally adversarial and agonistical. Positive and negative pairbondance are not mutually exclusive but may be episodically coexistent in the same pairbondship. In the proverbial love-hate relationship, two people who live with one another also feud with one another.

In the human species, pairbondance is phyletically (i.e., phylogenetically) mandated for the survival of the newborn, and for the mating of the species. Among all mammals in the wild, if the mother and newborn do not become reciprocally pairbonded, the infant is not suckled and, deprived of nourishment, perishes.

The establishment of an animal mother's pairbond with her newborn baby has very recently been demonstrated, in experiments with sheep, rats, and voles (Pedersen et al., 1992), to be contingent on postpartum binding of the hormone oxytocin to receptor cells of the bed nucleus of the stria terminalis (BNST) and of the ventromedial nucleus (VMN) of the hypothalamus in the brain. Oxytocin is a peptide hormone that the pituitary gland secretes when it receives the instructions to do so from nearby cells of the hypothalamus. Carried in the bloodstream, oxytocin stimulates the uterus to contract at parturition, and the mammary glands to let down milk when the newborn infant suckles. Thus oxytocin has three related functions associated with birth: parturition, milk ejection, and affiliative pairbonding. The extent to which its role in affiliative bonding might apply also to mating, and to nonsexual social bonding is in the early stages of investigation.

Among the four-legged mammalian species, mother-infant bonding is contingent predominantly on smell. For the mothers of subhuman primates, the eyes are important also. For the mothers of human babies bonding is contingent, although partly on smell, predominantly on touch and sight. The unanesthetized mother, when her baby is presented to her as soon as it has been delivered, explores it visually and with her fingers. The baby rapidly develops to the stage of recognizing her as the primary mothering person. Subsequently, it recognizes other consistent caregivers including the father. In the contemporary era of infant formula and prepared baby foods, the father may fill the role of primary caregiver.

A baby's health and well-being are contingent not only on nourishment, but also on stimulation of the skin senses, as in suckling, cuddling, rocking, and caressing. Deprived of such haptic (that is, tactile) stimulation, the baby fails to thrive and may die of inanition. Animal experimental evidence indicates that secretion of growth hormone from the pituitary gland is contingent on regular skin stimulation (grooming) of the infant. When baby rats are deprived of maternal licking, they die (see Money, 1992b).

The principle of pairbondance that guarantees individual survival guarantees also species survival. Developmentally, the bonding of the infant to the mother serves the dual purpose of being also preparatory for, and prototypical of the bonding of that same infant, when older, to a mating partner. The parallelism between the two manifestations of pairbonding is remarkably close. Both involve eye contact and visual exploration. Both involve extensive haptic or tactile stimulation in close body contact. Both involve smell, taste, and sound in variable degree. In addition, both include explicit sexuoeroticality. Customary prudishness notwithstanding, some women do report the occurrence of orgasmic climax while the infant is suckling at the breast. In the case of baby boys, it is possible to see that there is at times a genital component of being suckled, namely, erection of the penis.

Intense sexuoerotical bonding of the type identified as being love-smitten or limerent (Tennov, 1974) usually has its onset after puberty, though a long-lasting love affair may begin as early as age eight. There is no upper age limit to the emergence of a new love affair. For an individual, the total number of limerent attractions ranges from zero upwards, and the continuity of each ranges from transient to a lifetime.

In human donor insemination and in vitro fertilization, as well as in stud livestock breeding by donor insemination, it is evident that breeding may take place without contact with the sperm provider. Breeding may also take place in the context of an arranged marriage, without the limerence of having fallen in love. Reciprocal falling in love, however, pretty much guarantees that two people will be entranced with one another long enough to guarantee parenthood. Then the two-way bond enlarges to a three-way bond to include the baby, without which the baby, unbonded, may perish.

If the parents' own two-way mating bond weakens or breaks, then the baby may survive by becoming bonded primarily or exclusively to only one of them. If abandoned, the baby may bond to a surrogate parent. The familial bond of two parents and one or more than one child is qualitatively different from the bond between two sexuoerotical partners, but not necessarily either inferior or superior.

Healthy and pathological pairbondance have sequelae that may themselves be, respectively, healthy and pathological. In either case, the sequelae may be either temporary or long-lasting. The persistence and pervasiveness of these sequelae are multivariately determined as a product of the developmental age when they were initially induced, and of the duration, magnitude, unpredictability, and inescapability of the conditions that induced them.

The earlier the age of onset of conditions of pairbondance that are either healthy, pathological, or both combined, the more long-lasting and immutable their outcome as, respectively, healthy, pathological, or ambivalent, either in general or in particular with respect to the pairbonding of erotosexual mating.

In the years following childhood, pairbondant disorder is widespread among those with an earlier history of such disorders as for example a history of extremely abusive neglect, deprivation, and cruelty. Abusiveness includes systematic social isolation and sensory deprivation, neonatally and subsequently, as well as injurious cruelty. Abusiveness includes systematic negation of manifestations of sexuoeroticality in infancy and childhood. Juvenile rehearsal play includes sexuoerotical rehearsal in preparation for the pairbonding of mating when older. Abusive deprivation of such play, or abusive retribution following its occurrence, paves the way for impairment and pathology of sexuoerotical pairbonding subsequently.

Troopbondance

Troopbondance, from the verb "to troopbond," signifies the reciprocal allegiances among individuals within an aggregation or cluster in mutual interdependency and, conversely, lack of allegiance toward members of rival aggregates or clusters.

In the human species, as in many primate and some subprimate mammalian species, troopbondance is phyletically mandated for the survival of both the individual and the aggregation of individuals as an organized community rather than an amorphous assemblage. The minimum size of a troop is a family consisting of parents and their offspring. For the offspring, troopbondance is phyletically mandated for survival. Siblings are dependent on troopbonded caretakers for at least as many years as there are between the birth of the oldest sibling and the attainment of puberty of the youngest one.

Within a troop, individuals distinguish themselves from one another on the basis of two principles. One is the principle of a dominance hierarchy of leadership and followership. The other is the principle of the division of labor for the maintenance and perpetuation of the troop on the basis of age, sexual dimorphism, and specific capabilities.

In babyhood, troopbonding begins as pairbonding with the mother and then progressively extends to include bonding with other members of the troop—first with those old enough to be caregivers, and eventually with agemates in the peer group. Juveniles rehearse in play the roles and alliances of troopbondance in adulthood. Many rehearsals are sex-segregated—boys with boys only, and girls with girls only. The pervasiveness of sex-segregation in childhood is in response, at least in part, to sanctions of the adult society against male-female social interaction in childhood and youth. Juvenile sex segregation is also a rehearsal of adult sex segregation to the extent that it is practiced in recreational, vocational, and social activities.

In the late adolescent or early adult years, individual bondedness within the troop of origin may undergo a phylogenetically ordained breakaway contingent on mating and possibly also on competition for position in the dominance hierarchy of the troop. Although females may break away, in most primate species those that depart are males. The breakaway individual may seek membership in another troop, or assemble the nucleus of a new troop of its own. In the traditional patriarchal society, it is the male who leaves home, woos a woman, and with her establishes a new family troop. In matriarchal society, by contrast, the male joins the female who may remain within her extended family troop.

In the human species, in the years of childhood, the constancy or inconstancy of an individual's troopbondant network of loyalties and disloyalties, fealties and defections, constitute a feedback: the troop influences the individual and the individual influences the troop. Rank and role in the network in childhood also carry over to, or at least have an influence on rank and role in the network in adulthood. For instance, to take an extreme case, an adult with a history of childhood autism, the deficiency of troopbondance carries over from childhood into adulthood.

The continuity of a troop's existence supersedes that of its individual members. Hence the distribution of allegiances and ranks within a troop are impermanent and subject to revision. Although revisions are multivariately induced, one constant source of change can always be counted on, namely, the succession of the generations.

Abidance

Abidance, from the verb "to bide," is derived from the Anglo-Saxon *bidan*, meaning to stay in place, or dwell. Abidance means being sustained in one's ecological niche or dwelling place, and not being destroyed by other species or inanimate substances.

Plant and animal species that exist in proximity to one another, the human species included, sustain their ecological resources partly in mutual dependency and partly in competitive rivalry. The ecological resources that ensure human sustentation are animate, namely, various plant and animal species, and inanimate, categorized in early Greek philosophy as earth, air, fire, and water. Replenishment of plant and animal resources is contingent on harvesting without exterminating the species. It is contingent also on competition without exterminating the rival species, and on exploiting inanimate resources without exhausting them.

It goes without saying that the preservation of a species from extinction is contingent on the sustentation of individuals who transmit the genome across the generation gap. Individual sustentation is itself contingent on access to various ecological resources that constitute the phylogenetically mandated minimum for survival. For the human species, these mandatory resources are subsumed under three major categories, namely, food, shelter, and clothing, and under two conditions of periodicity, namely, diurnal (asleep and awake) and seasonal.

Conditions of abidance that are optimal and predictable are conducive to health and well-being of body and mind. These are generally recognized as positive conditions. Conversely, conditions of abidance that are not optimal and predictable but either deficient, exaggerated, or chaotic and unpredictable are not conducive to health and well-being of mind and body. These are recognized as negative conditions.

The sequelae of positive or negative conditions of abidance are, respectively, positive or negative. Sequelae may be either short-term or long-term. Their pervasiveness and duration in a person's life are multivariately determined from the age when they were initially induced, which may even antedate conception if either egg or sperm has been adversely affected before uniting. Sequelae are multivariately determined also on the basis of the immutability, magnitude, and predictability of the conditions that induced them. In general, the earlier the age of onset of either positive or negative conditions of abidance, the more long-lasting their outcome as, respectively, either positive or negative, and the greater its resistance to change at a later age.

Poverty and pestilence, famine and disaster—these are the great confrontations that jeopardize one's success in negotiating the requirements of abidance.

Ycleptance

Ycleptance, from the now archaic Elizabethan English verb *"to clepe,"* meaning to name or to call by name, is derived from Middle English *clepen* and Anglo-Saxon *cleopian*, meaning to call, or to cry out. The past participle of *to clepe* has three forms, *yclept*, *ycleped*, and *cleped*. Ycleptance means being named or known for some attribute according to which one is classified, branded, labeled, or typecast.

Ycleptance is phyletically rooted in the recognition of likeness and unlikeness in the identifying characteristics and attributes of the members of a species, either individually or collectively, as a group. Conspecific recognition between males and females is an essential ingredient of breeding. Individual recognition of one's mate and young ones is widespread across species. The recognition of each member of a troop by all its other members, whereas it occurs in species as different as, for example elephants and wolves, is noteworthy as a phenomenon of primate troops. Ycleptance, requiring as it does the classificatory use of language, is a specifically human phenomenon. Human beings have classified and typecast one another, presumably since time immemorial with names that compliment or ridicule; honor or insult; normalize or stigmatize; respect or reject; and so on.

The categories of ycleptance are many and diverse. They include sex, age, family, clan, language, race, region, religion, politics, wealth, occupation, health, physique, looks, temperament, skin color, gender orientation, legal status, and so on.

The terminology of ycleptance ranges from the haphazard informality of nicknames that recognize personal idiosyncracies of appearance, body language, or biography, to the highly organized formality of hierarchical titles, occupational typology, and medical diagnoses.

The names with which we are yclept shape our identities and our destinies. A genealogical name bestows on the recipient the right or obligation to match the reputation of the forebear to whom it formerly belonged. A nickname may be aggrandizing or mortifying and belittling. A title or rank dictates one's position, rights, and duties in a dominance hierarchy, and the name of one's occupation defines which hierarchy within which one belongs. A prison number transforms one from a person into a cipher. A medical diagnosis transforms one into the incarnation of a disease, and its prognosis is one's future tyranny.

"What's in a name?" Shakespeare asked in *Romeo and Juliet*, "That which we call a rose by any other name would smell as sweet." There are many who would disagree, even vehemently. They despise both the name they were given and the identity that goes with it. Some undergo a change of identity and with it a change of name also. Others undergo a division of identity, each with its own name—the two-names, two-personalities phenomenon. In the syndrome of transvestophilia there are two wardrobes, one for each name and personality. In the syndrome of transexualism, there may be two occupations as well.

A formal name change to match a change of status may be marked by a special ceremony. The ceremony of marriage, for example, marks a woman's transition from the status of spinster to wife, from Miss to Mrs., and in most instances from being known not by her father's but her husband's surname. With the ceremony of marriage, the personality of the bachelor or spinster may metamorphose into the personality of husband or wife. Not uncommonly, the metamorphosed personality is a remake of the husband-personality of one's own father, or the wife-personality of one's own mother, respectively. Similarly, after the birth of the first child, father-personality and mother-personality may be remakes of one's own parents, irrespective of one's earlier vow not to repeat their errors and deficiencies of parenthood.

A change of name, status, power, and prestige may be ceremonialized in the granting of a title, honor, or advancement in rank. Whether it be aristocratic, military, judicial, clerical, academic, or whatever, the change of name incurs a change in obligations and duties as well as in privileges. To a variable degree, such a name change may be marked also by a change in personality.

Foredoomance

Doom, the noun, and to doom, the verb, are derived from Middle English and Anglo-Saxon *dom*, meaning what is laid down, a judgment or decree. In today's usage, doom means destiny or fate, including tragic fate, ruin or death. To doom means to condemn, or to destine to a tragic fate, or to consign to suffering or death. Foredoom means to doom beforehand, to predestine, or to condemn in advance. Foredoomance is the noun that signifies existence in a state of being inexorably doomed.

The sword of Damocles that hangs inexorably over all our heads is the threat of infirmity and the inevitability of mortality. Sickness and a shortened life span may, in some individuals, be secondary to imperfections or errors encoded within their genome either fortuitously or by transmission from a forebear. Some individuals are more exposed than others to injury or death from dangerous substances, accidents, or catastrophes. No one, however, escapes from the risk that besets all life forms, from viruses and bacteria to insects and vertebrates, namely, the risk of being invaded or preyed upon, disabled, invalided, or killed by some other life form.

Aphoristically, one may say that the purpose of living is to die. Dying begins at conception. That one will die is a prophesy, but one that fails to predict the details of when, where, and how. Such predictions are, at best, only actuarial estimates or probabilities.

Actuarial data reveal that, at all ages, the death rate for males is greater than that for females. The male:female birth ratio is $111\pm1:100$ (Tricomi et al., 1960). It equalizes at around age forty. For each subsequent age, the survival rate for women remains higher than for men. Thus, for women who survive into their eighties, there is a shortage of older men.

Until death overtakes us, ourselves, we suffer not only our own infirmities, but also the infirmities of those near to us. Finally, we suffer their dying as our own grief and bereavement.

Death, together with creation and the cosmos, is vastly imponderable. The very vastness of its imponderability has promoted the construction of vast systems of explanation in mythology, religion, and philosophy. The full human intellectual enterprise, one might venture to say, was initiated by pondering the imponderable mystery of death. Death is a monster in all of our lives.

· 3 ·

Programatics

Ideation and Imagery

L ike a virus in a computer program, an unspeakable monster in one's life is able to infiltrate the maps and programs encoded in the human mindbrain, and alter their format and presentation in ideation and imagery.

It is a conceptual convenience on some occasions to have mindbrain as a unity, and on others to have the unity divided as mind and brain. The present policy is to have the unity undivided.

There are some occasions also when it is a conceptual convenience to analyze mindbrain functioning sequentially from dormant through stimulus and response to dormant again. Another convenient analytic sequence is from sensation to perception to cognition. The present policy is to conceptualize mindbrain functioning as a continuity of recognizing, matching against what is already there, screening, deleting, and hierarchically organizing new input, finding similarities and constancies, forming explanations and predictions, and sequestering archival information in memory storage.

It is a conceptual convenience of another sort to analyze mindbrain functioning into conscious and unconscious, and to postulate an unconscious, subconscious, or preconscious mind as well as a conscious one. It is not the present policy to utilize this convenience, insofar as whatever becomes knowable becomes ipso facto conscious, and whatever may be unconscious is ipso facto unknowable.

Still another conceptual convenience is the very ancient one, dating from Plato and Aristotle, of analyzing mindbrain functioning into knowing, emotion, and will (or cognition, affect, and conation). This convenience also is not in accord with present policy. One knows or cognizes whatever one experiences as an emotion, and one is not utterly without the emotion that belongs specifically to the experience of being cognizant of something. Correspondingly, one is not energized with conation in the absence of concomitant knowing and feeling.

Mindbrain function varies in the degree of its proficiency on the basis of individual difference, developmental age, and the intervention of deleterious impairments and senescent deterioration. Individual differences include insufficiencies and deficiencies like color blindness, tone deafness, space-form dysgnosia, anosmia, and pain agnosia. Conversely, individual differences include specific talents, like perfect pitch and aural memory, eidetic imagery and photographic memory, synesthesia, ambidexterity, computational excellency, polyglotism, and aptitude for impersonation.

In cases of the syndrome known only by the French term "idiot savant" (skillful idiot, or foolish scholar), deficiencies of mindbrain functioning usually attributed to either mental retardation or autism, or both, coexist with a specific and prodigious proficiency in, for example, calendar calculation, rote memory of lists and numbers, musical performances, clay modeling, and precociously self-taught figure drawing, alphabetic writing, and rote reading.

Not only are there different degrees of mindbrain functioning, but also different states. The difference between the waking and sleeping state is universally experienced. It serves as a criterion against which to define and compare other states that have a lesser frequency and prevalence of occurrence, like delirium, narcosis, toxicosis, hallucinosis, fugue, trance, hypnosis, and crowd mania (see below).

The imagery and ideation of mindbrain functioning varies qualitatively. The eidetic vividness of the nightmare or of the post-traumatic flashback differs from the constrained orderliness of logical thinking and planning. The furor of creative excitement as the mindbrain synthesizes new conceptualizations, insights, or creative inspirations is different from the ruminative obsessiveness and overinclusiveness of the schizoidal pursuit of thoughts and ideas for a perfection never found. It is different also from the scrupulosity and circumstantiality that is sporadically associated with temporal lobe epilepsy (Trimble, 1991; Waxman and Geschwind, 1975).

The maps or programs into which ideation and imagery are organized also vary according to the state of mindbrain functioning. Thus, while it lasts, prolonged sleep deprivation impairs concentration, sensorimotor performance, reaction time, and judgment. Correspondingly, prolonged sensory deprivation, as in an isolation tank, prepares the way for hallucinatory elation and grandiose schemes that later prove to be hare-brained and silly.

The maps and programs of mindbrain functioning are matched in polarized pairs, one negative, one positive. Thus, for example, every individual possesses a gendermap for masculine and one for feminine, one of which is coded "mine," and the other "thine." Both are prerequisite to negotiating everyday existence in the company of men and women, boys and girls. In dealings with boys and girls, there are age-reciprocal maps, one that maps how to be an adult with a juvenile, and one that maps what to expect reciprocally.

Language maps are another example. To be able to use one's native language syntactically, it is necessary to have not only a built-in map for correct usage, but also one for incorrect usage, so as to know how to recognize error and to avoid it. Similarly, food maps are polarized into edible and inedible, and moral maps into permitted and prohibited.

Under special circumstances, the positive and negative coding of mindbrain maps may become switched or transposed, as happens in gender transpositions, for example.

Maps and programs of human mindbrain functioning that stand out with special prominence as a distinguishing characteristic of the human species are those in which causal scientific explanations are formulated and communicated in words. Regardless of their recency or antiquity, all causal explanations, scientific and otherwise, possess a history of having originated as an insight, conjecture, or hypothesis formulated in a human mindbrain.

Causal Explanations

One of the two genera of causal explanations is the dogmatic or apocalyptic. The other is pragmatic or probabilistic. Dogmatic causal explanations carry an ideological or doctrinal promise of being able to prophesy, or of having been able to prophesy, without provisos, the occurrence or recurrence of an event or consequence. Pragmatic causal explanations carry a statistical or stochastic promise of being able to predict or of having been able to predict, with statistical provisos, the likelihood of the occurrence or recurrence of an event or consequence. The difference is between prophecy and prediction.

It is on the basis of its acceptability to other people, that a causal explanation, whether prospective or retrospective, is differentiated on a scale that ranges from delusion through belief to certainty.

A causal explanation is rated as **delusional** if it is maintained tenaciously by its original proponent despite its rejection by other people as untenably eccentric and bizarre. A delusion fails to yield to empirical evidence or logical argument. It may be diffuse and overly inclusive, or it may be concise and conceptually restricted.

A delusion held with intense and unyielding tenacity is characterized as paranoid. There is no fixed criterion by which to distinguish paranoid suspicion—of being the victim of cabalistic intrigue and conspiracy, for instance—from cautious suspicion or wariness. In loose usage, paranoid is a synonym for suspicious. It is often applied contemptuously, as an insult.

A causal explanation that comes close to being delusional may have sufficient plausibility to be classified not as a delusion but a fixated idea (**idée fixe**). Thus a man (or woman) may have a fixated idea of being in need of an aphrodisiac to offset a diminution in the intensity of orgasm. The apperception of a person's orgasm being that person's own exclusive monopoly, there is no basis for disputing whether its intensity has or has not diminished. The fixation may persist in an unending round of clinic shopping for an aphrodisiac.

A causal explanation that is an expediency designed to fit a specific event or state of affairs, without critical examination of alternatives, is a **rationalization**.

A causal explanation is rated as a **belief** if it is accepted by a group of adherents or converts irrespective of how implausible or unconfirmable it appears to be to the members of other groups. Beliefs may be simple or compounded into complex belief systems. A belief becomes a **dogma** when it is held as an absolute, never to be relinquished. In the history of philosophical thought, causal explanations that are dogmas have been the special intellectual property of religion, and of law and politics as well.

A dogma may become not only an explanatory cause, but also the only true cause, one for which believers will fight, kill, and die. The religious wars of history attest to that, as do the secular wars. So also do acts of self-immolation undertaken by either individuals or groups in the service of a cause.

A causal explanation that is rated as a **factual certainty** is one from which reliable predictions can be made and agreed upon by all. Such predictions may derive from folkway empiricism as evidenced in the formulas, calculations, and practices of, for instance, house-building, crop-farming, or food-making. Alternatively, they may derive from scholarly empiricism as evidenced in the formulas, calculations, and practices of the investigations and experiments of professional science and its applications.

Empirical causal explanations have a long history of association with the everyday pragmatics of providing food, shelter, and clothing, and a short history of association, mostly since the Renaissance, with the academic investigations of pure and applied science.

Before an explanation gains the status of certainty, it has first the status of being a hypothesis. The predictive reliability of a hypothesis is tested mathematically and graded on a probability scale from less certain to more certain. According to the most rigorous canons of science, there are no absolute certainties. Any scientific proposition, no matter how revered, is subject to revision when new data topple it from its pedestal. It is part of the credo on which science is built that all of its propositions are open to challenge. None is sacrament. None has the privilege of eternal verity.

Dreams

Dreams bespeak the continuity of mindbrain functioning as a perpetually ongoing process that does not require starting and stopping with stimulus and response. It is a process that includes monitoring and recognizing of incoming stimuli. When a person is asleep, the entry of incoming stimuli is reduced to a minimum. The imagery and ideation of the dream is a display of what happens when mentation is left more or less to its own devices, undisciplined by the input of additional stimuli.

The autonomy of dream mentation is such that the dreamer has the sense, and sometimes the conviction, of being not the source of the dream, but its recipient from, perhaps, a supernatural source. Hence the ancient theory of the migration of the soul while asleep to observe and participate in a spirit world of dreams. Hence also the special significance of dreams as auguries and of seers as their interpreters.

Before they can talk, children may wake at night showing signs that strongly suggest they have been dreaming. As soon as they say words while awake, they may say them also while asleep, presumably as an accompaniment of dreaming. As soon as they exchange dialogue, children are able to talk about dreams. They are not nonplussed by the concept of dreaming, even when they claim not to remember any dreams.

Dreaming occurs following the stage of deep sleep, during the REM (rapid eye movement) stage. REM sleep can be observed in animals, for example cats, so that it can be presumed they also dream.

In human beings dreaming is universal, with the possible exception of patients who have undergone prefrontal surgical lobotomy. The symptomatology of dreaming in relationship to other syndromes has been anecdotally rather than systematically recorded. One example is the phenomenon of hallucinatory, hypnagogic dream imagery at the time of going to sleep. Hypnogogic imagery may occur alone, but may also be associated with the syndrome of narcolepsy. Narcolepsy is a syndrome of brain disorder marked by pathological lapses into brief periods of sleep. It may coexist with cataplexy (Chapter 5, Derision) and be accompanied by the phenomenon of sleep paralysis at the time of waking.

Mostly dreams are a hodgepodge of images and ideas the coherency of which is fragmented by ellipses, tangential associations, kaleidoscopic scene changes, abrupt inclusions, and overinclusive rambling. The message of such dreams is not lucid, logical, and readily decipherable, but muddled and disconnected. Like a message written in rebus code, it needs to be deciphered by a code-breaker if it is to have any meaning at all.

The code-breaker, following the example of Freud, may regard a dream as a source of information about an old issue or challenge retrospectively retrieved and encoded. Alternatively, following the example of Jung, the code-breaker may regard the same dream as a source of information about a present issue or challenge prospectively solved or being solved, with the solution being encoded in the dream.

Solutions to problems in some dreams are not encoded but are presented quite logically and coherently. Thus a poet may dream the stanzas of a new poem, a composer the theme of a new composition, a novelist the completion of an unfinished novel, a mathematician the solution to an unsolved equation, a scientist the design of a new hypothesis, and so on.

For the majority of people, dream messages which are solutions for problematic stresses and puzzlements are of a rather mundane and perhaps trivial nature. A member of a mountain rescue party dreams that the lost climbers he is searching for walk into his camp and are saved. A bereaved wife dreams that her husband is back with her again, returned from among the dead. Problem-solving dreams are sometimes associated with physiosomatic happenings that occur during sleep. A starving explorer dreams of sitting down to a lavish banquet and temporarily solves his hunger problem. A sleeping child with a full bladder dreams of getting up and going to the bathroom, and then wets the bed. An adolescent boy has a wet dream in which ejaculation may be preceded by imagery that provides an index of sexuoerotic outlook and orientation.

In nightmares, frightening and imponderable challenges are struggled with, but not resolved. A soldier, strategically powerless in the midst of an enemy bombardment, survives while all his comrades are killed. Thereafter, he has recurrent flashback nightmares of being rendered powerless by overwhelming catastrophe. A child, lone survivor among a group of taller adults struck down by lightning in an open field, subsequently has nightmares of unresolved catastrophe. Childhood, when small size is incompatible with superior prowess in encounters with angry adults, wild animals, and menacing mechanical contraptions, is the period of life when nightmares are most prolific.

Fantasy

Fantasy exists in either the past tense or the future. In the past tense it is a mental replay of the imagery and ideation of what once was, with or without revision. In the future tense, fantasy is not a replay, but a rehearsal of something new. The new fantasy is cut and spliced from old imagery and ideation derived from multiple and perhaps incongruous sources. It is from their rearranged sequence and juxtaposition that the newness of the fantasy is created.

In one of its guises, namely, daydreaming, when attention is diverted away from assigned work, fantasy is characterized by those in authority as escapist, ephemeral, and unproductive. Not so, however, when fantasy in the guise of reverie gives birth to an entire poem, novel, drama, movie, painting, sculpture, or other original work of art. It is then characterized as inspiration or insight.

Original works of fine art are not alone in having their roots in fantasy. All original products of the human mindbrain, scientific hypotheses included, are rooted in fantasy. So also are prospective solutions of many personal problems. It is what grows from the roots, and how focused or untrammeled that growth is, that gives fantasy either a good name or a bad name.

There are fantasies of mastery and fantasies of defeat, of love and hate, despotism and martyrdom. The themes and topics of fantasy are shared or secretive, borrowed or original, rare or prevalent. Prevalence varies according to time and place. Masturbation fantasies, for example, featuring explicit sexuoerotical themes, are prevalent in pubertal and teenaged boys, if not universally, then certainly in the culture of Christendom. Among girls, the corresponding fantasies are romantic rather than coitally explicit—at least according to presently available data.

The more the product of fantasy deviates from established usage, the greater the likelihood that it will be publicly criticized as insane. The correct criterion of insane fantasy lies not in its content, however, but in either its overinclusiveness, its internal incompatibilities, or in some instances its monomaniacal and fixated resistance to developmental change.

In the developmental mentation of very young children, there is initially a fusion of the imagery and ideation that adult observers characterize as, respectively, fantasy and reality. The two become unfused as experience with the law of recognitional constancy progressively accumulates. Recognitional constancy signifies the persistence of a core of sameness amidst a periphery of manifold differences. Developmentally, recognitional constancy of imagery and ideation is the law according to which the mindbrain developmentally construes reality. The constancies of reality are shared by others. They are in the public domain. The imagery and ideation of fantasy and dream, by contrast, are recognitionally inconstant, idiosyncratic, and not shared by others. They are in the private domain.

For most children, the make-believe world of imaginary playmates and personages sooner or later becomes distinguishable from the actual world of peers and people. For others, the distinction fails. Among them are those whose thinking is characterized as pseudologia fantastica (fantastic false logic). They fabricate elaborately fantastic stories as if they were entertainments for an audience, but they tell them as if narrating an account of actual happenings.

There are some instances of pseudologia fantastica in which the narrator tells a story that is self-incriminating even to the extent of being ostensibly a confession of a crime that the narrator did not commit. The crime may not itself be fictional, but a crime committed by someone else. For example, soon after the suspect in a case of serial lust murder was taken into custody, his room mate, himself a bit of an outlaw, phoned the police. On the basis of what he knew of the case, he then confessed in detail to being himself the murderer. His confession, however, did not match the evidence, which the imprisoned suspect's own confession did match. In such a case, it would appear that the false confessor's own prior fantasy matches so closely the actual history of what has happened that he is unable to separate the history from the fantasy.

Although false confessions, like other examples of pseudologia fantastica, are sporadic in occurrence, they are not unique or rare. Typically, they arise spontaneously. Pseudologia fantastica may, however, be the outcome of bullying and indoctrination, as in the case of children who, under investigation for signs of having been sexually abused, make false confessions.

Being held under conditions resembling virtual house arrest as captives of the investigative bureaucracy, children can, under the pressure of relentless interrogation, all too readily be brainwashed into agreeing with their tormentors, if only to please them and escape. If the investigators appear more pleased by added fabrications, then still more are added to produce an extravagantly complete narrative composed entirely of pseudologia fantastica. Though false, this narrative may subsequently be adduced as evidence against the accused abuser.

Fabricated responses, technically known as confabulations, are encountered also as improvisations to fill in memory gaps in the wake of degenerative brain disease. They are particularly associated with Korsakoff's psychosis, which is one of the possible outcomes of advanced alcoholism.

The degree to which, in adulthood, the mentation of fantasy maintains its own autonomy is individually variable. The therapeutic technique of guided fantasy is based on the presupposition that fantasy is amenable to being scheduled, and that its content can be ordered on command. In large part, however, fantasies come and go on their own timetable, and dictate their own content. Like dreams and nightmares, they have an autochthonous life of their own. They may completely defy interruption until intruded upon by an outside intervention.

Hallucination

Hallucinatory ideation and imagery resembles that of fantasy, reverie, and dream. It takes place chiefly, if not totally, in the absence of concurrent sensory input into mindbrain functioning. Contrived sensory deprivation in an experimental isolation chamber is one way of inducing an hallucinatory state.

In illusion, as compared with hallucination, there is a sensory stimulus that is misconstrued, as in seeing the mirage of a base camp in the white glare of an Antarctic ice field, or in seeing the reversible image of a graphic optical illusion, or in having the experience when exploring a place for the first time of having been there before (déjà vu).

Hallucination may be induced by taking in a hallucinogenic pharmacologic substance or plant product. The delirium of high fever is a form of hallucination. Excessive sleep deprivation or advanced starvation may also be associated with hallucination. So also may an epileptic seizure, as in the hallucinatory imagery of the aura that may signal an impending attack. There is also the specific quasi-hallucinatory phenomenon of phantomism in which an absent or nonfunctional limb or organ continues to be represented as a phantom in the body image. It is projected into the void of the missing part.

Historically and transculturally, those who hallucinate have been both feared and revered—feared as demon possessed, and revered as shamans and medicine men. Among some North American Indian tribes, shamanistic candidates would demonstrate their suitability for their calling by inducing visual hallucinations by social isolation, fasting, and self-torture. It is a speculation of science-fictional history that religions had their origin in the ideation and imagery of trance states induced by hallucinogens or by sensory isolation.

In our own society, someone who is not classified as insane, but who has an hallucinatory type of experience, may be characterized as a religious mystic having a divine revelation; a spiritualist or medium channeling a telepathic or occult message; a creative artist or thinker experiencing an inspiration or *idée donnée*; a susceptible person misperceiving an illusion or mirage; or, perhaps, a prophet receiving dictation from a higher power either by ear, or directly through an automatically writing hand.

Like dreams, hallucinations may be brief or long, simple or complex, convoluted or coherent, and looking backward or looking forward. They may be recapitulating old problems, or rehearsing the solutions to present ones. A seldom understood function of hallucinogenic drugs and drug addiction is that, for those whose philosophy of life provides no solution to the problems that are closing in on them, they promise a new solution in the visionary imagery and ideation of the hallucinatory state. The visionary solution may be quite impractical. Nonetheless, it holds out the promise of hope.

Recognition of what is and what is not contingent on concurrent sensory input is one of the unsolved mysteries of mindbrain function. For some hallucinators extreme vividness of imagery of the type known as eidetic is a criterion of what is real. Their experience of hallucinatory imagery may be so vividly eidetic that it is, for them, indistinguishable from nonhallucinatory imagery. There are some who would say it is "more real than reality itself." This very saying implies, however, a distinction between what is reality and what is not reality. This is a distinction that, sooner or later, many if not all hallucinators are able to recognize. In other words, they are able to say that they have heard voices, seen visions, or had the smell, taste, or tactual perception of something for which no sensory stimulus was present. False attribution of hallucinatory imagery and ideation to concurrent sensory input does, however, occur.

Monomania

An unspeakable monster in one's life may maintain its silence and concealment by metamorphosing into its polar opposite. Thus the offender becomes the aggrieved, the victim the tyrant, the nonentity the ostentatious flaunter, the battered the batterer, the survivor the killer, the male the female, the female the male, and so on. The list has no fixed ending. The proposition expounding the legitimacy of the metamorphosis is a delusion or a fixated idea.

The bipolar logic by which a proposition becomes a fixated or delusional idea may be as simple as the binary logic of reversing inside and outside—projecting from within outward, and introjecting from without inward. Projection is illustrated in the example of a seminary student who has homoerotic dreams in which he is engaged in explicit sexuoerotic interaction with a fellow seminarian. As a sequel, he develops a fixated or delusional idea that there are students who, as undercover agents in the seminary, are secretly plotting to convert him into a homosexual.

In the counterpart of projection, a causal agent or power beyond oneself is introjected and accredited as an agent or power acting within oneself. Thus a student in training in an espionage academy also has an explicit homoerotic dream. As a sequel, he develops a fixated or delusional idea of being the unique possessor of an "erotobionic power" with which to conduct a supersecret surveillance espionage and to detect and expose closeted homosexuals among his superiors.

The polar reversals that produce delusions and fixated ideas are examples of what the psychologist Richard Solomon (1980) conceptualized as opponent process. According to opponent process theory, that which was negative, aversive, and abhorrent undergoes a rapid transformation and becomes positive, attractive, and addictive. Solomon quoted an example of rifle practice, which initially he found frightening. Very soon it became ecstatically exhilarating, and he became as if addicted. It is possible, though still to be proved, that the switch is contingent on the release from brain cells of their own opioids, the morphine-like endorphins.

After the flip-flop of opponent process, the ensuing delusion or fixated idea, although not totally incapacitating for the affairs of daily living, may commandeer exorbitant amounts of time and attention. It is then characterized as a monomania (Greek, *monos*, single + *mania*, madness). When French psychiatric terminology was in vogue, there were dozens of terms for monomanias of which only a few remain in current usage. They are listed with their Greek derivations in the following: dipsomania (*dipsa*, thirst), meaning alcoholism; dromomania (*dromos*, a course), meaning running away; erotomania (*eros*, love), meaning morbidly exaggerated sexuality; kleptomania (*kleptein*, to steal), meaning uncontrollable stealing; megalomania (*megas*, big, great), meaning excessive conviction of one's own greatness; nymphomania (*nympho*, nymph), meaning exaggerated sexual desire in a female; and pyromania (*pyr*, fire), meaning compulsive fire setting.

In the syndrome of transexualism, there is a fixation or monomania to change the body to be concordant with the body image—in other words changing from male to female, or from female to male. The fixation is particularly insistent with respect to surgical change, which is less easily achieved, than is hormonal change and cross dressing.

In the Skoptic syndrome, the fixation or monomania is not to change sex, but to become a eunuch, which is achieved in some instances by self-castration. In another of the sexual body image syndromes, the fixated idea is on foreskin restoration, either by surgery or stretching. Fixated ideation is characteristic also of the paraphilic sexological disorders which are discussed further in Chapter 11.

For professional killers, mercenaries, terrorists, death squads, hit men, bank robbers, and state executioners, slaughtering human beings may be equivalent to slaughtering animals. Even among these, however, there may be some for whom the job of killing other people represents a homicidal fixation or monomania as a stratagem for coping with an unspeakable monster in their lives.

One of the manifestations of homicidal monomania is in the exorcism syndrome as represented in, for example, gay bashing or racial lynching. Either alone or in groups, murderers with this syndrome stalk individuals who overtly symbolize an unspeakable monster within themselves. In sacrificing their victim, they symbolize the killing off, by proxy, of the monster within. Some patricide and other close-kin homicides also exemplify this dynamic of symbolic exorcism and self-cleansing.

Another manifestation of homicidal monomania is in the paraphilia of serial lust murder, also known as erotophonophilia (Chapter 11). In this syndrome, the murderer decoys his victims under circumstances that initially appear legitimate. Very often the victims have the appearance of being near replicas of one another. One component of this paraphilia, which is exploited in horror fiction and horror movies, is to risk one's own entrapment, and then to stage a near-miss escape.

Homicidal monomania with serial killing is predominantly, if not invariably, paraphilic in type. By contrast, homicidal monomania with mass killing is more likely to be paranoidal in type. In some cases, the killer has a fixated grievance against a particular person whose killing may entail the fortuitous killing also of bystanders. In other cases, the killer randomly shoots into a crowd of strangers as though they were enemy guerillas disguised for attack. This kind of mass killing may be a manifestation of a post-traumatic stress (shock) disorder originating in a history of mass killing on the battlefield. It becomes reactivated in eidetically vivid, nightmarish flashbacks, and is re-enacted in a shootout of civilian surrogate enemies. The paranoidal killing spree may, for the killer, end in suicide, but serial lust murdering seldom does so.

Homicidal monomania, as for example in shootouts and killings of colleagues, associates, or family members at their place of work, or at home, may be secondary to fixated or delusional ideas or suspicions of having been wronged. In such cases, homicide is superimposed on the basis of paranoidal grievance collecting.

Collecting grievances, and to some extent engineering them, is itself a fixation in its own right among those who may be characterized as grievance collectors. They fail to recognize the unspeakable monster concealed behind their treasure trove of grievances. Grievance collectors may become adepts at litigation, repeatedly using the courts to seek redress for their suspicions and grievances. Grievance collecting devastates family relationships. It sets people up as targets for mutual accusation, nagging, and denigration.

The counterpart of the grievance collector is the collector of boastful and egocentric exaggerations of prowess, wealth, and status. Monomanic grandiosity diverts attention from the monster it conceals, but in the long run it is, like grievance collecting, self-sabotaging.

Egocentric intolerance of rivalry may express itself in a monomania of sabotage, attack, or eradication of the rival. Or, if the allegiance of a third person is involved, it may express itself as a monomania of disputed allegiance. This is what happens when, for instance, a parent violently punishes, deprives, or disinherits an unmarried daughter for having an affair, or a son for being gay. In each instance, the parent's rival is a newcomer, vying for the child's allegiance. In each instance also, the parental maneuver is counter-productive. It induces alienation, and rules out the likelihood of reconciliation and the resumption of allegiance on the basis of a new, revised contract. The destruction of allegiance is total and irrevocable if, in obedience to a cultural tradition, a daughter who becomes pregnant out of wedlock must be killed by her father or one of his male kin.

In the era before contemporary acculturation began, Aboriginal Australian society of the central north coast had the age-old custom of the blood feud with which to settle a disputed allegiance. According to the fixed rules of the totemic kinship system, whoever would be eligible to be one's promise man or promise girl was preordained and could be predicted, even prenatally. In teenage, one might anticipate having an illicit love affair with someone else's promise person, but with the understanding that the rightful promise man of the girl in this illicit affair then had the socially sanctioned right and obligation to kill his rival, and possibly his promise girl also. It would then be obligatory for the kin of the deceased to avenge the death of their kinsman by killing the killer. This institutionalized merger of the love affair with death and vengeance altered the sex ratio in favor of polygyny and served to curtail population expansion.

The love-death theme is found also in romantic troubadour tradition of unrequitable love ending in death by murder or suicide—a tradition still kept alive in grand opera, and in contemporary versions of Romeo and Juliet.

A fixation or monomania over the allegiance and fidelity of a spouse or betrothed is an extreme manifestation of jealousy. In some instances, the rival exists only as a figment, constructed from suspicion. In some societies there is a culturally fixated stereotype that all males are promiscuous, and all females potentially unchaste and unfaithful. Therefore, daughters and wives are jealously possessed and oppressed, subjugated and beaten, so as to ensure obedience and fidelity. To some extent, this stereotype is present and exerts an effect on lovers and spouses in our own society, serving as camouflage for the unspeakable monster of an allegiant monomania. Its paradoxical outcome is not allegiance, but estrangement and alienation.

In the converse of allegiant monomania, one partner stage manages a relationship with two, or possibly more than two partners, each of whom is ostensibly unknown to the other. The hidden agenda in the dynamic of this drama is the unpredictability of what will happen if the partners discover the existence of one another. A turmoil of incrimination and feuding is likely to ensue. The outcome may be decided in the courtroom or, in a worst possible scenario, in homicide plus or minus suicide.

Allegiant monomania may express itself as erotomania, the condition of love unrequited, in which one of two people is morbidly love stricken and the other is present only in absentia, or is indifferent, or is responsive only enough to be tantalizingly unattainable. Erotomania is also known as the Clérambault-Kandinsky syndrome. The monomaniacal fixation is on the unrequiting lover, and on the absolute imperative of obtaining or regaining that person's undying love. The person may be one's former date or spouse, a stranger onto whom one projected love at first sight, or an unapproachable celebrity in sports, entertainment, politics, or high society. A student may be fixated on a teacher, a patient on a doctor, a client on an attorney, but always the fixation is one-sided. It may dictate a monomania of spying, stalking, threatening, suicide, and assassination. Some celebrities have met their death in this way.

Complicity

A fixated idea or delusion may perhaps be held in solitude, utterly private and unknown to anyone. Hence the shock of disbelief when the well-mannered, respected next-door neighbor, or the class president of the senior year, is the one who is apprehended as a sex murderer, or captured as a serial killer.

If a fixated idea or delusion is not totally shrouded, it may be transmitted in replica to only one other person. One then has a *folie à deux* (French, foolishness or lunacy of two). Rather than be perfectly replicated, however, a fixated idea or delusion is more likely to be shared as the common denominator of a mutual complicity. Such complicity may be exemplified in the collusion of an abused child with his abusing parents. As if addicted to abuse, the child covers for the parents and, if rescued, begs and connives to return to them.

Another scenario of a mutual complicity might conceivably be as follows: A fixated idea or delusion takes hold quite fortuitously in more than one person. Two of them adventitiously meet each other and, upon meeting, recognize their mutual compatibility—not unlike the recognition of love at first sight. Only later do they discover that each has brought the same fixated idea or delusion to their adventitious first meeting. They construe that they are living proof of the aphorism that they are made for each other, just as dominant and submissive, leader and follower, or hero and hero worshiper are made for each other. Their attachment to one another may be, if not frankly erotic, then subliminally so. Alternatively, it may replicate a parent-child attachment or, conversely, the breakaway from parental attachment to a new charismatic attachment to a messiah.

A paired collusional attachment on the basis of a shared fixated idea or delusion may remain limited to the same two partners exclusively. Or the collusion may enlarge to include the complicity of more than two people. The larger group may be the domestic unit or family in which each member operates on the basis of the same fixation, even though it may not be articulately spelled out in propositional form. Like actors on a stage, each member of the group has a specific role to enact in the group complicity, and each role is contingent on every other player's role. If one changes, then it may be incumbent on all the others to undergo compensatory change. Thus when the healthy one falls sick, the invalid recuperates and takes the helm. When the abused child is rescued, a younger sibling becomes the victim. When the alcoholic is in recovery, the spouse becomes the addict.

Complicity in the sharing of a fixated idea or delusion extends beyond pairs and small groups to include large masses of people. When a crowd assembles, the whole may become greater than, or different from, the sum of its parts. Then there emerges a superordinate phenomenon which has variously been called the group mind, crowd psychology, and mass hysteria. It is contingent on bodily closeness, on hypnotic rhythmicity of motion, as in clapping, dancing, or swaying, and on hypnotic rhythmicity of singing or chanting a slogan which is the crowd's mantra—an abbreviation of the fixated idea or delusion which has been supplied by the master of ceremonies.

Religious mysteries, as in the Eleusinian mysteries or the Dionysian ecstasies of ancient Attica, or in the Christian Pentecostal rapture of being possessed of the Holy Spirit, are in large part the mysteries of crowd hypnosis, so-called. More specifically, they are the mysteries of the hypnotic power of rhythmicity of motion and chanting to bond an assembly of individuals into a cohesive troop. Then individual autonomy is surrendered to the troop, and the troop acts as a unity. The sign of an individual's complete surrender is a collapse from a state of ecstasy into a state of syncopal faint or swoon. This surrender is defined as being possessed by the spirit. In Pentecostalism, it may include "speaking in tongues." Although men as well as women may undergo the experience, it is more likely to be a sanctioned form of surrender for women than men.

Assimilation of either a religious or secular fixated idea or delusion may, after a period of build up, be transformed quite suddenly into the momentous enlightenment of being converted or born again. Alternatively, conversion may be more gradual and the outcome of persuasive, perhaps even sophistic indoctrination.

If persuasion fails, either with crowds or individuals, ascendancy of the fixated idea or delusion may become ensured by being made contingent on the techniques of behavior modification. With a long history in the taming and training of wild animals, these techniques have a long history also in the enforced conversion of heathen to the true faith and in the Inquisition. They have likewise a long history in the brainwashing of captives, slaves, prisoners, novitiates, and school children, so as to indoctrinate and enforce declarations of error, wrong-doing, guilt, and repentance. The techniques of indoctrination include accusation, threat, and humiliation; enforced mutism; deprivation of clothing, hygienic facilities, and privacy; sleep deprivation; sensory, motor, and social isolation; starvation and dehydration; and brutality and torture.

The virtuosos among masters of indoctrination are politicians, preachers, and orators. They plan and rehearse their indoctrination ceremonies in detail. They program the timing of crowd participation so as to maintain orderliness while maximizing frenzied adherence to a slogan. Hitler was a supermaster of that art. He showed, even in the age before television, that an entire nation can be orchestrated into mass mania. At the present time in the United States, the nation is being insidiously indoctrinated into a mass mania regarding the existence of Satanistic cults dedicated to sexual child abuse and the sacrifice of fetuses.

The fixated idea or delusion of a mass mania may be quasi-military, as in stadium riots of soccer fans at international matches, and in street riots of communities enraged by police and political injustice. It may also be military, religious, or political. It may be celebrated at public lynchings, floggings, or executions. Mass mania may spread through a community in the form of a socially contagious undiagnosable epidemic, its disappearance as unexplained as its appearance.

As in the Salem witch hangings of the 1690s, mass mania may set neighbors against neighbors. Accused as Satanists and child sexual abusers in today's heresy trials, neighbors are inquisitioned, persecuted, and imprisoned, even though falsely accused. Paradoxically, the fixated delusion of a mass mania may also set believers against themselves in mass suicide as at Jonestown.

On the night of November 18, 1978, nine hundred expatriate American men, women, and children, black and white, died in Jonestown, the commune of the People's Temple in Guyana. They drank from a tubful of a deadly potion concocted of strawberry Flavor-aide laced with tranquilizers and cyanide. They had been rehearsed for this White Night in several previous religious drills, but no date had been set for the ultimate act of obedience. In the late afternoon of that fateful day, Jim Jones, the self-appointed messiah of the cult, ordered the mass slaying of several departing members of an American legislative team of inquiry. He then assembled all his followers and from the temple pulpit orchestrated their self-immolation. When the carnage was completed, he shot himself. This abomination terminated the unspeakable monster of his drug-fueled, delusion-fixated life.

Inconsistency and Double-speak

There is no way to guarantee that the utterances and writings of anyone will always be logically consistent and not contradictory. On the contrary, the juxtaposition of beliefs and prophesies, on the one hand, and practical formulas and predictions, on the other, guarantees that everyone's explanatory thinking will be to some degree inconsistent. Scientists whose thinking about their own specialty may be logically consistent are notorious for being unscientific and dogmatic in some of the moral, religious, and social beliefs and values to which they adhere.

Logical inconsistency may be part of a program of planned deception, prevarication, and lying. No one is completely free of a certain amount of knowing duplicity, even if only in resorting to little white lies as a customary form of social politeness. For some people, duplicity is virtually a way of life, as in impostoring, for example. Even an impostor, however, may be blurry-visioned as to the difference between deceit as confabulation and role-playing theatricality, and deceit as denial and lying. The difference is even more blurry in the case of pseudologia fantastica (see above).

In infancy, saying no as a denial is like saying no as a refusal. Both are tactics of self-assertiveness and are prerequisite to the development of a sense of selfhood. Bigger and more powerful people are inconsistent in their response to the negations of smaller and less powerful people. Thus the infant and young child must formulate from experience a mindbrain map of etiquette and morality that includes this inconsistency, namely, a map of situations and occasions when denial and refusal are practiced, and when they are not. If all the members of a child's society are consistent in applying their rules of inconsistency, then the child's own map of morality and etiquette incorporates those rules without further ado, and the child becomes a social conformist. Confusion arises when different people in the child's society use different rules of inconsistency. There is even more confusion when the same people are inconsistent in applying the rules so that a yes now converts to a no next time, even though the situation is identical on the two occasions, except for the passage of time. Confusion leads to the chaos of double-speak.

In the logic of double-speak there are no contracts, for what is said with one breath is taken back with another. A typical example is one of the type used to illustrate the principle of the double bind: A husband traps his wife in a double bind by agreeing to her going away to summer school for graduate studies and then, within her hearing, launches into a tirade on everything he finds wrong with women's liberation. The wife, in turn, traps her husband in a double bind by initiating and then withdrawing from sexual intimacy. Her assertiveness bears no relation to women's liberation, as he surmises, but with her unmentionable phobia of vaginal penetration which, being an unspeakable, is never spoken about.

For teenagers, another typical example of double-speak is that of a parent who agrees in principle to teenage dating, but on the occasion of each date plays the role of suffering martyr who will be sleepless until the teenager returns.

A double bind is not limited to double-speak, but sometimes may be expressed as actions that speak louder than words. To illustrate: By phone, on a Friday morning, a stranger with a femininely modulated masculine vocal tonality, self-identified as a hermaphrodite who lives as a female, requested an appointment for the following Monday. She was in the area visiting her brother.

As a child, she said, about twenty years ago, she had written for help, but her father had intercepted the reply. Years later she read the letter. Ostensibly, it invited her to stop by the clinic any time she might be in the vicinity—and now here she was with no time available except on Monday.

Upon inquiry, it became evident that her history was consistent not with a diagnosis of birth defect of the sex organs, but with a diagnosis of gender identity disorder, probably transexualism. Despite the short notice, it was possible to arrange a Monday appointment with one of the clinic doctors in his private office.

On Monday, at around the time of the appointment, there was another phone call. Agitated and distraught, the patient was in the emergency room of another hospital, having been overtaken by an asthma attack while driving. She had lost the name and phone number of where she was supposed to go. Although the information was again supplied, she did not keep the appointment, nor phone to cancel or reschedule it. In this kind of double-speak in which the second proposition cancels the first, it is not surprising if the cancelation is, in turn, itself canceled—in which case such a patient sooner or later turns up again, almost certainly without an appointment.

Another example of double-speak carried out in deeds as well as words was that of a father-son struggle over the son's academic underachievement in preparation for high school. The father punished him with various deprivations and coerced him into hours of isolation with homework assignments that did not get finished. He requested another round of psychological testing so as to assure himself that the earlier ones had not given the boy a false-positive high IQ. Reiteratively, he insisted that the boy must be motivated to achieve. Otherwise he would forfeit a career. He considered the situation urgent, as the boy was on a downhill course that would require repeating a grade.

The boy's own remedy was to transfer immediately to another school where he would no longer be subject to schoolyard harassment, but the father insisted he remain in the school where he was failing. Three times, over a period of weeks, the father failed to keep clinic appointments that were scheduled for himself and his wife as well as for their son. His double-speak message to the boy was a demand to not fail and, superimposed on it, a veto or neglect of intervention to prevent failure. The background to the father's double-speak was that, as a child, he himself had been required to undergo long-term clinical follow-up for very early puberty that rendered him permanently deficient in stature, though not in intellect. His son who at puberty had already outstripped his father in height was too great a threat should he also outstrip or even equal him in intellect. The punch line was that the father was, unknown to himself, engineering his son's failure intellectually.

In the clinic, there is a double-speak syndrome informally known as the most famous patient syndrome. People with this syndrome are among the so-called clinic shoppers. One proposition of their double-speak is the search for a cure. The other proposition is that not even the most famous doctors can diagnose the condition, let alone cure it. The symptoms in some, though not all such cases are factitious and self-induced as in Munchausen syndrome (Chapter 5). In other cases, the symptoms are not factitious but are confabulatory elaborations and embellishments of lesser ones. The closer the approach to a correct diagnosis, the greater the likelihood that the patient will take leave and disappear.

Double-speak is readily apperceived after its two contradicting propositions have been recognized and reciprocally matched. They do not come packaged in pairs, however, but separately. Hence, after becoming acquainted with the first proposition, one must be alert to the possible existence of its polar opposite, so as not to miss it or disregard its significance. In other words, when things are not as they appear to be on the surface, reverse the sign from positive to negative, and see if the resulting proposition might be applicable.

· 4 ·

Scissilics

Selective Inattention

The dominant principle of mindbrain function is recognition. Accordingly, the mindbrain operates not in aleatory stop-go-stop sequences. Instead, it operates as a perpetual monitor that matches incoming data against those which are already in storage. The first matching is simplex. It distinguishes background data that do not require further processing from foreground data that do. The second matching is multiplex. It compares foreground data with stored data systematized and coded in mindbrain maps and programs until, with split-second timing, their reciprocal matching locus is found. Their significance or meaning is thereupon recognized.

The threshold for background data that are given no relevancy is higher when asleep than awake, so that the sleeper in familiar surroundings is protected from being awakened. Being asleep is not, however, the same as being in hibernation, nor the same as being in deep anesthesia or coma. Some sensory stimuli do break through the threshold of recognition. Some, like the stirrings of a small infant, immediately alert the mother or whoever else is finely attuned to register them while asleep. Other sleepers, not so attuned, sleep on undisturbed.

Proprioceptive (Latin, *proprius*, one's own + *-ceptus*, take in) stimuli may also transcend the sleep-wake threshold and warn the sleeper against falling off the edge of the bed, for example, or of a full bladder that requires getting up to micturate. Instead of waking the sleeper, some proprioceptive stimuli, like those of impending orgasm, or of being cold and shivering, or of being overheated and sweating, may be incorporated into the contents of a dream. The contents of a dream may also incorporate distant stimuli like the wailing of a siren or an ultrasonic boom. The sound of a midnight railroad train, for example, became incorporated into the dream of a boy at the age of puberty. In the dream, his penis became a giant coupling rod that attached the cars to the locomotive. As the locomotive hauled the train toward the depot, he ejaculated.

Not only while asleep, but also while awake, selective attention and inattention are attributes of mindbrain function. The threshold level for stimulus recognition is, however, lowered while awake, and the scope of attention is greater. The degree of lowering is individually variable. Thus some students, far from being distracted by a television or radio program, say that they study better with it playing. They attend selectively to specific items only. By contrast, some scholars are unable to be selectively inattentive. Easily distracted by any sensory input, they require sound-proofed silence.

People who are easily distracted may become much less so when extremely fatigued. Attending a lecture or performance, they may listen and look, only to discover subsequently that nothing had sunk in, nothing was retained, and nothing could be recalled.

Selective inattention, not only while drowsy but also while wide awake, may be a blessing for those who possess it. But talk that goes in one ear and out the other is a curse for those who are not attended to. Being tuned out may not only thwart, but also enrage when, say in a marriage, only one of the two partner's is selectively inattentive, and literally does not register the other's complaint.

Selective inattention may be manifested as drifting off into daydreaming and reverie, a bane of schoolteachers and work supervisors. The ideation and imagery of the reverie may constitute, in effect, a plan for eluding whatever it is that constitutes a present monster in one's life, namely, monotony and punishments of the classroom; child abuse at home; sickness and death in the family; sexual deprivation; the urgency of unrequited love; athletic failure; social rejection; being physically unattractive, and so on.

Recognition Failure and Depersonalization

Loss of recognition once extant is a phenomenon in which sensory stimuli are not tuned out or selectively not attended to but, having been registered, are falsely recognized or misconstrued. A spouse or child, for example, may no longer be recognized, but falsely construed as a total stranger and intruder. A much publicized case is that of *The Man Who Mistook His Wife for a Hat* (Sacks, 1987). This man, a musician, had an extensive brain lesion that impaired recognition of visual stimuli belonging especially in the conceptual category of living and human. Hence, instead of reaching out for his hat, he took hold of his wife's head, and tried to lift it off as though to put it on his own head. Although he could no longer read music, performing and hearing music was not impaired, so that he was able to continue teaching as a professor of music.

Loss of recognition leaves an illusory phantasm in the place of whatever has been misconstrued. Phantasms belong in the general category of agnosia (Greek, *a*, no + *gnosis*, knowledge) and aphasia (Greek, *a*, no + *phasis*, speech) and are most readily demonstrated when they occur as a sequel to strategically localized damage to brain tissue from a stroke, tumor, or head injury.

The range of recognitional impairment may be either diffuse or quite specific. An example of specificity is prosopagnosia (Greek, *prosopon*, face + *a*, no + *gnosis*, knowledge), a variety of visual agnosia characterized by inability to recognize faces, either one's own face in a mirror, or the faces of other people. In the context of more extensive visual agnosia and dysgnosia, the man who mistook his wife for a hat experienced prosopagnosia also.

Loss of recognition applies not only to the face, but also to other organs or limbs of the body whose function has failed or been impaired as a concomitant of damage to brain tissue. Thus a patient with hemiplegia (Greek, *hemi*, half + *plege*, stroke), following a stroke that paralyzes one side of the body, may lose the capacity to recognize the arm or leg, or both, on that side. This loss of recognition goes under the name of anosognosia (Greek, *a*, no, + *nosos*, disease + *gnosis*, knowledge), meaning loss of ability to recognize or acknowledge one's own bodily impairment. A patient bedridden with hemiplegia and anosognosia may push the paralyzed leg from under the covers, saying that it belongs to a stranger or that it is a third, superfluous leg. If loss of vision also occurs, as sometimes it does, then the patient may fail to recognize blindness, and to explain it away as the result of being, for example, in a dark cellar.

In the absence of known damage to brain tissue, an organ or limb may fail to be rightfully recognized as belonging to one's own body. This type of failure belongs in the category of body-image fixation which may include a fixation on getting rid of the organ or limb. Self-mutilation, for example self-castration, may be resorted to. In some instances of self-mutilation there is pain, and some pain agnosia.

Recognition failure without identifiable brain-tissue damage may apply not to a single organ or limb, but globally to the entire body. Such a failure is experienced subjectively as depersonalization, known also in the vernacular as an out-of-body experience. In a state of depersonalization, one has the sense of being a spectator of one's own body, as if it were inhabited by someone else other than oneself. Should that someone else take on an independent identity, then the condition that exists is known as dissociated personality (see below).

Amnesia is the phenomenon of being unable to recall either a lengthy or brief part of one's past history. For example, the severe concussion of a head wound may leave a person unconscious or in a coma. Following recovery, and forever thereafter, that person may have no recall whatsoever of the incident or accident that produced the wound. The amnesia may be retroactive, so that there is no recall of what happened during the hours, or even days or weeks, immediately preceding the onset of unconsciousness.

Repeated blows to the head, as in prize fighting or constant assaultive abuse, may bring about a partial amnesia of the agnosic or aphasic type. Then the person has trouble in recalling and associating details of the past rather than failure to recall an entire episode or period of existence.

Recallable details as well as episodes from the past are retrieved from long-term storage in the mindbrain. They are screened and processed from recognition through short-term memory into long-term memory storage. On a daily basis there are myriads of short-term memory items that, like food menus for instance, have very short-lived usefulness and then are discarded. There is a possible short-term memory pathology in which too much is discarded, as in so-called amnesic shellfish poisoning from eating mussels contaminated with domoic acid (Culotta, 1992). With no new input, long-term memory becomes frozen in the past.

In syndromes of progressive cerebral degeneration, like Tay-Sachs disease in young children, and Alzheimer's disease in older adults, there is also progressive amnesia. One's past becomes progressively dissociated from one's present history, and one's present regresses until even the reflex habits of eating and continence become lost in amnesia for the image and function of the body.

Amnesic Dissociation

There is a syndrome of dissociative amnesia that has no special name and is not, so far as is currently ascertainable, concomitant of brain-tissue damage. In this syndrome, dissociative amnesia may be progressive or acute in onset. Characteristically, the recall of one's past history and identity become dissociated from one's present existence. The amnesia is not so pervasive as to require the person to begin life again as a newborn infant who must repeat all the stages and achievements of growing up. Rather the dissociation bans all specific information that might link one's present history with one's preamnesic past and betray one's original identity. Being amnesic in this way is somewhat like being a spy or fugitive operating under an alias. It requires not only failure of recall, but also selective inattention to any stimuli that might inadvertently resurrect the past.

Dissociative regression occurs when there is reversion, either transient or lasting, from a more mature to a less mature level or phase of development. Mostly there is no discernible concomitant regression of brain tissue. In young children, transient regression to more infantile ways is observable when developmental challenges become insurmountable. Thus a toddler unable to cope with being displaced by a newborn sibling may regress for a while to baby talk, nipple feeding from a bottle, and other babyish behavior.

Dissociative regression may occur at any age. It may apply to a specific segment of development, for example sexuoerotic development, or economic autonomy and independence. Age regression may apply to an entire stage of earlier development. Thus the complete juvenile stage is unmistakable when, in the syndrome of dissociated personality, one of the personalities represents a regression in entirety to boyhood or girlhood.

In dissociative regression, there is a discrepancy between the chronological age and the maturational age. The same discrepancy is evident also if maturation fails to progress and becomes prematurely fixated. Physically and mentally, developmental fixation is a characteristic of the already mentioned Kaspar Hauser syndrome (Chapter 2) before rescue. On the basis of symptomatology alone, and in the absence of a developmental record, fixation and regression may not be distinguishable.

Amnesic dissociation may apply to the performance of one of the body's sensory or sensorimotor systems. In popular parlance, it is said that one becomes blind with fury, as if the eyes or more precisely the visual brain has forgotten how to see. In being paralyzed with fear or rage, it is as if the limbs and motoric brain have forgotten how to move; and in being speechless with terror as if the vocal organs and language brain have forgotten how to talk.

The biomedical wisdom contained in these everyday sayings is that when the sensory or motor services of the body are aroused to a crisis level of fear, rage, sexuoeroticism, or other state of urgency that has no negotiable outlet, the outcome may be a complete functional failure or shut-down of one of those systems. The failure is manifested as, among other symptoms, paralysis, blindness, deafness, mutism, tactile anesthesia, and pain agnosia. The list might include also agraphia (writing blockage) and alexia (reading blockage), both of which may be highly specific. Thus a translator may have a writing block specific only to a foreign language; or a psychoanalyst in training may have a reading block specific only to the works of Freud and psychoanalysis; or a religious may have a reading block specific only to Scripture.

In the nineteenth century the name given to this kind of dissociative amnesia was conversion hysteria. In the era of World War I, battle-derived conversion hysteria was renamed shell shock; and in the era of World War II it was again renamed, this time as combat fatigue. After the Vietnam War it entered the official psychiatric nomenclature in *DSM-III* (*Diagnostic and Statistical Manual of Mental Disorders*, Third Edition, American Psychiatric Association, 1980) finally as post-traumatic stress disorder (PTSD) or syndrome.

Discovery of the phenomenon of conversion hysteria and its first publication by Breuer and Freud (1895/1955) was the beginning of psychoanalysis and of the theoretical formulation of the psychogenic cause of illness. Initially Freud attributed the symptomatology of conversion hysteria to child sexual abuse, including incest. In 1897, with a change to the theory of infantile sexuality and the Oedipus complex, conversion hysteria was attributed to infantile fantasy of incest. Today Oedipal theory has fallen from grace and child sexual abuse has returned as a dogma with which to explain conversion hysteria and other dissociative phenomena including dissociative personality.

Dissociative Personality

In the way that the mindbrain functions, some incoming information is coded as superfluous or suitable for brief-term storage only, and some as suitable for incorporating into the maps and programs that are already in the mindbrain library of long-term storage and retrieval. Mindbrain maps and programs are catalogued conceptually and systematically. One of the systems is that of bipotentiality or bipolarity (Chapter 3). There are, for example, age maps in reciprocal pairs. The maps for grandparentalism are matched by those of grandchildhood in infancy, prepuberty, puberty, and adolescence, each one of which is additionally gender-coded for male or female. Age and gender codes are also cross-coded on such criteria as kinship, occupation, education, social status, ethnicity, language, religion, morals, health, and whatever other categories may be of regional, communal or kinship significance.

There is a principle of conformity whereby people at large expect one another to grow up matching their progress from one developmental map or program to the next in a more or less predictable and orderly way. Thus the wild-oats map of adolescent invincibility gives way to the more settled married map, and the map of being a parent takes over from the map of being an offspring. Although changes are expected, even if they are of considerable magnitude, they are expected to be predictable. Predictability is equated with constancy, and the person is said to have a stable personality or, in the jargon of psychotherapy, to be well integrated.

Inconstancy signifies irregularities such as having an age map out of synchrony with chronological age, or a gender map at odds with one's genital and morphological sex; or having two moral maps, one piously religious, the other diabolically evil, and so on. Inconstancy signifies the dissociation of one map, or more than one, from its polar opposite. If they alternate, each appears to be a contradiction of the other.

Children know from an early age that dissonant maps are, in some instances, societally tolerated. Deceitful evasiveness is both morally reprehensible and lauded as shrewdness and acumen in business and politics. Taking the Fifth Amendment so as not to incriminate oneself is a solemn rite in the courtroom.

To at least a minor degree, everyone has the experience of alternating two dissonant maps. For example, the map for engaging in a ding-dong fight with one's partner or spouse may be disconnected in the time that it takes to answer the doorbell, whereupon the friendly welcome map takes over. This type of change is usually named a change of mood, not a change of personality. The more pervasive the degree of change, and the longer lasting, the greater the likelihood that it will be regarded as a change of personality.

The primary personality may be wholly dissociated, and be superseded by the new one. The other possibility is a partial dissociation, so that a residual of the primary personality coexists with a now subsidiary personality, neither of which alone is complete. Thus, in the case of male transvestophilia with two names, two wardrobes, and two personalities, the residual personality may be one in which stereotypic macho cruelty and treachery is ascendent, and the new subsidiary personality one in which stereotypic feminine simpering seductiveness is ascendant. Neither of the stereotypic extremes is able to exercise a leavening influence on the other, except perhaps partially when the macho dresses in women's lingerie so as to get an erection and copulate with his wife. The other possibility is that over a period of time a merger is effected and consolidated with a complete sex reassignment.

Another example of dual personality is that of a self-righteous adult television evangelist coexistent with that of the sinning adolescent patron of whores; or of the highly successful business executive coexistent with that of a masochistic victim of juvenile parental abuse. The famous example of dual personality in literature is that of R. L. Stevenson's Dr. Jekyll and Mr. Hyde.

Two or more personalities are distinguishable on the basis of such criteria and stereotypes as age, name, sex, race, speech, schooling, occupation, clothing, health, religion, morality, and social conformity.

After a lapse of half a century, multiple personality disorder (MPD) is in vogue again and is associated with sexual child abuse and the revival of early Freudian seduction theory. Historically, MPD has been closely associated with the theory and practice of hypnosis in psychotherapy, and with the concept of hypnotic suggestibility. One must differentiate, therefore, between evidence of two or more personalities in existence before the onset of any type of therapy, and evidence that appeared only during therapy. In view of the mindbrain's multiplicity of maps and programs, it is not surprising that some of them might be fused into a new subsidiary personality in response to therapy. It should be clearly labeled, however, not as inauthentic, but as an authentic artifact of therapy and given only limited credence, accordingly.

Although each of two or more dissociated personalities may have some degree of amnesia for the affairs of the other, there is some interchangeability and not a complete blockage of reciprocal recognition. The frequency and duration of the appearance of each is individually variable. In the diphasic alternation of dual personality, it is not atypical for the emergence of the subsidiary personality to coincide with manifestation of an altered state of consciousness, namely, a fugue state (Latin, *fugua*, flight).

Phenomenologically, a fugue state bears some resemblance to a trance or trance-like state, including an hypnotic trance, and to the trance-like state of a temporal-lobe, psychomotor epileptic seizure. A paraphilic fugue state is named for its occurrence in conjunction with episodes of paraphilic sexual behavior.

A fugue state may be precipitated by exposure to a toxic substance. One example is the state of hallucinatory mania, dangerous recklessness, and assaultive violence known as pathological alcoholism and also as a *mania à potu* (drinking mania). It is precipitated in those rare individuals who are excessively sensitive to even small quantities of alcohol. After a recovery period of sleep, there is complete amnesia for the episode.

Fugue states may be contingent on a prior history of brain injury. They may be activated or exacerbated by disruption of brain rhythms and/or neurochemistries as a sequel to sleep deprivation or other noxae of unremitting stress.

The role of rhythmicity in the maintenance of orderly mindbrain function has barely had its surface scratched in contemporary research, although its importance is indubitable. It is feasible to implicate rhythmicity of the blood supply to the brain as the flywheel of consciousness. There are unofficial operating room reports from the 1950s of an anesthesiological error in which, in two instances, a patient was totally immobilized by a neuromuscular blocking agent, but without being unconscious. Both could not signal that they were still conscious while undergoing open-heart surgery. They lost consciousness after being transferred to the heart-lung machine which pumped steadily, without a pulsating rhythm. After the machine was disconnected, consciousness returned.

Phobia

Whereas dissociation shuts out or excludes, phobia (Greek, *phobos*, fear) assiduously avoids. Should avoidance fail, the outcome is a state of anxiety which may escalate to a full-blown panic attack replete with respiratory, circulatory, digestive, excretory, and exocrine symptoms of an agitated autonomic nervous system.

Between some species phobic avoidance may be a matter of life and death that is phyletically in-built. Thus cats avoid dogs, chimpanzees flee from elephants, and human beings avoid tigers and potentially venomous things that creep and crawl, notably snakes and spiders. In these instances, avoidance is prudent and situational. That is to say, the phylism of avoidance of creepy, venomous things is dormant, except when the stimulus appears. Avoidance in a genuine phobia, by contrast, is persistent and incapacitating, even when the stimulus has permanently disappeared and exists only as an unremitting, potential threat.

In the professional literature, phobias are named etymologically according to the Greek or Latin name for what is feared, as in claustrophobia, the fear of closed spaces, and agoraphobia, fear of open spaces, and so on, with no fixed limit. Accurate naming of its phenomenon is the necessary first stage of any science, after which follows the search for regularities in their antecedents and origins. Regularities can be discovered only from the detailed studies of many clinical cases in each of which the overlay of details may be quite individualistically specific. Specificity is well exemplified in the following case of agoraphobia.

The phobia in this case kept the patient not only housebound, but also entrapped in the solitude of her upstairs room in the family home. She was unable to eat with family members at mealtimes, and so would prepare food for herself at night when they were asleep. She was unable to leave her room for essential health care at the hospital, except at times of emergency, and then only with special arrangements with an accompanying relative for private transportation and avoidance of public waiting rooms. She had neither explanation nor apology for her behavior, and neither the term nor concept of phobia. She had no joy from being agoraphobic, but even less joy from the terror of confronting the future without it. For fifteen years, she was completely unable to talk about it. Any attempt to converse about it evoked the silence of elective mutism. It was an unspeakable monster in her life.

Although the fine details are missing, the outline of the unspeakable monster could be found lurking in the details of the history recorded in the patient's medical chart. Born with ambiguous genitalia and initially declared to be a boy, the baby was soon redeclared to be a girl. The diagnosis was female pseudohermaphrodite with the syndrome of congenital virilizing adrenal hyperplasia (CVAH). The sex and name were not changed on the hospital chart, nor in the state office of vital statistics.

The mother was not convinced that her baby was no longer a son, but a daughter, especially in view of the evidence of a grossly hypertrophied clitoris. It looked exactly like a penis, but with a hypospadiac misplacement of the urinary orifice at its base. Since this baby was one of the first two ever to receive the newly discovered cortisol treatment for the CVAH syndrome, surgical feminization of the genitalia was delayed in the hope that hormonal treatment alone would shrink the enlarged clitoris.

In the meantime, the baby was tied by ankle and wrist constraints to a metabolic bed designed to collect twenty-four-hour urine specimens for hormonal analyses—a procedure that today would be prohibited as abusive. The clitoris did not shrink. Clitoridectomy was decided upon, but the child, now old enough for a simple preparatory explanation, was given no preparation.

When she was six, she warned her eight-year-old nephew, who was due for an opthamalogic examination, not to let her own doctor get hold of him, or he would cut off his "bunny," too. At around this same time, the child, left alone with her mother in an examining room, opened her chart to the section on medical photography showing her clitoris looking like a penis, and confronted her mother with lying. "Why," she asked, "do you tell me I never was a boy? I can see I was."

Having once been a boy became the unspeakable monster in this child's life. The monster would for several years keep a low profile until, suddenly, a precipitating event, itself unspeakable for many years, gave birth to a monstrous agoraphobia.

The precipitating event was the hate-filled gossip of a vindictive and locally ostracized next-door neighbor. This woman, seated on the front porch of her home on a street lined with row houses, proclaimed for all to hear that the patient was a sex freak who had been born a boy and changed to a girl. The patient herself heard this talk, and it was from this day onward that she was unable to emerge from her own home to be seen by any of her neighbors. Even after the gossiping woman moved away, the phobia continued. It resisted any plans for therapeutic intervention which entailed travel to and from home. It showed signs of remission only when, after many years it became necessary for the patient to confront the problem of a place to live after the imminent death of her aged parents.

In this particular case, as well as generically, one may speculate that agoraphobia has its phylogenetic origins in the phylism of troopbonding: There is safety in the intimacy of only the very small family or household troop. Danger lies beyond. In the present instance the danger that lay beyond included also the threat of pairbonding. A potential romantic partner, man or woman, would inevitably discover the genital abnormality and the horrific history of having been born with indeterminate sex.

Disengagement

One way to avoid a struggle is to become disengaged and quit. So also, one way of coping with an unspeakable monster in one's life is to become disengaged.

An inordinate degree of disengagement is manifested as catatonic stupor which entails nonresponsiveness to sensory stimuli accompanied by mutism and by waxy flexibility of the torso, neck, and limbs. They all remain motionless in whatever position they are set. Over an extended period of time, stupor may be interrupted by stereotyped gesturings or vocalizings, or by phases of agitation (catatonic excitement) and negativism.

Another way of becoming disengaged is by falling asleep. When danger threatens from cataclysm or catastrophe, there are some people who become agitated and sleepless. There are others who become fatigued and sleep through it. The longer a period of prior sleep deprivation, as in battle for instance, the greater the likelihood of falling asleep, despite the danger.

Daytime sleeping spells of sudden onset may be symptomatic of sleep apnea, a condition in which sleep is seriously interrupted by grossly irregular breathing and snoring. Sleeping spells of acute onset are also a primary symptom of the syndrome of narcolepsy, plus or minus cataplexy.

The brain dysfunction that produces the convulsions of a grand mal or epileptic seizure produces also the ensuing period of sleep. Brain dysfunction induced by insufficient cerebral blood flow, possibly in response to shock, may produce fainting (syncope) with its temporary suspension of consciousness. In Victorian times, swooning, feeling faint, and calling for the smelling salts was a fashionable way for a lady to feign moral shock or a headache, and so to become disengaged from an offensive situation.

The more worn down the defenses of the body by exhaustion or disease, the more frequent and longer the periods of sleep. The ultimate sequence may be to go to sleep and never wake up, or to pass from sleep to a comatose state and death. The transition from wakefulness to coma may, as in acute brain injury, be abrupt. The coma itself may be transient or very long lasting. When irreversible it is synonymous with brain death, in which case it becomes an unspeakable monster in the lives of surviving kin.

Death is the ultimate disengagement. For some people death means suicide, which may be the culminating expression of depression. Depression itself is a form of disengagement, often marked by a self-conviction of worthlessness. Profound depression may be unremitting, or it may be punctuated by periods of well-being which may or may not escalate to phrenetic euphoria and hyperactivity.

The attempt to attribute depression to a precipitating event or situation becomes an exercise in circularity, like trying to prove whether the chicken or the egg came first. On the one hand, if depression is of endogenous onset, then it may become retrospectively attributed to a prior tragedy. On the other hand, if depression is attributed to a present tragedy, then its precipitation may have been possible only in an individual rendered vulnerable by a brain already neurochemically predisposed to depression. In acute bereavement, the typical mourning response of depressive sadness and grief eventually resolves, except in those who are vulnerable to the persistence or recurrence of pathological depression.

The vulnerability factor in depression is, in some way yet to be fully ascertained, related to hormonal function. The relationship may be particularly to sex-hormonal cyclicity—witness the occurrence of menopausal depression, postpartum depression, and the mild depression that may be associated with premenstrual tension. Depression may possibly be related also to hormones in the birth-control pill, and the changes they bring about in the levels of sex-steroidal hormones circulating in the bloodstream.

The hormone-depression relationship is confounded by the possibility that hormonal dysfunction may be secondary to the stress of being depressed. The hypothalamic pituitary adrenocortical axis responds to stress by increasing the output of the hormone cortisol from the adrenocortices.

Survivors of those depressed people who have successfully suicided, impelled to find an explanation for the death and finding no signs of overt depression, may fall back on the idea of masked depression. Masked or unmasked, depression does not, however, apply to all suicides—not, for example, to ritual suicide, seppuku, in Japan to disengage oneself and family from official disgrace; nor to suicidal disengagement from a lingering, painful death from terminal cancer; nor to suicidal disengagement from what is for some young people the unbearable agony of unrequited love.

Disengagement from a personally insoluble life dilemma is the formula that all suicides share in common. The suicidal person has the experience of being entrapped in the dilemma of living not one's own life but someone else's prescription for it. Enforcement of the prescription is too overpowering to allow of escape, and the more so the younger one's age. The outcome is a sense of oppressive worthlessness in which identification of the aggressor is metamorphosed into identification with the aggressor. Then, according to the formula of "if you can't beat them, join them," you do it to yourself before they do it to you. In some instances there is a dreamlike quality to the formula, as though the ending will be to wake up, as from a dream, reincarnated; or to come back on stage for the curtain call at the end of the performance.

The person who might commit suicide lives every day, sometimes for many years, with detailed imagery and ideation of death reiterated to a degree seldom suspected by others. Suicide is a secret weapon for use against those from whom one will become disengaged. Thus stealthiness and cunning are among the defining characteristics of suicide. Part of its fatal attraction is not to initiate talk about it in advance. In counseling, therefore, one of the first maneuvers is to discuss the detail of the imagery and ideation of the impending suicide as explicitly as the patient rehearses it. The drama that unfolds may be minutely detailed, so that a single unplanned incident may abort the entire process. For example, in one case a woman was unable to plunge from a vertical cliff into the sea when she saw that her shoes had become covered in mud. She had not planned to die wearing dirty shoes.

In another case, unsurpassed academic achievement was, for a college student, no compensation for congenital testicular deficiency which rendered him the last male heir of his line permanently doomed to have no progeny and to a lifetime of hormonal replacement treatment. In fantasy, he planned the tableau of his final leap and the procession of his remains to a waiting ambulance. With all his papers neatly in order, and his alarm clock set for a seven a.m. suicide, he slept a sound night's sleep. Showered and dressed, he raised the blind, ready to open the window and leap. The yard beneath was blanketed with snow. He was immobilized. In his mental tableau, dying in snow was not included. He lived, the demon of suicide permanently exorcised.

Those whose first suicide attempt fails may try again a second or third time. But there are those for whom a near-miss serves the function of a reincarnation. They survive and live their allotted life span.

From an early age, children absorb the concept of reincarnation from television entertainments in which shootouts and killings are known not to be terminal. Juvenile and adolescent street killings, as well as suicides, may reflect the televised philosophy that death is an act in a drama that is not terminal.

Martyrdom and Debility

In colloquial usage, a martyr is not one who is put to death for the sake of a principle, but one who is a constant sufferer. The constantly suffering martyr does not abdicate a responsibility or disengage from a no-win situation or relationship, but stays with it, entrapped, and pays the price in saintly sacrifice, ill health, and loss of well-being. Being a martyr is not synonymous with being a masochist, despite careless usage to the contrary.

The master monsters that make martyrs of their victims, like poverty, war, and tyranny, are inexorable, remorseless, and implacable. When their victims are children, the stage is set for them to become self-sabotaging martyrs as adults. The devastating victimizations of childhood are impositions from which there is no escape, and for which there is no appeal, no redress, and no appeasement. Isolation, deprivation, starvation, humiliation, threat, brainwashing, cruelty and torture are such impositions. Victimization by those like parents, guardians, or mentors, who should offer one the only hope of rescue and protection, is the most devastating of all.

Paradoxical though it may seem, one of the characteristics of martyrdom is the complementarity of folly (*folie complémentaire*). That is to say, the martyr may become affiliatively bonded with the oppressor and become dependent on returning for more oppression. Thus abused children return to their abusing parents, prisoners to their jailers, and spouses to their partners. An often-seen example is that of an oppressed and exploited spouse who remains bonded, in the role of the persecuted martyr, to an alcohol or drug-addicted wife or husband. In much the same way, in the Stockholm syndrome, so-called, a kidnap victim becomes bonded to the kidnapper (Money, 1986a).

As their grievances mount, martyrs become grievance collectors. They absorb their suffering which, concealed at first, eventually undermines their own health and well-being until, as the weakest link in the chain yields, health is impaired.

The symptoms that appear, despite their diversity, all share in common the characteristic of being opportunistic. That is to say, they take advantage of the opportunity provided by impairment of the body's resistance and defenses against them. In some instances, they may be attributable to a viral or bacterial infection, or to an allergic pathogen. In other instances, they may be related to a dysfunctional predisposition, possibly genetic, within the circulatory, pulmonary, endocrine, immunological, excretory, or other organ system. In still other instances, they may be symptoms, like tension headache or lower back pain, that cannot presently be attributed to any specific etiology other than to be more or less stress-related.

In the psychiatric and psychoanalytic nomenclature, it was formerly more fashionable than it is today to name stress-related disorders psychosomatic. The strong implication was that somatic symptoms were psychogenically originated. Today the terminology more likely to be used is somatization or somatoform disorder, and the implication is more likely to be that somatic symptoms are exacerbated but not originated psychogenically.

In the language of everyday use, there are phrases and sayings that indicate age-old understanding of health and stress. Their significance is readily comprehended by everyday people who know at first hand about having a sinking feeling, or butterflies in the stomach, about swallowing resentment, and being made sick to the stomach with disgust. They have their hair stand on end with fright. They get annoyed with others who give them a headache, a pain in the arse or a pain in the neck, or who get under their skin. They understand the infidelity of someone with the seven-year itch. Their faces turn as red as a beet with embarrassment, or as white as a sheet with terror. They have the wind knocked out of their sails by an unexpected confrontation, and are held breathless with awe and spellbound with wonder. They get hot under the collar when falsely accused, and feel their blood pressure rise. Their hearts pound like a sledgehammer when they make a narrow escape.

There are some cases in which one of these sayings applies to the symptoms of an illness of martyrdom. The saying may then be used as a way of explaining, without being offensive, the possible relationship of the symptoms to the stimulus that evoked them. One example is that of a high-steel construction worker who was a martyr to the demands of a dangerous job and family responsibilities. His symptoms were severe abdominal pain and digestive upset of unexplained origin.

Having been told that his symptoms were emotional in nature, he felt humiliated that anyone would consider his complaint "imaginary and all in his mind," and worse still that, at age forty, he would be declared a failure by being advised to make a complete change of occupation. Without working as a high-construction welder, he argued, he would no longer be able to support his family. He resolved not to be the victim of an "imaginary illness," and became a martyr for yet another year of suffering.

Thereupon, with new-found understanding of the meaning of the sinking feeling and the butterflies, he conjectured a relationship between his symptoms and his work. A terrifying loss of nerve had overtaken him as he hung suspended in precarious positions, welding the steel girders of a bridge from which several workers had fallen to their deaths. He did not find it humiliating to grant that a human being may take risks and tempt fate for a limited period in youth, but not indefinitely. With the support of his family, and having reconciled himself to a cut in pay without loss of manhood, he changed to ground-level work. With the change, he experienced a remission of symptoms.

Another category of symptoms, namely, those in which the infirmity that afflicts its victim simultaneously protests against the victimizer, is also recognized in everyday sayings and phrases. They include, for example, being sick with envy; being scared shitless; being as tight as a hen's behind; having the piss frightened out of oneself; being piss-shy in public; and telling someone to fuck off or go fuck yourself.

These colloquial sayings recognize disorders that involve desynchronization of a functional coalition of the autonomic and the central nervous systems. These two systems, instead of working together, work out of synchrony in response to either a persistent or an acute crisis in the patient's life. From the patient's vantage point, the existence of the monster responsible for the crisis cannot be formulated in words. It exists incognito.

The presenting symptoms in disorders of this type include the following: either inability to swallow food or, having swallowed it, vomiting; either urinary sphincter spasm with inability to release urine, or urinary incontinence as in enuresis; either constipation or bowel incontinence as in encopresis; and various inadequacies of sexuoerotical interaction with a partner, as in impotence, ejaculatio precox, vaginisimus, and anorgasmia. In some though not all instances, the symptoms represent a regression from a more mature to a less mature level of bodily function.

The coalition of the two nervous systems represented in these disorders generates the paradox that the various bodily malfunctions are simultaneously under the control and not under the control of the voluntary musculature, as for example in encopresis and enuresis. These two disorders follow a general principle, namely, that the bodily malfunctions do not readily remit, and the symptoms are not readily ameliorated by either pharmacologic or behavioral intervention, provided the monster that generates them continues to exist unabated.

· 5 ·

Pragmatics

Atonement: Self-Mutilation and Imposture

Since the dawn of recorded history, and undoubtedly before that, human beings have construed the tribulations of war, pestilence, famine, and other sources of suffering as retribution for their offenses against supernatural beings with whom they peopled their universe. To appease these supernaturals, and to atone for their offenses, they performed penances and made sacrifices.

There are remnants of the rite of sacrifice still evident today in such practices as deforming or mutilating various parts or organs of the body, as in circumcising the penis, infibulating the vulva, piercing the flesh, and scarifying or tattooing the skin.

The three-part proposition of offending a spirit, personally suffering the spirit's retribution, and making amends sacrificially is an ideological formula that, insofar as it can be applied in many different contexts, is called a paradigm. A paradigm of extremely ancient vintage is a paleodigm. Paleodigms as ideological formulas are incorporated into sacred narratives, folklore, and parables and rhymes recited to children. Thus, from infancy onward, they become integrated into the propositional functioning of mindbrain. Like the principles of grammar and syntax, they function incognito, without having to be explicitly recognized or attended to.

The paleodigm of sacrifice when applied to appeasement of an unspeakable monster in one's life is expressed in one of its manifestations as self-mutilation. The self-mutilator tells of experiencing unexplained foreboding and apprehension that builds to a climax that can be relieved only by an act of self-mutilation. The climax may occur while the person is awake and unable to concentrate on anything else, or it may occur as a nightmare while asleep. The act of self-mutilation is followed by an uncanny state of relief and peacefulness. The type of self-mutilation is individually specific rather than indiscriminate. The varieties include: cutting, piercing, burning, or flagellating the flesh; banging the head; amputating a digit or limb;

excising a genital or other structure; and inserting a noxious object into a bodily orifice.

There is a rare syndrome that offers future researchers a glimpse of where to look for the vulnerability factor that predisposes some people more than others to self-mutilation. It is the Lesch-Nyhan syndrome which, being an X-linked recessive disorder, occurs in boys. It is marked by a depletion or absence of HPRT (hypoxanthine-phosphoribosyl-transferase) and a consequent excess of uric acid. Although neuromuscular dysfunction resembling cerebral palsy is severely disabling, the most striking disability is self-mutilation which begins in infancy with biting and grossly destroying the lips and fingers. According to parents' observations, self-mutilatory practice increases under stress (Anderson et al., 1992). Although self-mutilation may be accompanied by painful screams, it does not stop except by the application of restraints.

Self-mutilation may be performed or exhibited in public as a religious act of penance, as a rite of initiation into a cult, gang, or secret society, or as a ceremonial paraphilic scenario. Although self-mutilation is not denied as a personal pathology, information about its existence is withheld as much as possible from those whose response might be judgmental and chastising. By contrast, in the syndrome named after the fictional Baron von Munchausen, renowned in German literature as a teller of tall tales, secrecy, deceit, and prevarication about self-mutilation and the self-induction of symptoms is pathognomic. In Munchausen syndrome by proxy, there is secrecy, deceit, and prevarication about mutilating or inducing symptoms in someone too small or feeble to resist or escape—as when the proxy is a parent's own child.

People with Munchausen syndrome of either variety are medical impostors. They may be medically naive, as when a mother attributes a child's cuts, bruises, and bone fractures to clumsiness, falling, and collisions despite unequivocal evidence to the contrary. Impostors may also be medically sophisticated to the extent of being able to misuse pharmacological or other substances to produce symptoms of an apparently mysterious and undiagnosable disease. Thus it requires some medical sophistication first to know how to obtain a supply of, say, insulin and insulin-injection needles, and then to know that secret self-injections of insulin will induce a state of insulin shock (circulatory insufficiency with tremor, sweating, giddiness, double vision, convulsion, and collapse) that cannot be explained without knowledge of the exogenous source of the hormone. Likewise, it requires some medical sophistication to know that powdered aspirin secretly sprinkled under the eyelid everyday will produce undiagnosable corneal ulceration and eventual loss of the eye.

Medical impostors suffer their symptoms, or those of their proxy, with angelic patience and stoicism in cooperation with their doctors and nurses until they recognize that their impostoring is under suspicion. Thereupon they disappear never to return. Sooner or later, they turn up at another clinic or hospital, and the cycle is repeated. Thus there is rarely an opportunity to ascertain what manner of monster is being appeased by the sacrifice of their health and well-being.

Among the exceptions, one is the case of a girl in late adolescence. She had been under long-term follow-up with a diagnosis of Cushing syndrome which became progressively more serious. She had a history of prolonged endocrine admissions during which she had been considered a model patient. When signs of impostoring were uncovered, it was therefore with much professional consternation. These signs were unexplained elevations of temperature that proved to be the product of heating the thermometer on the bedside radio or in warm coffee; and unexplained bruises on the legs that proved to be the product of self-beating.

The girl's admission at this time had been in preparation for what she knew to be a life-and-death measure, namely, complete surgical removal of her malfunctioning adrenocortical glands, and subsequent daily dependence on treatment with the life-sustaining hormone cortisol. It was not known at the time that, during brief leaves of absence from the hospital, the girl's grandmother took her to the cemetery where her mother had been recently buried after an agonizing death from cancer. At the mother's graveside, the two cried and prayed for the girl's deliverance from death. Death was the monster to be appeased and also, through the tricks of impostoring, possibly held at bay. Although it was life-threatening not to undergo surgery, it was perhaps even more life-threatening to do so. That is what the girl heard from her grandmother. From her doctors she heard the opposite.

All impostoring is by its very nature contingent upon having someone who is deceived. In the imposture of Munchausen syndrome, deception is directed toward outmaneuvering health-care professionals, especially physicians, so that they order diagnostic tests, medications, and treatments, including surgery that the impostor, acting alone, could not obtain. It is not essential, however, for a patient to be an impostor so as to obtain services that would not otherwise be obtainable. It may simply be sufficient for the patient to have a talent for manipulating the responses of other people in accordance with the patient's own agenda.

The medical manipulator exalts one professional at the expense of another and, if successful in appealing to his Hippocratic vanity, beseeches deliverance from the consequences of prior neglect, negligence, or professional incompetence. In the case of the manipulative polysurgery patient, after each surgical intervention there are either residual or new symptoms. With or without surgery, as prescriptions are multiplied, symptoms that are pharmacologic side effects become confused with those that are not. Infatuation with patienthood conceals the unspeakable monster in the medical manipulator's existence. The longer the concealment is maintained, the longer the infatuation continues, unless it becomes terminal.

Serial surgery is in some cases an attempt to revise the body so that it matches the idealized body image (Chapter 11). For instance, the idealized body image of a morphologically normal male was that of a hermaphrodite with ambiguous genitalia and an otherwise male morphology (Money and De Priest, 1976). He became a self-taught amateur urological surgeon so that he could, with self-surgery, construct an opening in his urethra at the penoscrotal junction. With dilation, he hoped to enlarge the bulbous urethra into a substitute vagina. He had had no alternative to self-surgery, he claimed, as the urologist who had promised to help him had been killed in a car crash. He succeeded in creating an artificial vaginal cavity, but it was too tight and would not yield to dilation so as to be able to accommodate the full length of a "host penis." More self-surgery was thwarted as the necessary surgical supplies could not be obtained, and the quest for professional help failed. He died without having proved his theory that the orgasm from the bulbous urethra was a lost secret of the alchemists.

Forfeiture: Fasting and Failure

A counterpart to the paleodigm of sacrifice is the paleodigm of forfeiture, that is, of placating an offended spirit by giving up something, or denying oneself something, especially a pleasure of the flesh. Relinquishing food or fasting has a long history as a method of atonement and spiritual purification.

Fasting may be also a technique of nonviolent political protest. It is also part of a dietetic method for weight reduction, so as to match the body morphology with a fashionable idealized body image. Girls as young as five or six years of age, identifying with a mother who is a fashion model or ballet dancer, have been known to adhere to a diet of self-imposed, partial fasting (Money, 1994).

Self-imposed fasting not scheduled as a political protest nor as a fashion statement that proceeds to a state of emaciation and death is diagnostically identified as anorexia (Greek, *anorexia*, want of appetite) nervosa. As in all cases of severe starvation, in anorexia nervosa there are changes in hormonal function, particularly with respect to the hypothalamic and pituitary regulation of adrenocortical and gonadal hormones. In females, menstrual cyclicity ceases, in males erection and ejaculation diminish or cease, and in both sexes sexual arousal goes on hold. Through lack of decisive evidence, the argument as to whether changes in brain chemistries precede fasting, or vice versa, remains circular.

Restriction of nutritional input may, in anorexia nervosa, be effected not only by fasting but also by vomiting that is self-induced either reflexly, or by poking fingers down the throat. Intravenous feeding, resorted to as a life-saving necessity, may be thwarted, as the patient may turn off the valve or otherwise disengage the tube.

Anorexia nervosa is more prevalent among adolescents and young adults than older people, and among females more than males. In both sexes, although the prestarvation appearance is sexually attractive and even seductive, behind the appearance lies the renunciation of sexuality and fasting to grow pure. The personal sexuoerotic biography is a forbidden topic of discussion. Therein lies the unspeakable monster, and the spiritual offense which is atoned for through fasting.

The fasting of anorexia nervosa may be punctuated by episodes of bulimia (Greek, *bous*, ox + *limos*, hunger) or binge eating. Metaphorically, the saint of renunciation loses ground to the sinner of indulgence. Here is yet another example of the periodicity that exists in the dissociative phenomenon of dual personality (Chapter 3). Bulimic binge eating may occur also in people who are consistently overweight.

Anorexia in its literal sense of lack of appetite has sometimes been applied to sexual appetite. Sexual anorexia is popularly referred to as lack of sexual desire. Those who have never experienced sexual desire have no standard of comparison against which to make a complaint. Those who do complain are therefore complaining about a change from more to less which, in some cases, signifies a forfeiture. The monster who is placated by a forfeiture of sexual desire maybe one who, in the form of, say, a heart attack, threatens death. The threat may turn off sexual desire not only in the patient, but in the spouse also.

Sexual anorexia may placate not only the monster of death but also a monster that is itself sexual, with origins in an earlier period of the sexually anorectic person's life. The possibilities include exposure to sexual cruelty, tyranny, punishment, or humiliation, or to a traumatic sexual incident, injury, surgical procedure, or other sexually noxious experience.

Sexual forfeiture may be partial rather than complete—a forfeiture of genital functioning, say, as in vaginal-penetration phobia, or phobia of putting the penis in the vagina. Forfeiture may also be manifested as a vow of sexual abstinence. Abstinence is more inclusive than celibacy, which entails only the forfeiture of marriage.

Nonsexual forfeitures include, for example, forfeiture of career. Thus an aspiring young actor goes drunk to an audition and blows his chance for a leading role. An exemplary young military officer inexplicably goes AWOL and destroys the possibility of an otherwise certain promotion. A high-ranking financial officer crash lands in prison after dabbling in crooked transactions. A famous sports star already on probation returns to using drugs and is permanently banned from all future competition. A brilliant graduate student procrastinates ad nauseam until he misses the deadline for submitting his dissertation, and so forfeits his doctoral degree forever.

Academic forfeiture may take the form of deterioration to an earlier level of achievement. For example, a medical student who was destined to become a professor began, much to the consternation of his teachers, writing dysgraphic clinical reports laden with misspellings and incomprehensible passages. It was touch and go as to whether he would be permitted to graduate. The deterioration reversed, however, when the messy, political, religious, monetary, familial, and marital complexity of a pathologically love-stricken, limerent attachment was finally resolved. That resolution in turn resolved the threat that impotence would persist as a deterioration of virility.

Deterioration from a higher to a lower level of academic achievement may be observed in children diagnostically labeled with learning disability or one of its specific manifestations, e.g., dyslexia (which is Greek for "can't read"). There is, for example, the case of a boy whose reading deteriorated to the preprimer level and was mostly gibberish on days when his mother brought him to reading clinic, whereas on other occasions it became congruent with his age and grade. Entangled in divorce and custody recriminations, he was one of three siblings (one a girl) who had dyslexia and were drawn into the mother's gravitational field. The fourth sibling, a brother, was in the father's field. Like his father he did not have dyslexia and was not learning-retarded like his siblings. The father was a financier, and the mother a partly trained specialist in learning disability.

In a reading clinic, it is not uncommon to find that cases of reading disability are more accurately identified as cases of reversible academic deterioration. Thus, in one summer, a boy of eleven in a remedial reading program with a tutor of whom his mother approved progressed from preprimer to third-grade level. The next summer exactly the same thing happened. In the intervening months, at a school where the mother was a constantly antagonistic parent, his reading level regressed to preprimer, at which level it persisted. It failed to improve when his mother removed him from school and taught him at home. He was embroiled in a network of family multipathology. The parents feuded endlessly in a bitter and acrimonious sexual dispute, with the father as the underdog.

Parental sexual incompatibility of severe and pathological degree turns up with uncanny frequency in the families of children with reversible academic deterioration. The same might very well apply in cases of academic underachievement in which the evidence of reversible deterioration has been neither observed nor searched for. More often than is given credence, although not invariably, a sexual monster lurks in the lives of the parents of underachieving children and dropouts.

A different type of relationship between academic nonachievement and sex was exemplified transculturally thirty years ago among Aboriginal Australian children who lived in a newly established settlement at Elcho Island, on the north central coast of Arnhem Land, in Australia's Northern Territory. They were children of the first generation to come in from walkabout in the bush. Their ancient customs forbade intermarriage between various apposing totemic clans, so that boys from one of these clans and girls from another were forbidden to fraternize or talk to one another. In the school classroom, seating was allocated alphabetically, so that boys and girls who should avoid one another were placed in close proximity. In obedience to the avoidancy taboo, they hung their heads in shame, unable to pay attention and unable to learn.

Forfeiture of achievement may be a manifestation of self-sabotage attributable to the so-called guilt of success—the guilt of surpassing one's forebears, or rising above them, of being accused of making them feel inferior, and, if they have died, of not having settled the unfinished business of emancipation before it was too late. Forfeiture of achievement also serves to postpone the obligations and duties incumbent upon one who has already achieved.

Forfeiture may also take the form of arbitrarily and capriciously divesting oneself of one's possessions, property, or wealth. Divestiture may be accomplished by having too many hangers-on, by entering into ill-advised partnerships, or by entrusting one's earnings or fortune to reputed impostors. In one case, a young woman was on the verge of signing away her inheritance to a relative stranger, ostensibly so that she could start her life afresh, completely alone and independent. Her explanation was that the money she had inherited was, at least in part, tainted. This explanation overlooked two other points of biographical significance. One was that her mother overtly attributed her own disastrous and irreversible disablement to her pregnancy when this child was in her womb. The other was that the daughter had been born with the androgen-insensitive form of internally concealed intersexuality and infertility that, despite her stunning appearance as a woman, sabotaged her sense of self-worth. The monster to be placated by divestiture of her financial worth was the monster of self-worthlessness.

Reiteration: Rituals and Tics

Like the paleodigms of atonement and forfeiture, there is a third one for which the human species has an age-old memory. It is the paradigm of reiteration, according to which an offended spirit can be placated by the reiteration of rituals and chants.

Repetitiousness preserves that which is repeated. Young children delight in hearing the same rhymes and tales told and retold, and in recognizing and repeating the words themselves. Repetition is the fish trap of memory. That which it captures it preserves intact, resistant to mutation. Ancient Polynesians kept their genealogies intact because students who failed to recite them error-free did not graduate to the priesthood and might even forfeit their lives instead.

One of the errors of preservation is perseveration, as in giving to the second of two unrelated questions the same answer given to the first. In mental testing, when perseveration is inappropriate for age and educational history, it is taken as a sign of intellectual pathology.

Another pathology of preservation is overscrupulous and pedantic repetition of the same words or movements again and again. The person is obsessively and compulsively unable to desist, and violently distraught by any attempted interference.

Obsessively repeated behavior varies in complexity and elaborateness. One child's bedtime scenario entailed checking under the bed three times, times three, times three ($3 \times 3 \times 3$), then checking within the clothes closet $3 \times 3 \times 3$, and behind the bedroom door, $3 \times 3 \times 3$—all of this not only once but $3 \times 3 \times 3$. Who did the checking? A young girl who at the time had recently returned home after three years of isolation in a glass-walled, ostensibly germ-free hospital cubicle, in accordance with now-outmoded pediatric practice. Whom did she suspect? She had no answer. Her monster was, by inference, an unspeakable amalgam of the threat of death from kidney disease, if she stayed out of the isolation cubicle, and a threat of being sent back into the cubicle if she became germ-infected in her own home. She could not sleep without the ritual reassurance that the monster would remain absent for at least one more night.

Obsessive rituals vary not only in their elaborateness, but also in their duration, frequency, and interference with daily living. A ritual to avoid touching coins and dollar bills that might have been contaminated while in the possession of unknown strangers required a young professional man to accept change with abhorrence and toss it rapidly into a carrying bag or onto the back seat of his car, and to leave it there. This obsessive ritual ruled out a career in banking and merchandising, his family's business, but not in law, medicine, or religion. By contrast, a compulsive hand-washing obsession that is activated three or four times hourly interferes with any career. It is pathologically dangerous to the skin as well.

Compulsive washing may apply not only to the hands or other parts of the body, but also to utensils, furnishings, and household linens. Instead of washing, the obsession may be with cleaning and dusting. One woman's obsession compelled her to follow behind guests as they entered the house, brushing their footsteps with a feather duster.

The monster that lurks behind anticontamination rituals is quite likely to be sexually derived, perhaps from a juvenile history of tyrannous and cruel punishment or humiliation for masturbation or sexual rehearsal play.

The less elaborate an obsessively repeated act, the more likely is it to be known as an automatism. Thumb sucking is an example, and so is biting the fingernails and cuticles. Other examples are: twisting and plucking the hair so as to leave a bald patch (trichotillomania); stroking the beard; rubbing the eyes or lips; pulling or playing with the fingers; wagging the foot;

smoothing the clothing; adjusting the crotch; straightening the neck tie, and so on.

From an ethological point of view, many automatisms are adaptions of an innate releasing mechanism at work in the absence of the key stimulus or sensory cue that normally is necessary for its release. For example, twisting or pulling the hair and bunching it under the nostrils is a form of nuzzling, just as an infant nuzzles against the breast. The releaser stimulus of someone to nuzzle up to is, however, missing.

Tactile automatisms and hand rituals are common symptoms of the syndrome of infantile autism. So also are rocking and twirling automatisms that provide proprioceptive self-stimulation. Autistic infants recoil from grooming, so that their history of insufficient grooming may be attributed to their disease. By contrast, developmental deficiency, as in the Kaspar Hauser syndrome of abuse dwarfism (Chapter 2), is induced at least in part by deprivation of grooming as an outcome of either parental or institutional neglect and sensory isolation. Children with this syndrome also manifest tactile automatisms, hand rituals, and rocking. The same symptoms appear also in monkeys reared experimentally in social isolation. The monkeys also manifest self-mutilatory picking, biting, and scratching.

As simplified as the motions of an automatism are, those of a tic are even more so. A tic is a rapid and repetitious twitching of a small group of muscles. The jerky movements, even though complex, do not belong to a prolonged coordinated plan of behavior, but are autonomous and divorced from the releasing stimuli to which they might originally have been an appropriate response. Jerky motoric tics are named choreic (Greek, *choreia*, dance) when they are symptoms of neurological impairment in various syndromes such as Sydenham's chorea and Huntington's chorea. Slower, writhing movements are characterized as athetoid or choreiform.

Motoric tics that are not choreic include eyebrow flicking; eyelid batting; grimacing, sneering, and grinning; sniffing and snorting; teeth baring; lip licking; tongue darting; chewing; and throat clearing.

In addition to motoric tics, there are also vocal tics. A vocal tic may be simply a monotone, like a murmur of assent, ums, ers, or and-ers, obsessively repeated; or it may be the stutterer's reiteration of the initial consonant, syllable, word, or words, of a sentence the completion of which is obsessively delayed. A vocal tic may be also an incessantly repeated vocalism that punctuates one's conversation as an irrelevant interjection, such as the questions keh? (for okay) or y'know (for you know) or you know what I mean?; the exclamations wow! or wow man!; and the claimants like, like I said, actually, in fact, or as a matter of fact.

Vocal tics are pathognomonic of Tourette syndrome. They are heard as plosive barks, yelps, or grunts, unexpectedly and in public places, or as declamatory strings of words, publicly censored as being too profane or obscene.

With evidence such as the symptomatology of Tourette syndrome, there has in recent years been a reconsideration of the old issue of an organic versus a psychogenic etiology of obsessive-compulsive disorder. Here as elsewhere, today's most likely formula is that there is a primary vulnerability and a secondary triggering factor. This formula is illustrated in a case of complex psychopathology of which one symptom was a facial tic, namely, a sniffing grimace that bared the top incisors like those of a rabbit. Another symptom was a vocal tic, namely, a noise like the squawk of a chicken. Eventually, in this case, the patient was able to explain the grimace as an obsessional gesture that betrayed her humiliation at having decayed, broken, and discolored teeth and having also too powerful a dental phobia to get them attended to. The squawk was derived from a childhood memory of her mother in the chicken yard, capturing a fowl, and wringing its neck. This memory coalesced in adulthood into a nightmare and horror fantasy in which she herself became the chicken being chased for the cooking pot. After some years, both tics disappeared not in isolation, but along with the other symptoms of the illness as it went into remission.

The principle of interplay between a vulnerability factor and a triggering stimulus applies also to stuttering. Thus a person who stutters in a face-to-face conversation may not do so when talking on the telephone, singing, or as an attorney arguing a case in court. The situational contingency between the presence and absence of stuttering is illustrated in the developmental history of the hermaphroditic patient (Chapter 4) with severe agoraphobia. This girl lived in a household that included a nephew, an anatomically normal male, two years older than herself. He had a severe stutter until, at age eight, it abruptly disappeared. More precisely, it was transferred to his niece whose speech until then had been clear. At this age she showed her mother the pictures of her penoclitoris in the photography section of her medical chart, wanting to know why people denied that she had once been a boy. Had she remained as she once was, she would have been a boy like her nephew, who stuttered. By the magic of transfer, gaining a stutter might also have led to regaining a penis—and possibly to his losing the one he had, witness her warning him to avoid her own doctor lest he take off his "bunny" as he had taken off her own. The monster in this girl's life was the monster of a history of ambiguous sex and all that it had entailed. When the magic of stuttering failed to return her to boyhood, her speech became fluent again, and remained so during forty years of follow-up.

Retention: Pedantry, Hoarding, and Stealing

According to the retention paleodigm, it is possible to appease an offended spirit and to obtain a favor or concession provided one has retained and conserved a venerated relic to which is attributed the power of intercession.

In orthodox psychoanalytic doctrine, the so-called anal-retentive type of personality is characterized by obstinacy, orderliness, pedantry, frugality, and hoarding that is ostensibly derived from the anal stage of infantile psychosexual development. Regardless of their derivation, these characteristics are not, per se, pathological, though in excess they become so. In persons responsible for collecting and preserving books and artifacts in tombs and temples, libraries and museums, they have been prerequisite to the development of our civilization. Without perfectionism in collecting, systematizing, and preserving data, there would be no science.

When orderliness and tidiness become pathological they are manifested as obsessional pedantry. Then the ordering, saving, and retrieving of peripheral minutiae and trivialities far surpass the attention given to perfecting the main assignment. In some students this obsessive pedantry becomes "library disease"—an unending search for just one more publication, the one in which the holy grail may, at last, be found. Alas! it is not found, and the assignment is never completed. Pedantry and perfectionism are, although related, far from identical. In many tasks and situations, the slightest deviation from perfection spells failure and, maybe, catastrophic disaster. Pedantry is itself an imperfection, and is incompatible with success.

Tidiness and orderliness may take the form of ritualistic and obsessional retention and maintenance of the status quo. Thus, at every meal time, a bereaved mother would set a place at the table for years and years after the disappearance and death of her son. Thus also, in a case of epilepsy combined with pedophilia, having everything in its place at home was so great and obsession for an adult son that an ash tray even an inch out of its proper alignment would precipitate a ranting and raving temper tantrum. Children and adults with a history of childhood autism are among those who are exceptionally dependent on the retention of sameness and predictability of things in space and events in time.

Across species, retentiveness is varied in its expression. Ants, termites, bees, and wasps are fabled for their industrious hoarding of food. Birds of some species are orderly and tidy in building nests. In Australia and New Guinea, male bower birds build not nests but courtship bowers by arranging an arcade of twigs along a runway. The satin bower bird paints the twigs with a mixture of charcoal and saliva, and decorates his bower with blue objects and flowers. The spotted bower bird covers a play area at each end of the arcade with pebbles, bones, and other small objects. The bird plays in his bower throughout the year, prancing and tossing items from his collection, sometimes alone, sometimes with company. In late winter and early spring a female is attracted to a male in a bower, and before her he performs courtship rituals in his playhouse. In New Zealand, the flightless weka collects miscellaneous shiny things that unsuspecting picnickers may leave unguarded, and adds them to its secret cache of pebbles and other odds and ends.

Among mammals, pack rats leave a miscellany of objects as well as nesting and food materials in their underground middens. Squirrels hoard winter food supplies. Hibernating species like bears hoard nutriment in the form of body fat. Hamsters have cheek pouches for temporary food storage. Seasonal food hoarding may well be one phyletic origin of human retention as manifested in hoarding, stealing, and pedantry. Building nests and shelters may be another. Using objects and territories for various forms of display may be yet another.

There is no fixed criterion as to when collecting and hoarding become pathological in human beings. There is also no specific name for pathological collecting and hoarding, and no categorization on the basis of the type of material or object hoarded. One type of hoarded material is monetary, in the form of bullion, coins, or bank notes. While hoarding a fortune, the pathological hoarder lives a frugal, miserly, self-depriving life, perhaps only to have thieves steal the hoard, or to have it discovered only posthumously.

Another type of hoarded material is domestic garbage, debris collected from the streets, outdated newspapers and magazines, and detritus that most people do not keep. The pathological hoarder saves them all until they may literally usurp all living space. For compulsive shoppers, merchandise may take the place of trash—a home-choking hoard of anything and everything purchased solely on the basis of its availability or having been a bargain. Large or small, the bargains are stashed unopened in every available space from floor to ceiling. One of the characteristics of hoarding of this type is that it is unsystematic, unclassified, and unlabeled, so that retrieval of specific items is not possible.

Another type of hoarding pertains to small animals, mostly stray cats or dogs, that are rescued and housed, as many as twenty to a hundred together, in an inner-city apartment, without proper hygienic or health care, and subject to epidemic diseases (Worth and Beck, 1981). The carcasses of those that die may not be discarded. In one case, when her cats had died, an elderly woman eviscerated them, dried them on the fire escape, and, calling them "cat boards," hoarded them in cupboards. In another case, a man hoarded canine carcasses in the walls of his house. Tied into a chair in one room was the carcass of his missing brother. It had been there for about six months. In a third case, a woman conjectured that, having not coped well with her own adoption, she was attempting to do so by adopting animals. Usually, however, the monster being appeased by hoarding animals remains unconjectured and unknown.

Hoarding may be a correlate of paraphilia, as in the case of a sadomasochistic law student who bragged about his hoard of bathroom supplies, soap, and household cleaning products. He also bragged about hiring unsuspecting young prostitutes, subjecting them to brutal sadistic practices, and then cleaning up the blood and filth.

Hoarding is a frequent correlate of paraphilia. For example, a pedophile might keep a self-incriminating list of names, addresses, descriptions, and photographs of all the partners with whom he has achieved an orgasm. He might maintain also a computerized list of the names and addresses of other pedophiles he has met or corresponded with, and a catalogue of pertinent library and media material that he has collected. Paraphilic collectors and hoarders are quite unable to divest themselves of their collectibles, no matter how great the risk of self-incrimination should they be discovered.

Not all paraphilic or sex-related collections are self-incriminating. One young man had become conjointly obsessed with restoring his foreskin and restoring antique electrical appliances, both of which he talked about with a wry touch of self-mockery. With a program of stretching, he achieved unusual success in becoming equipped with a foreskin, and passed the test for admission to an "uncut" society. Thereupon he broke from his parents, who had converted to Protestantism, by converting from secular to Orthodox Judaism. He was unique among Jews as one who had once been circumcised, but now was foreskinned. He lived alone within his appliance museum as in a harem of surrogate sexual partners, each one lovingly given a turn to function in the course of a month.

Materials hoarded or collected may be stolen. Paraphilic stealing is kleptophilia (Greek, *kleptes*, thief + -philia, love), also known as klepolagnia (Greek, *lagneia*, lust). In a case of pubertas precox, a six-year-old boy had reached the stage of ejaculatory maturity. Neighbors feared that an adult sex prowler was at large until they discovered that their neighbor's young son was the one stealing ladies' brassieres from backyard clotheslines. He hid them in his tree house, and used them as masturbation accessories. After he was discovered, the erotic excitement of stealing became transferred from brassieres to ladies' handbags, which he obtained while hiding underneath the bleachers at the local college football games.

In kleptomania, the theft is not of erotic excitement, but of something else. In one case, the something else was being pregnant, and the thieving took the form of shoplifting baby clothes and other paraphernalia of the newborn. The shoplifter was a woman with Turner syndrome, predestined by congenital absence of the ovaries never to be pregnant, but desperate for motherhood in the days before ovum donation and in vitro fertilization. She was totally oblivious to the possibility of a connection between the two variables, sterility and shoplifting. In fact, she was mystified by her behavior. Kleptomania very often appeases a personal monster that is societally unidentified, as in such media headlining cases as that of a mail carrier found to have stolen and hoarded thousands of pieces of unopened mail in his house.

Thieving is a cultural construct specific to those societies that sanction the ownership of goods and property. Among nomadic Aboriginal Australians who retained no property, wore no clothes, built no houses, and improvised or manufactured artifacts as needed, there was nothing for an individual to steal except perhaps the small bag of articles of magic that a witch doctor wore at the back of the neck, suspended from a headband. In a communitarian society, as in much of Polynesia, using the property of other people is not stealing, but borrowing.

In some cases, theft may be part of a triad of stealing, lying, and sexing which may, indeed, constitute an unnamed syndrome. All three activities are carried out compulsively and are intrinsically exciting for their own sake. A typical scenario is one in which a very personable stranger, either man or woman, often with a strongly disciplined academic and religious history, finds a lonely benefactor, also either man or woman, who becomes a client in a business deal and/or a sexual arrangement. For the lonely benefactor, the sexual relationship is idealized as excitingly romantic and even lustful, but for the stranger it is a sham. Exaggeration and inconsistencies begin to show up in writing and in conversation. If challenged, they become more convoluted. Things begin mysteriously to disappear, ostensibly lost, misplaced, or taken by employees or guests. Mutual contacts are agreed upon and signed, or a loan is made. Then time is up. The stranger absconds with money, insurance, stocks, bonds, art, jewelry, or other assets. The benefactor may also lose his or her reputation, insofar as the stranger may move into impostoring no longer the role of friend, but the role of victim, engaging the benefactor in costly and career-ruinous litigation on false charges of breach of contract, sexual abuse, tax evasion, or whatever.

Redemption: Attachment and Addiction

Relief or deliverance from an offended spirit may be attained, according to the paleodigm of redemption, by entering into a state of ecstatic worship. Traditionally, there are two entryways. One is by addictive attachment to a charismatic leader. The other is by addictive attachment to a mind-altering plant, plant extract, or synthetic pharmacologic substance.

The discovery that there are, within the brain, receptor sites on nerve cells that take up the molecules of a mind-altering substance was first made only a few years ago. The substance, a naturally occurring neurotransmitter, an endorphin, is an opioid chemically related to the opium extracted from poppy seeds. Receptor sites are indifferent to the source of mind-altering molecules they bind. They may be secreted from cells within the body, or put into the body by inhaling, swallowing, inserting, or injecting. The ingestion of ferments and psychoactive herbs has been observed in avian and non-human mammalian species. In the human species, mind-changing alcoholic ferments and hallucinogens obtained from fungi and plants have an extremely ancient history and usage in medicine and in religious worship world-wide.

The concept of addictive attraction may be only a metaphor when applied to the bonding of a disciple to a charismatic leader or the bonding of a Cupid-stricken suitor to the Venus or Eros who is unrestrainedly adored. There may be more to the concept than mere metaphor, however, insofar as the ecstatic euphoria of becoming converted to a cause, or of falling limerently in love, is concomitant with changes in brain neurochemistries that may, in some future research, prove to correspond with those induced by addictive drugs.

In contemporary syntactical usage, addiction has two types of predicate. One is a noun, as in the usage: addiction to heroin, chocolate, or women's shoes. The other is a gerund or verbal noun as in the usage: addiction to running, hang-gliding, masturbating, or gambling. There are no syntactical restraints on extending the list of gerunds to encompass physiological processes, as in the usage: addiction to eating, breathing, drinking, urinating, coughing, or having sex. Physiological processes may become hypofunctional and hyperfunctional, but they do not become an addiction without the specification of a nounal predicate, as in the usage: addiction to eating chocolate, or addiction to wearing baby clothes concomitant with being erotosexually aroused and having sex.

The currently fashionable term "sexual addiction" is too overinclusive. It means having too much sex, but without quantitative criteria, and without differentiating what is engaged in. It fails to recognize that the only legitimate sexual application of the term "addiction" pertains to the paraphilias and, in particular, to whatever it is that the paraphilia is fixated on. Thus in acrotomophilia (Greek, *akron,* extremity + *tome,* a cutting + -philia) the fixation/addiction is to amputee stumps; in klismaphilia (Greek, *klusma,* enema + -philia), fluid from an enema syringe, and so on.

It is a paradox of addiction that its redemptive euphoric state can be induced by stimuli that, in folk wisdom, are cruel, abusive, punitive, and supposedly deterrent. Thus the prisoner may become addicted to the restraints of life in prison. The abused child returns for more abuse. The front-line soldier who has escaped the bombs that dismembered his companions plays Russian roulette with a loaded revolver. The paraphilic masochist achieves orgasmic ecstasy by being repeatedly bound, beaten, and burned. The addicted gambler rides the crests of the tidal wave of chance until it crashes with the loss of everything he owns. The shopping addict goes on buying sprees, buying more and more additions for already overloaded collections, ranging from personal attire and modest knickknacks to rare paintings, vintage cars, real estate, banks, retail stores, and billion dollar industries. Addictive shopping knows no limit on credit-card indebtedness or other risk of bankruptcy. The greater the risk, the nearer the approximation to addictive, big-time gambling. Go for broke, and start again!

The resolution of these paradoxes lies in the theory of opponent-process (Chapter 3) and in the hypothesis that the brain responds to trauma by releasing its own opiate pain killers and euphoriants.

Reparation: Exploits and Agitation

A reparation is an act of making amends for a wrong or injury. According to the paleodigm of reparation, it is possible to ward off the wrath of an offended spirit and to earn its favor by making amends for whatever one may have done, or neglected to have done, to offend it. Acts of reparative religious piety historically have included self-flagellation, living in monastic isolation, undertaking a long pilgrimage on hands and knees, donating a large sum of money, constructing a shrine or temple, dedicating oneself to good works on behalf of the sick and needy, and so on.

Prodigious acts of religious piety have their secular counterpart in prodigies of secular achievement like making the first ascent of Mount Everest "because it's there," to quote Sir Edmund Hilary. Exploits of great daring and success are the stuff of myths and history, and in them live the heroes whom we dream of and emulate. Great virtuosity of performance and achievement is valued for its own sake. It has audience and viewer value as entertainment, irrespective of its utility or morality. The mass slaughter of a thousand elephants is as much a cause for celebration by ivory poachers as is the mass rescue of a thousand live ones by endangered-species officials.

They who embark on prodigious exploits are likely to take prodigious risks. They confront the laws of chance not like those who cautiously go to Hartford to insure against them, but like those who recklessly go to Las Vegas to gamble against them. The grimness of their determination to beat the odds is evident in, for example, the man with prosthetic feet who is a champion rock climber, the blind man who crosses the Pacific in a sailboat alone, the one-legged woman amputee who becomes a ski champion, or the boy with progressive muscular dystrophy who takes up weight-lifting to prove that his doctors are wrong in their bleak prognosis.

Commitment to the perfection of physical or mental achievement in any endeavor may become enough of a monomania to exclude other endeavors, or to displace them. Thus the hermit monk has no place for ordinary social activities or pairbonding relationships. The full-time workaholic, so called, has no time for spouse and offspring. Vice versa, those who are inept with spouse and offspring become engrossed in work overload. Either way, the affected person's health is at risk for the burnout of a stress-related illness.

Work overload may be a sequel to what some have called the guilt of survival—the guilt of having been spared by fate to survive when others were wiped out by catastrophe, death squad, or holocaust.

Energy expenditure that lacks an organizing principle and that leaps grasshopper fashion from one thing to another becomes hypomanic, if partially constrained; manic, as in manic-depressive psychosis, if less so; and agitated if completely lacking in organization. Agitation with mental confusion is a concomitant of various deteriorative brain syndromes.

In school children, manicky behavior is usually characterized as hyperactivity or, in connection with short-attention span, attention-deficit disorder. Extreme hyperactivity together with extreme distractibility may have the appearance of being idiopathic. It may be an outcome of the stress of child abuse, including sexual child abuse. It may also be a concomitant of another syndrome—for example, an early, if not the earliest manifestation of juvenile hyperthyroidism (thyrotoxicosis). This endocrine disorder serves as a reminder that, although etiologies differ, symptoms may be the same. In addition, etiology is more often unknown than known in attention deficit disorder.

Retaliation: Surrogates and Delinquency

Like spirits, unspeakable monsters in one's life are, by definition, intangible and insubstantial so that they cannot be defended against by overt attack. According to the paleodigm of retaliation, an offended spirit can be defended against by an attack on a surrogate that is construed by the assailant to be one of the offended spirit's own enemies.

The phyletic basis of an attack on a surrogate is attack on a nonsurrogate. In carnivorous hunting species, eating entails attacking and killing for food. In troopbonding primate species, nonsurrogate attack entails also defense of the young, and territorial defense against predation and marauding.

In the human species, although both males and females are able to prey on other species for food, the division of labor has long been an accepted paleontological doctrine, namely, that far-ranging, large-game hunting and fishing are man's domain, whereas near-ranging, small-game hunting, fishing, and gathering are woman's domain. Similarly, protective defense of infants and children is woman's domain, and territorial defense against invaders is man's domain.

It is possible that the male-female division of labor is phyletically derived from the expendability of the male. Only a very small stable of stud males is sufficient to guarantee the fecundity of a very large female population.

In addition to the foregoing, there are two other phyletic bases for nonsurrogate attack, namely, dominance rivalry and mating rivalry. Human beings share both types of rivalry with other primates that live in troops with a hierarchy of dominance. Maintenance of position in the hierarchy entails, for both sexes, having an alliance network and defeating or expelling challengers.

Retaliation against a surrogate has been recorded among great apes and other nonhuman primates, as well as among human beings. It is expressed in diverse ways. Among human beings, it may be vocal: screaming, yelling, blaming, accusing, insulting, or humiliating. It may be violent: destroying, abusing, killing, torturing, injuring, or maiming. It may also be expelling, or robbing. The surrogate may be inanimate or animate, animal or human. The surrogate may also be a single individual or a group. To be a candidate for surrogate retaliation, the only criterion may be proximity and availability at the critical moment. Hence the paradox that the individual victims of surrogate retaliatory attacks frequently are not enemies but personal friends or kin. Societally and politically, the corresponding paradox is that oppressed peoples war among themselves, not against the enemy; and when they riot, burn, and loot a neighborhood, it is their own, not that of the oppressor.

The more tyrannous the oppressor, the less the likelihood of retaliation against a surrogate individual or group. Hence yet another paradox, namely, that the closer the approach of emancipation, the greater the likelihood of retaliatory striking out against a surrogate enemy.

That the availability of surrogates against whom retaliation may be directed is situationally determined is well illustrated in the case of a boy who was dying with terminal nephrosis. For most of the three years of his life, he was one among many children hospitalized with the same syndrome who were protectively isolated, each alone in a glass cubicle. With a play doctor's kit and a flexible doll, after each time he was stuck with a syringe or injection needle himself, and with a face fierce with glee, he would jab his play syringe into the doll surrogate. With arms almost too weak to move, he did it for the last time only an hour before he died.

In this example there is a transparent reversal of role as the boy identifies himself as the doctor, and the doll as his surrogate self, a reversal known as identification with the aggressor. The psychologist Bruno Bettelheim (1947) provides another example of identification with the aggressor from his experience in a German concentration camp.

> A prisoner had reached the final stage of adjustment when he changed his personality so as to accept as his own values the values of the Gestapo. A few examples may illustrate this. . . . Old prisoners, when in charge of others, often behaved worse than Gestapo because they considered this the best way to behave toward prisoners in the camp. . . . Another example was the treatment of traitors. Self-protection asked for their destruction, but the way in which they were tortured by old prisoners for days and slowly killed was copied from the Gestapo. Old prisoners tended to identify with the Gestapo not only in respect to aggressive behavior. They tried to arrogate to themselves old pieces of Gestapo uniforms. If that was not possible, they tried to sew and mend their uniforms so that they would resemble those of the guards. When asked why they did it they admitted that they loved to look like one of the guards. . . . This identification with their torturers went so far as copying their leisure-time activities. One of the games played by the guards was to find out who could stand to be hit longest without uttering a complaint. This game was copied by old prisoners.

In countless hundreds of thousands of cases, situational proximity determines that it will be one's sexual partner who becomes the surrogate victim of misdirected retaliation. The organs of retaliation may then be not only the vocal chords or the limbs, but also the genitalia. Feuding with the genitalia may be manifested as one-sided sexual apathy and inertia, or as its converse, an accusation of one-sided sexual insatiability. Or it may be manifested as a phobia about penetrating or being penetrated. Alternatively, the fighting may be manifested as reversible impairment of genital function masquerading as permanent. Impotence, premature ejaculation, anorgasmia, or lubrication failure are typical examples. Whatever it is that the sex organs are feuding about may, behind a smokescreen of accusations, evade the couple's recognition.

The resources available for retaliation against a surrogate are age-contingent. Young children scream, whine, spit, vomit, bite, pinch, scratch, slap, kick, piss, shit, smear, smash, rip, cut, and tear. Even at a very young age they have as a powerful weapon a package of matches with which to set fires. Among peers, they begin early to vent their grievances on a surrogate by beating up a playmate, breaking or stealing the playmate's toys and other belongings, and lying to get the playmate into trouble. In a worst-case scenario, as in some cases of morbid sibling rivalry, an older child may suffocate or drown a smaller one.

With the juvenile years, there comes increased adeptness in attacking age mates, and skill in handling weapons—rocks, ropes, sticks, blades, broken glass, and guns. As surrogate retaliation and revenge increasingly offend the laws and values of the adult world, disobedience is changed in name to delinquency. In the prepubertal years, hard core delinquency, like torturing and dismembering animals, maiming or killing age mates, sexually abusing younger or weaker children coercively and getting high on alcohol or drugs, does not augur well for the future. The hard-core delinquent has almost always, if not invariably, an antecedent history of having been abusively neglected, assaultively brutalized, capriciously tyrannized, and sexually coerced, singly or severally. Institutional or foster-home placement may have increased, rather than lessened the likelihood of such a history.

Adolescence is the age of the declaration of autonomy—autonomy in matters of love, sex, and procreation, and autonomy in matters of earning and spending. If the realization of autonomy in either sphere is thwarted, whether by a personal disability, by another individual, or by society at large, then a potential for retaliative revenge against a surrogate ensues.

Children and adolescents are exposed to social codes in which it is honorable to direct vengeance against an enemy, but not against a surrogate or scapegoat. There is, however, no hard and fast dividing line between enemy and scapegoat in the power politics of society as encountered directly from childhood onward, as well as in recreational play and in mass media entertainment. In retaliation against a surrogate, the line between scapegoat and enemy may be crossed without explicit recognition of what has happened.

Derision: Humor and Humiliation

Political cartoonists and satirists ridicule and lampoon officials in high places too distant for assault or retaliation in person. Their motto is that the pen is mightier than the sword. According to the paleodigm of derision an offended spirit that is invincible can be assailed, belittled, and humiliated by means of mockery, scorn, joking, jesting, and being laughed at.

From the viewpoint of ethological gestural analysis, the smile is an infant-faced appeal that elicits a parental bonding response. Dependent on the native body language which an infant assimilates, the smile may come to signify happiness, deference, politeness, amusement, or sneering. The significance in each case is conveyed in part by vocalization—the happy gurgle, the polite or subdued tone of deference, the amused chortle or giggle, and the sneering snort of laughter. Laughter itself breaks the smile and spreads movement over the entire face and neck. The belly laugh involves the torso, and maybe the whole body in contortion. Laughter itself, like yawning, is socially contagious. Infants laugh along with adults whose jokes they do not yet comprehend. Social laughter unites a group against the person or group, present or in absentia, whom their laughter derides and excludes. Joining in with the laughter, instead of being offended, prevents exclusion and is a passport to becoming a good sport with a good sense of humor.

Paroxysmal laughter brings on a flow of tears and the person says: "I laughed till I cried." There are also tears of happiness, without laughter, as when a winner accepts an award. The proximity of laughter and weeping in the functioning of the limbic brain and autonomic nervous system is evidenced in such phenomena as laughing at funerals and weeping at weddings. Correspondingly, laughter and rage often go together—witness the taunting laughter of the tormentor, and the maniacal laughter of the killer.

A proximity of laughter, sleep, and muscular collapse also occurs in the brain and nervous system. The evidence of this proximity is found in that syndrome (Chapters 3, 4) marked by an abrupt transition from laughing, in response to a humorous stimulus, to loss of muscle tone and falling down (cataplexy), and then passing into a state of deep sleep (narcolepsy). In some cases there is eidetically vivid hypnagogic imagery during the transition from wakefulness to falling asleep at night, and temporary sleep paralysis in the transition to waking up. The syndrome is attributable to seizure-like dysfunction of sleep regulation in the brain.

The autonomy of laughter is exemplified in the phenomenon of laughing spells, also known as gelastic epilepsy, the occurrence of which is associated with a nonmalignant tumor, a hamartoma, of the hypothalamus. When a person with gelastic epilepsy has a laughing seizure, the experience is one of chuckling in amusement, as if in response to something funny, except that the funny something is a blank nothing.

Joking relationships are formally institutionalized and prescribed in the social code of some societies. Kluckhohn and Leighton (1947) write of the Navaho Indians of New Mexico: "Much Navaho humor is expressed in a patterned kind of teasing that is supposed to be carried on between different classes of relatives. . . . With some relatives one is not supposed to joke at all, with others one may not 'joke bad,' while with certain relatives one is expected to make jokes of sexual or obscene connotation." Navaho society is matriarchal. Not only does a man not joke with his mother-in-law, but he is supposed never to be looked upon by her. Maternal uncles traditionally hold a position of great importance for nieces and nephews in this matriarchy; they assume many of the disciplinary, instructional, and bequeathing functions which fall to the lot of the father in white society. One male informant, after narrating several examples of buffoonery, some of it physically painful, between brothers and grandparents and grandsons, commented about erotic joking: "But the only one you can tease about girls is your sister's son." Jokes about mothers-in-law and mother-in-law avoidance are an informal part of the social code of our own society.

Adversarial tension is present to some degree in all situations and anecdotes characterized as humorous. For example, in the sexually risqué joke, there is the tension of acutally giving expression, albeit obliquely, to subject matter that according to moral principles of one's opponents is unmentionable and forbidden, and perhaps punishable.

Joking in the face of the monster of adversity, as when a prisoner on the way to the gas chamber quips, "Let's get this show on the road," may relieve other people of the guilt of survival. For the prisoner, however, gallows humor simply affirms the futility of either rage or crying and the inexorability of his fate. In numerous inexorable situations, people encounter their fate with joking, laughing, or nervously giggling about it. Playing the clown is a coping tactic for some people with a chronic disablement—for example, children who are dwarfs. Behind the smile, one should look also for the sadness, and also for the rage.

Desertion: Runaways and Abandonment

According to the paleodigm of desertion, an alternative to resisting or surrendering to an offended enemy spirit is to flee and escape into hiding. But an unspeakable monster is not so easily abandoned. It travels with one. The strategy of desertion is unsatisfactory. It leaves unfinished business unfinished until it may be too late. Thus it is too late to complete unfinished business with, say, one's parents after they are dead.

Dromomania (Greek, *dromos*, running + *mania*, madness) is the technical term for a fixation on being unsettled, moving from place to place, leading a life of vagabondage, or repeatedly running away.

Dromomania in the life of an individual has its counterpart in nomadism and seasonal migration in societal life. Gypsy society, for example, is nomadically organized, even in the high-tech, industrialized societies of Europe and America in which some Gypsy communities travel. The wandering of dromomania and nomadism may both be conjectured to have its phyletic origins in the widespread, cross-species phenomenon of migration.

Dromomania in infancy and early childhood is more likely to signal exploratory roaming rather than running away from someone or something. In middle childhood and later, however, it is more likely to signify escaping from a domestic or academic situation for which the child has no other available coping strategy.

Running away may be an outcome of abusive cruelty and violence from other children or from adults. It may also be an outcome of imposed or coerced sexual participation that, if disclosed or discovered, would bring intolerable retribution. Another possibility is that a runaway child has been caught in the crossfire of a divorce and custody battle and/or has a new stepfather or stepmother as an adversary.

A runaway may have also more intimate torments, such as doubts and fantasies concerning a history of adoption, or puberty that is too soon, too late, or sexually ambiguous, or being attracted toward and falling in love with a partner of the same sex.

Ethologically, dromomania in adolescence has a basis in the primate phenomenon of leaving the natal troop to join another one, or to form a new one. Either the male or female adolescent of a particular species may leave kith and kin, though in the majority of species that have been sufficiently documented it is the adolescent male who is the one that leaves.

Among human beings, adolescents who run away from an intolerable home situation with no fixed destination and no source of support for food, shelter, and clothing may find new troop membership only among other vagrants, hustlers, prostitutes, thieves, and dealers in illicit merchandise, including illicit drugs. Otherwise they become homeless and dependent on eliciting private or public sponsorship.

Being a runaway may converge with a fixation on being a hideaway, lost in anonymity, or lost under the cover of an alias as an impostor. Running away from one imposture to another is for some a repetitious compulsion of such intensity that it precludes a legitimate way of life. An example is that of a surgeon who, without ever having gone through medical school, is nonetheless acknowledged as an expert. Then it is discovered that his professional documents and certificates are forgeries. Unmasked, he flees from an arrangement that would enable him to take a special examination and become legitimately certified. Years later, he turns up, again highly esteemed and re-established as surgeon impostor at another hospital. Alternatively, he may have impostored his way into an entirely new career.

Running away from something or someone means leaving that thing or person behind, abandoned. Thus a parent may abandon children and their other parent. A single parent may abandon a child or children to the care of relatives or a public charity. In worst scenario cases, a newborn is abandoned in a trash can, or older children are abandoned in an untended dwelling to die of cold and starvation, or to be burned to death. In some large impoverished or war-torn cities, abandoned children number in the hundreds of thousands, and are banded together in a quasi-tribal existence of self-support by scavenging, pilfering, commercial sex, and illicit merchandising.

Abandonment of the young has its counterpart in abandonment of the aged. Adults who are age-mates also abandon one another. In countries that have no legal divorce, the partner who leaves a marriage in effect abandons the other partner. Without legal or economic rights, a woman who leaves her marriage has virtually nowhere to go, so that leaving is virtually the prerogative of men.

· 6 ·

Interviewer

Adversarialism vs. Nonjudgmentalism

In the archaic and irretrievable history of the human race, the doctrine of taboo was discovered and used to ensure compliance to the authority of the lords of taboo. The principle of taboo is the same as the principle today called behavior modification. First, take some aspect of the repertory of species-typical behavior that, although engaged in by all, is amenable to restraint or being put temporarily on hold. Second, promulgate restrictions on when the behavior may be engaged in, with threats of penalties and punishments for nonconformity. Third, apply the threats of penalties and punishments, now and in the afterlife, with abusive thoroughness from childhood onward. Fourth, appoint officials and devise techniques and procedures for ferreting out infringements. Fifth, demand respect not only for the taboo, but also for the over-all authority and tyranny of its guardians and lords.

In history up to the present day, the great taboos world-wide have applied to manifestations of sexuality and eroticism; eating, cooking, fasting, and range of menu; corpses and their burial places; speaking or writing decreed to be heretical, blasphemous, obscene, or unfit for specified company; depicting the naked human face or genitalia; nudity and bathing; and disposal of fecal, urinary, menstrual, and parturitional excretions.

It may well be that the originators of taboo were ruler priests. In any case, the principle of taboo has long been assimilated into the world's great religions and has traveled with them. Hence the ubiquity of the sexual taboo which outperforms all the others.

From its inception, the doctrine of Christendom has defined infringement of its taboo, along with other infringements, as sin. Sin is the monster—the devil, or the demon, in one's life. The responsibility for being in cahoots with the devil is one's own. So also is the responsibility for confessing and repentance. To make the unspeakable monster speakable, the Church provided the confessional. The system is judgmental—guilty or not guilty. It is also adversarial—God and forgiveness through penance, versus Satan and damnation, possibly eternal damnation in a fiery Hell.

In the ecclesiastical trials of the Inquisition, from the twelfth century onward, the confessional was converted into a gruesome torture chamber. Truth was decreed to be synonymous with what the prisoner confessed under torture, provided it coincided with a preordained verdict of guilty. The monster, tenuous and occult, was the sin of heresy and witchcraft, for the proof of which witnesses were sworn to give testimony.

With the secularization of Renaissance Europe, the judicial system became progressively secularized, and the name of the monster was secularized to offense, felony, or crime. The system maintained the philosophy and practice of adversarialism, and to a certain extent, in pre-trial police investigations, it retained also the philosophy and practice of extracting confessions, even under torture.

Before the end of the eighteenth century, lunacy and criminality were not differentiated in the judicial system. Both were judged and penalized according to the adversarial system of the law. In the nineteenth century, as psychiatry developed into an independent medical specialty, some offenses were attributed to mental illness rather than to criminal intent, and transferred from the judicial to the medical system. However, psychiatry did not free itself from either the adversarial or the confessional system, but absorbed from both the philosophy and practice of judgmentalism. Judgmentalism became absorbed in turn, unofficially and insidiously, into psychology and various systems of psychotherapy—and into other institutions of society as well, for example, the entertainment industry in which programs and shows are prevalently adversarial in content.

The adversarial philosophy of judgmentalism owes its insidiousness to its embeddedness in the very language that we speak. We speak idiomatically of needs, wants, wishes, and desires that refer responsibility to the self. Others hold us personally responsible for them, and pass judgment on us for manifesting them. Pressed for an explanation of any motivation, and of why we did what we did, we come up as empty-handed as a child who cannot advance an explanation further than the conjunction: "Because." To fill the blank, vernacular explanations are invoked. They are derived from the pulpit or the bench, not the laboratory. The precision science of mind, motivation, and intents, and of its synchronies within the neurocomplexities of the brain, has hardly even begun. The divinations of psychology today betray their origins in astrology. To read motivations from inkblots or from the profiles of personality inventories is not far removed from reading auguries from the entrails of sacrificial birds.

English without the idioms of motivation is English devoid of the implication of personal responsibility for behavior that does not yield to voluntary control. Simultaneously, it is devoid also of the implication of accusatory judgmentalism. Nonjudgmentalism in talking with a patient is indispensable to the establishment of a sense of trust and of an alliance between the doctor and patient against the syndrome, not an alliance between the syndrome and patient viewed as if a confrontation with the doctor. Syphilis is a straightforward example. The patient and the doctor enter into an alliance against the spirochete, but not if the patient is judgmentally antagonized into breaking away.

If syphilis is, for the most part, an example of an unspeakable monster in some people's lives, then a second example, pedophilia, is all the more so, insofar as it is one of the paraphilias that is subject to widespread and severe condemnation. Pedophiles are condemned simply by being named child molesters and child sexual abusers. Except for members of their own kind they have no one in whom to confide and no one who will listen nonjudgmentally. Even doctors are by law, in a majority of jurisdictions, obliged to report them to the authorities.

As for pedophilia, so also for all the paraphilias and, indeed, for all the sexological syndromes, it is necessary that some members of society be officially nonjudgmental. Otherwise there will continue to be an insufficiency of data for the eventual scientific explanation of sexological syndromes and for the epidemiological control of their occurrence. Nonjudgmentalism has big implications for society, as well as for the individual.

For the individual, nonjudgmentalism may be a matter of life and death. Among the paraphilias, autoerotic asphyxiophilia is estimated, at a minimum, to account for the deaths of a thousand, if not more, young American males annually. It is as ineffectual to be judgmental with such a young man, warning him of the consequences of his relentlessly repetitive ritual of self-strangulation, as it is to expect that chastisement will be effective in curbing the seizures of a temporal lobe epileptic. The asphyxiophile knows about the risk of dying if he becomes unconscious before the strangulating cord is loosened. He knows he could tell someone to intervene, but that would entail speaking about the unspeakable monster of masturbation combined with self-strangulation. He knows no one on whom he can count to not judge him guilty for engaging in behavior that he cannot explain, and that is beyond the bounds of his voluntary control. If alone and unaided he could have desisted, he would have done so long ago. His salvation rests on what is still fortuitous rather than guaranteed, namely, finding a professional trained to talk with him nonjudgmentally about his syndrome and its treatment (Money et al., 1991). Otherwise he will remain deprived of the possibility of amelioration.

Professional nonjudgmentalism applies to the conduct of one's profession. It does not apply to one's conduct in general. It does not signify an absence of personal standards, or a licentious policy of "anything goes," not even a policy of anything goes in a relationship provided it is consensual. Many medical students, among others, have not been able to assimilate the concept of professional nonjudgmentalism. Their morality is absolute. They judge their patients by the same standard as they judge themselves.

Antecedent Biases

In the folkways of the Hippocratic tradition, the role of the physician is to relieve pain and suffering and to save life from untimely death. The good doctor knows his patient well and is self-sacrificing on his behalf. The good patient is respectful and compliant in following instructions. So much for Hippocrates. His tradition, although not dead, no longer stands alone. It is augmented in contemporary medicine by a new tradition of addressing not the well-being of the person as a whole, but the functioning of only one organ system, or even the readout of a lab report. The latter is sufficient in, for example, wiping out an epidemic.

Preventive public-health measures in the twentieth century turned the role of the patient topsy-turvy by coercing the healthy into being patients, namely, in programs such as immunization, contraception, and water purification, for their own and the public good. Compliance, in many instances, was replaced by resistance and rebellion.

Resistance has other origins. According to the medical folklore of some people, hospitals are places where those who are too sick to live are put to death—the converse of a contemporary folklore that hospitals entrap the terminally ill in apparatus that prolongs their death. Another source of resistance is the folklore that hospitals are places where doctors use patients as guinea pigs for experiments and tests.

Resistance, if not outright rebellion, is a likely concomitant of coercion from any source. People with a treatable disease resist family or community pressures to undergo diagnosis and treatment, perhaps until the disease becomes terminal. The stigma of mental illness is for some a deterrent not only to hospitalization and treatment, but also to a diagnostic workup. Even in childhood, referral for psychological testing may be responded to as an infringement of the personal right to be left to oneself. The shame and disgrace attendant upon having a sexual syndrome keeps many people away from a diagnostic evaluation. The same formerly applied to tuberculosis and was a carry-over from the era when consumption of the lungs was falsely attributed to degeneration induced by loss of semen, the most vital of the vital fluids, through masturbation.

One of the defining characteristics of the various paraphilic sexual syndromes is incorporation of orgasm into the syndrome. Subjectively, orgasm is strongly positive for most people. Thus so far as the paraphile is concerned, subjective inclusion of orgasm as the climax of a paraphilic episode disqualifies the syndrome from being an illness requiring diagnosis and treatment—even in the case of paraphilic lust murder or erotophonophilia (Greek, *eros*, love + *phonein*, to murder + -philia).

Noncompliance expressed as neglectfulness as compared with resistance is attributable in many instances to the frailty of memory when a routine must be followed regularly for as long as a lifetime, for example, in using a condom for protection against HIV, or taking insulin for diabetes. The principle underlying noncompliancy is very often the principle of inexistence, namely, that a risk or condition that is no longer recalled no longer exists. This principle applies especially to conditions that are symptom-free provided medication or other treatment is never interrupted. It is a principle particularly evident in teenage.

Noncompliance originates also in the principle of magic—simple possession of an unfilled prescription or a bottle of pills has a talismanic value of its own. There is also a magical value in using the talisman—swallowing a pill or applying a medication—only to counteract a symptom only after it has appeared, not to prevent its appearance.

In some cases, compliance serves as a masquerade behind which lurk self-induced symptoms that make a mockery of the Hippocratic role and the self-image of the healer. As already noted in Chapter 5, medical impostoring is named eponymically for a boastful teller of tall tales as Munchausen syndrome. When symptoms are induced not in oneself but in a surrogate, for example by a mother in her own child, the condition is Munchausen syndrome by proxy. Professional training in the art of healing generally omits reference to medical impostors, professionally self-trained to near perfection in the art of being undiagnosably and incurably sick. As a model of courage and compliancy, the patient with Munchausen syndrome readily coopts the healing professional into a collusional relationship. When the correct diagnosis is finally made, the typical reaction of doctors, nurses, and other personnel is one not of professional impartiality but of moral judgmentalism and outrage at their own culpability for having been duped.

Munchausen syndrome plain or by proxy is not alone in being inherently sneaky and deceitful. The intermingling of historical accuracy with prevarication and pseudologia fantastica occurs also as a pathognomonic feature of some cases of the supernumerary Y (47,XYY) chromosomal syndrome and, to some extent, syndromes of paraphilia. Pathognomonic means a sign or symptom on which a diagnosis can be made. Condemning the symptom does not eradicate the diagnosis. It is an exercise in futility, therefore, to become moralistic and judgmental when confronted by the sneakiness of a syndrome that is pathognomonically sneaky and devious. Rather, one puts the responsibility on the impostor to provide confirmation of statements that are presented as historically accurate. Otherwise they will be accepted only provisionally and with skepticism. That saves much wasted time.

Standard diagnostic and treatment procedures that professionals view as clinically routine may be procedures that patients view as clinically humiliating or abusive. Abuse that pertains to or originates in a clinic or hospital is nosocomial (from the Greek, *nosos*, disease, and *komein*, to take care of) abuse. The greater one's ignorance of the rationale for a procedure, the greater the likelihood that one will misconstrue it as abusive—as, for example, when an eight-year-old girl with idiopathic pubertal precocity misconstrues an unexplained genital examination as nosocomial sexual abuse, a vaginal or rectal probe as nosocomial rape, and medical photography as nosocomial pornography. The outcome may be not only future noncompliance, but also escape from follow-up.

Another potential outcome is litigation that is contrived, in some instances unscrupulously, with a specialist in compensation claims. False accusations of nosocomial abuse are particularly difficult to defend against in today's political climate of antisexualism (Money, 1992a).

Defining the Situation

"My mother said we'd be going to the circus, but I knew it wasn't no circus when I saw the building," said a young boy from out of state, in response to an initial inquiry: "Do you know why you're here today?" His mother's excuse was that he would have resisted her violently otherwise. For her the problem was one of disobedience, not that he had an intense phobia of injection needles.

Needless to say, the role of being a spectator at the circus does not compare with the role of being a patient, client, subject, or, to use a synonym applicable to all three, a proband or propositus (from Latin, *proponere*, to put on view) in a clinical workup. Especially in childhood, the role of being a proband in a clinic or hospital may be confused with that of being a student in school, or a parishioner in church. To familiarize a proband with his/her prospective role, a good lead-in question is: "How much do you know about why you have this appointment today." From here one may branch out into questions, briefly, regarding prior history and the referral source.

All people bring to the clinic or hospital their personal history of being in a role stereotyped according to the criteria of sex, age, race, social class, literacy, and so on. The role of being a patient, client, or subject in a clinical evaluation transcends these stereotypes not only ethically, but also legally. Otherwise the professional practitioner is open to being charged with discrimination.

An undeniable and deeply vexatious source of discrimination is ability to pay. A wider range of services is available to the wealthy than to the poor, though not necessarily always to their advantage as, for example, in cases of the polysurgery syndrome. In the absence of a prior contract regarding payment, if services received cannot be paid for, then those services are de facto charitable or pro bono. There are some people whose ploy is to offer themselves as interesting specimens in exchange for free services.

This is a prevalent ploy among applicants for surgery to change the body in cases of body image fixation. Applicants for sex reassignment surgery, for instance, not uncommonly request to be used as "guinea pigs" so as to be able to undergo male-to-female, or female-to-male sex surgery. Others are fixated not on sex reassignment, but on castration in order to become an asexual eunuch. Still others have an erotic fixation on having the stump of an amputated limb (the paraphilic syndrome of apotemnophilia). Volunteering to be a guinea pig for medical experimentation is futile, for it is rejected by institutional ethics-review boards.

The role of the proband in a professional relationship blurs easily when the proband is also a personal friend or kin of the professional. The outcome of such blurring is that the professional role becomes lax, and the personal role becomes austere. Especially with respect to members of one's close family, a wise safeguard against lax professional judgment is to consult with an independent professional colleague.

Friends and kin of a professional address him/her with informal familiarity on a first-name basis, whereas to be respectful and well mannered a stranger, a person of lesser rank, or a child use the formal terms of address. The line between familiarity and formality of address is not rigidly fixed. Some professionals are very informal. Some probands are very formal. Whether to be formal or informal may, however, become an issue, as when a patient addresses his doctor on a first-name basis, impostoring friendship in a bid for special consideration and privilege. At the opposite extreme is that of the socially inept patient with no living relatives and no close friends on a first-name basis except his doctor. In this case, informality of address would be justified, whereas in the former case informality might invite trouble.

For the professional, especially a pediatrician, it is awkward to change from the first name of childhood to the formal address of adulthood. It is belittling, however, if not insulting to call all adults, regardless of age, by their first names only—but there are some adults for whom being addressed by the first name is a reassurance of not being rejected.

The protocol for being professionally considerate and respectful is not the same as for greeting a colleague or chatting with friends. Children as well as older people know the difference. They construe staged or folksy friendliness as being talked down to, and not legitimate professional business. "I know why I came here," one youth said, "and it wasn't to talk about the baseball game."

The explanations given by a proband and the accompanying persons as the reason for the visit are, often enough, quite incongruent. Discrepancies between informants on "the reason for being here" may give the first clue that the wrong person has been designated as the proband, or that there is more than one proband as, for example, in a so-called dysfunctional family.

Whereas in the practice of veterinary medicine it is manifestly impossible to formally introduce the proband to the people responsible for the various scheduled procedures, it is not only impolite but also counter-productive to treat a human being like a veterinary animal and not to do so. Becoming oriented includes knowing who's who by name, what they do, and in language geared to the listener's age and comprehension, why it is done. One uses a similar etiquette in introducing a proband who appears before a class or audience.

The process of becoming oriented is a process of defining proband/ professional dialogue as being straightforwardly premised on the way things are, and not pompous, patronizing, evasive, or offensive.

Confidentiality

Everyone needs someone to confide in, a confidant in whom can be invested the utmost faith never to break the trust of confidentiality. Family members do not necessarily fill the bill, for information to be kept strictly confidential may pertain to them. Parents lament the lack or loss of their children's trust, but parents are morally and legally responsible for their minor offspring and cannot be entrusted never to take reprisals for what was told in confidence. Best friends, too, may betray one's trust through gossip. Even one's pediatrician is suspect, for his allegiance may be primarily to parents and guardians, not oneself. No matter how great the magnitude of the monster in the life of an underaged minor, there may be absolutely no one to talk to in confidence without fear of betrayal. Imagine, for example, the plight of a once agreeable and achieving child who takes to a life of petty delinquency and illicit drugs and is sent to a professional family colleague for counseling. For two years this child says nothing about the encroaching monster of puberty that is enlarging her clitoris and masculinizing her body. She was born a hermaphrodite, a fact which her parents have concealed from her and her counselor.

When eventually the evidence of a masculinizing puberty had become visible and undeniable, it was imperative that the girl be furnished with an unconditional guarantee of confidentiality by someone who could be entrusted with everything she could disclose about the unspeakable monster of whether she was a boy or a girl. Each of her parents also needed an unconditional guarantee of confidentiality, as they talked separately before uniting first together as a pair, and then in a joint session with their child.

To safeguard confidentiality it is imperative to have a closed room or cubicle that is adequately sound-proofed, and to have one for each person who will be interviewed concurrently. The interior design of inpatient wards of the majority of modern hospitals are woefully deficient in this respect. They do not have an interview room. In many instances, outpatient areas are equally deficient.

Ideally, the number of staff members will be sufficient to permit the scheduling of simultaneous individual sessions when family members need to be interviewed or tested alone. People disclose different information in each other's presence than when alone. If they spend time together between sequential interviews, one instructs or inculcates the other in what to edit, and what to disclose.

Those who participate professionally in an extensive workup increase the range of their experience if all of them come in contact with the proband and with the accompanying persons, if not in individual sessions, then in a concluding conference session. This plurality of contacts is mutually advantageous. It provides options to a proband whose response to individual professionals may differ on the basis of sex, age, and ethnicity. In addition, in the course of long-term follow-up, it allows continuity of personalized care to survive personnel changes. Children as well as adults rely on the assurance that at each visit to the clinic they will meet not only strangers, but someone who knows them.

Before separating proband and accompanying persons into private sessions, it is obviously necessary to ascertain that separation is feasible. It is not invariably so, as when a child clings to a parent, or when a relative must act as interpreter or signer. When separation is feasible, then the principle of privacy must be, irrespective of age, reciprocally consented to and respected, namely, that information given in confidence will be kept confidential until such time as it is agreed upon that it may safely be disclosed in the presence of, or by, the person giving permission for the disclosure. Thus parents may not invoke parental authority to coerce information from children. In time, most unspeakable monsters become speakable in part through the intervention of an intermediary, and the very act of speaking about them becomes an act of therapy.

As cited in the foregoing, the monster of masculinizing puberty created a moral quandary in the girl's life, but not a criminal one. As a moral quandary its resolution lay within the medical system, not the judicial system. Confidentiality was maintained. It would not have been, however, had the quandary been legally defined as criminal and mandated as reportable. Hypothetically, the case might have been argued as one of child abuse by reason of extreme medical neglect, and therefore subject to mandatory reporting. Had the case been reported, however, legal action would probably not have been taken, since the surface image of the child's family matches the iconical image presently popular in today's secular iconolatry of the traditional family.

By contrast, there are other monsters in which taking action is not dubious, but assured. These are cases, suspected or alleged, of sexual child abuse or molestation, biomedically named pedophilia. They are subject to mandatory reporting, with no provision for privileged communication. The paradoxical outcome of mandatory reporting statutes is that they have effectively outlawed the treatment of pedophilia. Even a fifteen-year-old pedophile is barred from being able to confide in his doctor or counselor. If he speaks of his unspeakable monster, namely, his sexuoerotical attraction to prepubertal boys, or girls, he must be reported to the police. The paradoxical outcome is that pedophilia has been legislated into being a crime for which arrest is the only treatment. Those who might otherwise apply for treatment are required to continue repeating their pedophilic offenses, until they are caught. Society has legislated itself into a corner from which it cannot escape.

Maintenance of confidentiality is, on the one hand, an issue of professional ethics, and on the other, obedience to the law. The former is an issue also of allegiance to an individual, and the latter of allegiance to a system designed to protect other individuals. The two allegiances are far from being congruently matched, for there are situations in which maintaining confidentiality on behalf of the individual proband is itself a criminal act, if there is a mandatory reporting law.

These two allegations create an insoluble dilemma in the proband/practitioner relationship. For the proband, the traditionally expected role of the professional practitioner is that of ally. In effect, however, if the ally fails to disclose his role in the system in which he must report, he is an undercover agent for that system. The dilemma surfaces on such issues as reporting that the proband tests HIV positive, that he has a positive history of taking illicit drugs, that he has a history of pedophilia, that he has a history of having been a paraphilic murderer or a paraphilic rapist, that he has a child or a wife whom he has violently assaulted and abused, and so on.

As of the present time, there is no set of working rules that give a proband the right to require a practitioner to give his signed, informed consent either to maintain confidentiality totally, or else to disclose the limitations beyond which confidentiality will not be maintained. Thus a proband is not in a position to give his own signed informed consent to procedures that will yield data that, if disclosed, will abolish confidentiality and possibly be self-incriminating. Unspeakable monsters may, therefore, be destined to remain unspeakable.

The alternative to not speaking is to be tyrannized into talking by the application of varying degrees and techniques of harassment, deprivation, and torture. Known in the twentieth century as brainwashing, it is a revival of the medieval Inquisition. In much attenuated form, it is the technique in vogue, under the auspices of the now professional cult of victimology, to elicit pseudological-fantastical testimony of sexual abuse and Satanism from infants and children to support false accusations of pedophilia and incest.

The converse of information obtained by coercion is that which spills out with no restraints on confidentiality or self-incrimination. This is information as entertainment. It is also information as imposture and confidence-trickstering. Its content, elaborated according to the gauge of the listener's response, merges history and fact with confabulation. The history can be distilled from the mix only by reference to documents and the independent testimony of others. In some cases the confabulation is history assimilated from someone else's biography, even to the extent of falsely confessing to someone else's crime. Theatrical confession and self-disclosure are a paradox not uncommon in all the paraphilias.

Confidentiality includes "housekeeping" details regarding the confidentiality of records. Itemized, they are as follows: Do not discuss any details of a case in public places like elevators, corridors, and cafeterias. Do not give out information by mail or telephone without identification of the authenticity of the recipient, and without informed consent. Do not reveal sensitive data, even a sensitive diagnosis, on insurance claims and other documents without informed consent. Beware of the potential misuse of computerized information. Sequester sensitive material, such as evidence of sex reannouncement and name change in infant hermaphrodites, from the medical record. Work on the assumption that all doors and walls in a clinic or other professional location have ears. Be advised that, in published material, confidentiality applies not only to data that may disclose a person's identity to others, but also to data that allow self-recognition, whereupon the individual concerned, despite having formerly given informed consent, may take action on the grounds that the material is personally sensitive and emotionally distressing.

In the United States, under the terms of the Freedom of Information Act, a person has the right of access to files that contain information about him or her. It is, therefore, a matter of simple expediency that, in professional reports, substantiated data are differentiated from hypotheses, conjectures, and speculations. An expedient rule of thumb is that one should write a report in conformity with two expectations: the first, that it will be read by and discussed in person with the person about whom it is written; and the second, that one will be called upon to defend its contents in a court of law.

Emergencies

It is not usual to think of the scheduling of an interview as an emergency, but there are some occasions when it is literally a matter of life and death. Consider, for example, the desperation of a mother who was denied an emergency appointment for her teenaged son on the grounds that she must pay the fee in advance. She was unable to raise the money. Her son, already known in the clinic with a diagnosis of pedophilic sadism, fulfilled her worst fears. He abducted the ten-year-old son of a physician and took him off on a pedophilic killing spree which ended in the pedophile's arrest and eventual execution.

In another example, with a better ending, an agitated young man appeared at the door of a secretary's office demanding an immediate appointment, or else. He also had no money, and had been unable to obtain an emergency appointment downstairs. His emergency demand was that he be cured of homosexuality so that he could join the military and eventually provide his family with a male heir. The topic of his interview was the distinction between homosexual and bisexual, and his own bisexual potential. Reassured, he expressed his thanks by displaying the handgun that, he said, he was fully intent on using, had he not that day found someone who would talk to him.

A different type of emergency arose in the case of a young man who was maintained in long-term follow-up from infancy until his death at age forty-six in status asthmaticus (Money and Lamacz, 1989, p. 109). He revealed that, in a state of what eventually proved to be acute hallucinosis, he elaborated a homicidal design on the life of his best friend and his best friend's wife. Intemperately resistant at first, he eventually agreed to listen to a telephone call warning his friend to safeguard himself against being knifed or stabbed, and to come in for an appointment without delay. In this way, the paroxysm of explosive irrationality was defused, and the friendship was eventually resumed.

Three Techniques of Interview

The technique of the interview dialogue ranges from interrogation to gossip. That range applies widely, from interviews in the media to interviews in the clinic. In the hard sciences, it has given the interview data of the soft sciences the reputation of being too capricious, fortuitous, and unreproducible.

The **interview as an interrogation** is known also as the forced-choice or closed-ended interview insofar as its questions require responses of the true-false, multiple-choice, rating-scale, or rank-ordering type. The interrogatory interview may follow a set inventory of items, or it may be chaotic and improvisational. Either way, true/false questions get yes/no answers. Too much information is lost in yes/no interrogation that excludes the respondent's provisos, exemptions and qualifications. Moreover, tormenting a respondent with a barrage of closed-ended questions for which he has no definitive answer has the negative effect of provoking alienation.

The **interview as gossip** is an undisciplined form of the unforced or open-ended interview. In clinical psychology, an interview may cross the line from professionalism into gossip when the declared procedural protocol lacks an agenda and becomes indiscriminately free associative or nondirective. That leaves the way open for the respondent to deprofessionalize the interview and change it into manipulative gossip that seduces the interviewer into collaboration with the respondent. To put the metaphorical brakes on the runaway train at this juncture, the technique is expository, namely, an interpretation of the injunctions of the code of professional ethics and, if applicable, the criminal code with respect to the penalties attendant upon the deprofessionalization of a professional relationship.

This expository technique is one of defining limits, not of passing judgment. For example, when doing a physical examination of a teenager who gets an erection and makes impudent sexual comments, a young doctor, male or female, does not report harassment, but responds by covering the genitals with a hand towel and commenting to the effect that the sexual reflexes are functionally normal.

Another application of the expository technique distinguishes between a friend/friend and a doctor/patient relationship. The latter being rarer and more societally privileged than the former, it should not, therefore, be lightly forfeited. It is with this distinction that one delineates the boundary between fondness and amorousness in the so-called transference relationship, but without hurt or humiliation.

There are degrees of transference which, in its greatest enormity, is manifested in the Clérambault-Kandinsky syndrome, also known as erotomania. This is the syndrome that accounted for John Hinckley's attempt on the life of President Reagan, March 30th, 1981. The attempt was a would-be (but failed) homicide/suicide signal to the actress Jodie Foster of the magnitude of his love unrequited. Newsworthy cases are likely to be those in which the target of erotomanic love unrequited surpasses the erotomanic lover in prestige or fame, and is unattainable. Correspondingly, a student's teacher, a patient's physician, or any other professional in the health-care hierarchy may be vulnerable as a target of erotomania. Those who know about the syndrome will seek the security and support of professional and legal consultants, whereas the naive target may all too readily become a victim.

An apparently innocuous question like "Are you married?" may be a first tentative sounding out of the possibility of a personalized relationship. Similarly, "Are you gay?" may signify more than a quest for a doctor who has "come out" professionally. In responding to such two-edged questions, the professional must explain that if they were relevant to professional competence, then an answer should be forthcoming. Otherwise they distract from the business at hand.

Unsolicited gifts are, metaphorically, another two-edged sword. Gifts impose, or at least imply, an obligation to reciprocate, perhaps with a personal favor. The technique for circumventing this burdensome obligation is to restrict the receiving of gifts to traditional gift-giving occasions. At other times, expressions of appreciation may be steered in the direction of a donation to a charitable or research foundation.

In today's legal and ethical climate, it spells professional ruin even to be accused, albeit falsely, of having sexual intercourse or other genital-erotic, breast-erotic, or mouth-erotic contact with a proband. To impress upon the uninitiated the gravity of transgression, the never-to-be-forgotten maxim is: "Don't shit where you eat."

In the guise of empowering potential victims, primarily women and children, against sexual abuse by professionals, protection has backfired to such a degree that the ancient concepts of the healing hands and the laying on of hands have become ethically suspect. It is nowadays ethically dangerous to comfort a crying child in one's arms or to reassure the grief-stricken with an embrace. It has actually happened that even the handshake of greeting or farewell may be misconstrued, as also a routine physical examination, or, in the course of taking a sexological history, routine inquiry regarding erotic fantasies.

As a safeguard against the interview as gossip and its possible repercussions, it is advisable, although not always feasible, to conduct an interview, if not with an auditor present, then within either earshot or view of other staff members; and to avoid scheduling appointments at a time when a building or suite of offices will be otherwise unoccupied.

In the dialogue of the interview, whereas exclusive open-endedness, like exclusive close-endedness is unproductive, the two in balanced proportion are not. At the outset of a workup, for instance, questions that fall into the general category of registration-desk statistics may be reasonably close-ended. However, there are pitfalls even here. Thus asking for a name is not enough; aliases are also required. Marital status—single, married, separated, or divorced—does not include polygamy or live-in cohabitation, or various combinations thereof. A question about number of offspring assumes the existence of a nuclear family exclusively, and does not allow for an extended family of step-children, foster children, adopted children, and grandchildren. The question should be about the composition of the household, with an added question about subsidiary households, and, in the present day and age, with still another added question about homelessness. The range of relevant registration-desk questions varies from one institution to another, and from one project to another, so that the registration questionnaire varies also. It is redesigned as need be, so as to be fail-safe and foolproof in accordance with the criteria of what it will be used for.

Close-ended questions have a legitimate place as a way of bringing open-ended inquiry on a given topic to a conclusion. This is when one may check specifics: names, ages, occupations, dates, times, frequencies, quantities, intensities, onsets, durations, estimates, documents, phone numbers, addresses, and such like.

The undisciplined rambling of the interview as gossip is transformed into the orderliness of the **interview as thematic inquiry** by adhering to a prepared schedule of inquiry. Unlike the interrogatory interview, with forced-choice responses, the thematic interview is an open-ended inquiry with unforced responses. The schedule of inquiry is not an inventory of questions, but an inventory of topics, a copy of which may be given to the informant, so as to expedite the interview.

In the era before recording machines, the least complete record of a thematic interview was that of the interviewer's own longhand notes. The most complete record was taken in shorthand on a court stenographer's machine. With the commercial marketing of electronic tape recorders in the 1960s, it became economically and technically feasible for an interview to be recorded and retrieved in full as a source of raw data available for independent verification, evaluation, enumerating, and scoring.

An essential discipline in taping a thematic interview is the keeping of a written list of headings by which to identify the sequence of topics and changes of topic in the transcribed version. The words seen by the transcribing secretary on the written list will be heard *verbatim* on the tape. The voice that speaks them may be that of either the interviewer or the respondent. In the headings, as throughout the transcript, the interviewer's voice is typed in upper case, and that of the respondent in lower case script. Too much upper case indicates that the interviewer was talking too much!

It is futile to record more data than can possibly be processed by the personnel and with the funds available. There are some thematic interviews that prove to be too wordy and to contain too many inconsequential and tangential digressions. It is then advisable, with the list of topics as a guide, to conduct a condensed summary interview to which interviewer and respondent both contribute. Only a small proportion of people are not able to quote themselves correctly in contributing to their own summary.

In an interrogatory interview, as in a written questionnaire, the criterion standard by which to estimate degree of magnitude on a rating scale, or of prevalence on a normative scale, or of incidence on a binary scale is the individual respondent's own, personal subjective standard. By contrast, in the thematic interview, the criterion standard is that of a panel or jury with a history of training and experience in applying the same criterion standard to all individuals. To illustrate, an individual's self-rating on consumption of alcohol may be light, whereas, from a larger data base, the panel would give a rating of heavy. The larger data base may be that of population statistics. Also, as is often the case in the thematic interview, self-data may be augmented from other sources, as when tests of blood alcohol level may alter a self-rating upward. Augmentation may come from other informants, as when a wife's ratings of a husband's impotence may or may not differ from his own estimate of its degree or frequency. In arriving at a rating, a panel is able to pool all sources of relevant information.

The interview as thematic inquiry, with its panel method of scoring, is the ideal procedure, and the most fair-minded one, in cases when an individual's destiny is at stake, as for example, in matters of education, career, or imprisonment. It is also the ideal procedure, and the one that yields the most information and loses the least, for initiating a survey of a small group of individuals all manifesting a phenomenon that has never previously been investigated—for example, the first-ever study of a pedigree of hermaphrodites concentrated in an isolated Stone Age tribe, the Sambia, of the Eastern Highlands of New Guinea (Herdt, 1981; 1984).

The interview as thematic inquiry is too time-consuming and costly to be used in large-scale surveys involving hundreds of people. Following the trail blazed by small thematic interview studies, it is possible to hybridize the thematic interview with the interrogatory interview to produce the semi-structured interview. The hybrid's structure is patterned after the Schedule of Inquiry to guarantee against omissions, but the majority of the Schedule's open-ended inquiries are analytically subdivided into a series of interrogatory questions, some of them with instructions such as: If you marked Yes, in box A, above, skip to Q.9. Some open-ended questions remain, however, and space is provided for respondents to add personal comments and provisos, and thus to add information that would be lost in a strictly interrogatory interview. The amount of time required to train interviewers to administer the semi-structured interview is considerably less than that to become adept at thematic interviewing. Thus there are more interviewers to match the large sample population. When Alfred Kinsey began his large-sample sex surveys at the end of the 1930s, in the era before machine recording, he and his interviewers used a semi-structured interview technique (Pomeroy et al., 1982). They committed the questions to memory and coded the responses as they were given, so that they could be unobtrusively recorded on code cards.

To Groom a Beginner

Tune in your TV to half a dozen news-show interviews and be assured of hearing a cardinal principle of interviewing being ignored. The interviewer will ask more than one question at a time. "What was it like to see the death chamber? Had you seen it before? What was your reaction? What was going through your mind about being executed? Were you prepared to die?"

A pile-up of questions like this one does not indicate whether all or only one should be answered. The respondent may come to the rescue by asking for specificity. Or he may attempt an over-all answer like: "My mind couldn't focus."

Then ensues the ignoring of another cardinal principle of interviewing, namely, never to be disingenuously benevolent, as in reducing a request for more with a diminutive: "Tell me a little bit about that." Alittlebitabout, telescoped into a single term, is a disingenuous banality to be avoided at all costs. Taken at face value, it evokes a reply such as: "Just that my mind was sort of blank," or "It wasn't anything."

In desperation to overcome the banal outcome of banal inquiry, an interviewer ignores another cardinal principle of interviewing and becomes undisciplined in body language. The hands in particular are flapped from left to right, revolved in circles, thrown apart and together, thrust forward and pulled back, and held outstretched, as though beseeching acknowledgement of the meaning of the words being spoken, and pleading: "You know? You know what I mean?" Words simultaneously cascade into long-winded, overinclusive sentences that put answers into the listener's ears, then end with a challenge to the listener: "Would you say it was like that?"

The language of gesture equals in importance the language of words and vocal intonation. The ideal technique by which to groom the beginner in the language of gesture is the videotape. Just as there is no substitute for listening to oneself on audio, there is no substitute for looking at oneself on video. Watching one's body language is the prelude to monitoring and using it as an actor does, electively and with optimal communicational significance. Excessive hand-waggling is distracting, if not distressing to the observer. So also are any of a variety of tic-like mannerisms that include head bobbing, stroking, twisting or pulling the hair of the head or face; scratching or rubbing eyes, ear, or nose; blinking too often, fluttering the eyelashes, and lifting the eyebrows; frowning; sucking the lips, tongue, or fingers; biting finger nails or cuticles; sniffing or snorting; throat clearing, grunts and other noises; playing with the fingers or a grasped object; tapping fingers or feet; adjusting the legs or crotch; adjusting hair, neckwear, or other clothing; nervous giggling and fatuous smiling; and other unspecified idiosyncracies.

Mannerisms are actions. Their converse is immobility: a face that is too often impassive and mask-like; arms folded closely to the body at times when being stretched apart would signify not exclusion but welcome; legs crossed as though poised to kick someone away; and the foot of one leg lifted onto the knee of the other, a posture that projects not a folksy image of informality but a foreshortened image of footwear barricading the person behind it.

For the grooming of a beginner, listening to one's own audiotape, preferably in synchrony with video, supplies in sound what is lacking in a typed transcript of words alone. It is by listening that one learns the do and don't rules of pacing, rate, loudness, and pitch or intonation of one's own speech.

The ungroomed beginner does not, as a general rule, do well with pacing the interview. Some beginners are far too long-winded, phrasing and rephrasing, as if straining earnestly to ensure that something quite simple can be made understandable. They usurp time that should belong to the respondent. Going at too fast a pace predominates over going too slow. For example, instead of being allowed enough time to complete a response, a respondent is cut short by a new, tangential question. The interruption may completely close off the topic of inquiry and change the course of the interview, as in the following. "I think I'm mostly submissive and masochistic, but I have this one girlfriend who's into being spanked, and . . ." How many girlfriends have you had like that?" "Well, it really depends on where I've been living and how much privacy. When I was at college . . ."

Gauging the frequency of pauses and the duration of silences is a specific challenge of pacing. At one extreme, silence is prematurely interrupted by intrusively rephrased questions, or ostensible reassurance that amounts to nothing more than inconsequential chatter irrelevant to whatever the silence is concealing. At the other extreme, silence unrelieved is a weapon of intimidation and tyranny when a respondent is in the throes of elective mutism. The silence of elective mutism means not that the respondent will not talk, but can not talk, so great is the power of a mental blockage. Responsibility for circumventing the mental blockage rests with the interviewer. A very telling example is that of the child with the female CVAH (congenital virilizing adrenal hyperplasia) syndrome and concomitant masculinized external genitalia (Chapter 2). Still living as a boy, he was afflicted with an extreme degree of elective mutism that prohibited the possibility of talking about changing to live as a girl, as noted in what follows.

> It was his mother's opinion that it would be easier for him to stay a boy. I took a sheet of paper and wrote two headings: man, woman. Under each was listed: yes, no, I don't know. After ten minutes of studying the page he almost furtively marked it and then, with embarrassment, allowed me to look. He had checked "I don't know" in both columns. . . . "It is necessary for him to discover," I wrote. "He is at a very immature state, psychosexually. Today was the first step in self-discovery. He will require more interviews and psychological sessions." They were scheduled weekly.
>
> In sessions three and four, an attempt to break the barrier of elective mutism with the help of hypnosis proved ineffectual. In session five, at the outset, he spoke briefly about having attended school for the morning session only and having made an easter basket. Then the trance-like state of silence returned. There was no mention of the written note that next morning I would find on the carpet, almost hidden under the sofa where he had been sitting. Though not quite literate, its message was unequivocal: "Dear DR. I do not wemt to Be a Boy. I wemt to Be a girl Just my sisters. FAEM STAMLEY B."

As with silence, so also with weeping, keeping quiet, and allowing enough time for a respondent to weep, but not too long without the reassurance of intervention. The common reaction is to intervene too soon with too much talk at too fast a rate. It is as if crying, like a fire, must be put out.

The experienced interviewer as well as the beginner who replays an audiotape of his/her interview listens to the intonation and timing, as well as the meaning of his vocalizations, and so learns what they convey about his subjective reaction to what he has heard—whether it be incredulous, jocular, flippant, bored, irritated, angry, or whatever. It would be dissembling to claim that such reactions do not occur in a professional relationship. What allows a relationship to be professional is that their occurrence precipitates not a judgmental response, but an analysis of what transpired. In the case of anger, for example, the interviewer might say: "I sounded angry after you had made a derogatory statement about all blacks, and therefore about me. If I sounded angry, then many other people would sound the same. How many angry-sounding people can you cope with before you have another rage attack?"

This particular explanation exemplifies a maxim as applicable to the grooming of the beginner in interviewing as to all and sundry: "Don't start a fight that you can't win." Like all maxims, this one has no guarantee of success. Nonetheless, maxims, like proverbs and parables, embody epigrammatic wisdom that predates logical and scientific wisdom by uncounted millennia of human history. The wisdom of maxims survives through their use as teaching devises.

Another maxim for the grooming of the beginner pertains to nonjudgmentalism. This one also has widespread applicability. It is: "Don't preach, teach, or judge; just talk." Telling means always telling about yourself. It means beginning sentences with the pronoun I. For example: "I can taste orange juice better than you can; and I defy you to prove otherwise." This I-sentence is declarative and noncontestable. It is neither right nor wrong, provable or disprovable, for I alone have access to my own taste of orange juice. If I assume that I can taste orange juice as well as you can, and if you do the same, and we both are correct, then our statements about the taste of orange juice will be convergent. Otherwise they will be divergent like the statements made about the color of oranges by two people, one color seeing, the other color blind.

I-sentences are about my reactions, and what I think, feel, dream, image, guess, conjecture, read into the future, and so on. My reactions are my own. I do not attribute them to anyone else. If anyone is to blame, it is I. The responsibility is mine. I am not accusing or passing judgment on anyone else.

Telling without the finger-wagging of preaching, teaching, and judging is an effective maxim for keeping open the channel of understanding between people who are important in each other's lives, whether intimately or professionally.

The exercise of monitoring videotapes of one's own performance as a beginner pays an excellent dividend insofar as the gestures and vocalizations that are self-monitored are monitored also in the person whom one interviews. They are a source of information that augments that of the words of the interview. Gestural information can be stored on videotape, just as intonation and other vocalizations can be stored on audiotape. It is not the storage, but the retrieval of gestural information that constitutes a problem, for there is no equivalent of an alphabet for transcribing them. Hence an essential part of the grooming of the beginner is directed toward the recognition and notation of nonlexical information. The notation is strictly phenomenological with no superimposed interpretation of what it signifies. To illustrate: immobilized facial muscles with a mask-like appearance is the phenomenon. The phenomenon in and of itself alone, however, does not declare its own significance or meaning. That requires additional, convergent evidence. Thus it would be unjustified to jump to the conclusion that a mask-like expression signifies apathy, indifference, or depression. It might signify that the person is in an unlifted hypnotic trance; or in an epileptiform, altered state of consciousness akin to a psychomotor, temporal-lobe seizure; or in the early stage of Parkinsonism or some other neurodegenerative disorder. By contrast, some anomalies of the face and of its expressions are diagnostically specific in some congenital syndromes.

As with the face, so also with other parts of the body and their functioning like squirming, athetoid movements, a stumbling or mincing gait, jaw movements, or hyperkinesis: recording of the phenomenon comes first, then a differential listing as to its diagnostic or other significance, and finally a convergence of data from other sources so as to confirm its most likely diagnostic significance. Hyperkinesis, for example, with its attendant distractibility and intrusive behavior, is written off by disciplinarians as naughtiness and disobedience in children for whom discipline is prescribed. Quite to the contrary, the agitated and restless overactivity of hyperkinesis may be a reaction to tyrannical and abusive discipline. It is seen also as a rebound phenomenon following rescue in children with a history of apathetic inertia associated with the Kaspar Hauser syndrome (Chapter 2) of dwarfism induced by child abuse at home. As a rebound phenomenon it is seen also in children recovering from hypothyroidism, in which case it resembles the hyperkinesis that is a primary, early sign of hyperthyroidism. Other syndromes of which hyperkinesis may be a manifestation include those induced by drugs, prescribed as well as nonprescribed, and by brain damage.

Giggling, smiling, and jocularity are worthy of special mention, for they may be misread at face value when in fact they should be construed respectively as nervous giggling, embarrassed smiling, and flippant jocularity. Then they are recognized for what they are, namely, cover-ups for distress and, as in the case of gallows humor, reactions to impending catastrophe.

The ungroomed beginner flounders helplessly in cul-de-sacs of silence, or improvises fatuous questions when he runs out of topics to pursue. That is why he/she needs to fall back on a Schedule of Inquiry (Chapter 8).

· 7 ·

Interview

Schedule of Inquiry

The existence of the Schedule of Inquiry as a document in manifold conveys to the respondent, who is entitled to have a personal copy, the message that the agenda of the thematic interview is not personalized, but routine. This message serves to define the situation as professionally reputable, and not in some way contrived to suit a personalized design of the interviewer. This distinction has importance particularly in lovemap biography interviews. The Schedule of Inquiry also allows the interviewer to move deftly from one topic to the next simply by saying, for example, "Lets move on to the next topic." Thus the beginning interviewer is spared the embarrassment of not knowing what to say next.

A straightforward way to begin open-ended inquiry is to indicate the topic on the Schedule with an invitation, such as: "Falling in love—tell me your ideas on that." Inquiry may be safely launched in this explicit way when the topic can be classified as belonging in the public domain, not the intimate and private domain.

Topics in the Public Domain

Topics in the public domain are those that are encountered in the print or electronic media, at church, school, or work, in sports and recreational groups, in family discussion, and so on. A short preamble ensures that a topic is located in the public domain. For example: "On television these days, there's a lot of talk about AIDS. What sort of information have you picked up about AIDS?" Or the preamble may be particularized as to time, event or person: "Everybody's basketball hero, Magic Johnson, said he has AIDS. What's your idea about getting AIDS?" Inquiry about AIDS provides a lead-in to inquiry about the meaning of being homosexual. An alternative lead-in might be a gay-pride march seen on TV, a local display of the Names Quilt memorial, gay attitudes at school, and so on. Other sexual topics in the public domain include teenaged pregnancy, unwed mother-hood, abortion rights, date rape, and sexual harassment.

Juveniles as well as adolescents and adults are exposed to topics in the public domain. For very young children, the public domain may be confined to the family domain. Then the interviewer may inquire about sexual information in the public domain of the family, for example, the pregnancy of a family member or friend; the genital appearance of a new baby relative to the informant's own; and the family custom regarding nudity.

In the thematic interview, information in the public domain is of value in approaching any theme that, in the private domain, is a source of shame, guilt, and the threat of reprisal, secondary to taboo, censorship, or criminalization. Sex is not the only such theme. Killing, especially homicide, theft, illicit drugs, and illicit finances are comparable themes.

Topics in the public domain provide information that has intrinsic value in its own right. In addition, they provide a gateway to topics in the private domain. They do not guarantee that the gateway will be used, but they do give the respondent a first-stage guarantee of the interviewer's ability to talk about, and to listen to potentially explosive material without having his/her ears explode. With this guarantee, the respondent may be able to entrust the interviewer with private and confidential secrets such as, for example, having one's baby born deformed following an unsuccessful attempt at abortion; or having not told one's husband that another man's sperm conceived one's newborn infant.

Explanatory Rationale

There are some topics that are neither in the public domain nor in the strictly private domain, but somewhere in between. Personal academic history or religious history are examples. Some people are able to give information on such topics without hesitation or restraint. Others are reticent. They are resentful of inquiry that is for them too inquisitive and personally intrusive. They are unable to justify the interviewer's curiosity.

The technique for dealing with this type of situation in open-ended inquiry is to introduce the topic with a preamble that offers an explanation of what use will be made of the respondent's information in the interviewer's over-all scheme of things. Consider, for example, the sexological history. The initial explanation might be simply that the sexological history has always proved sufficiently important that to omit it would be malpractice, but that particular topics may be put on hold, as need be, until the occasion is more auspicious.

There may be more that can be added to the initial explanation. It must invariably be genuine, not phony or patronizing. For example, one may be collecting information on male/female differences, if any, regarding which of the senses contributes most to sexuoerotic arousal (using vernacular vocabulary to ensure accuracy of meaning), namely, sight, hearing, skin senses, smell, and taste. Alternatively, one may be on the lookout for differences between two or more syndromes or conditions like blindness and deafness. It is for most people easier to give information about sensory imagery, either perceived or ideated, than it is about one's sexual history, even when the sensory imagery is sexual and erotic in content.

Inquiry about sensory arousal leads logically to inquiry about the age of onset of sexuoerotical imagery in sexual dreams and fantasies, with and without masturbation and/or orgasm. Here one's explanation, again genuine, might be that the information will be used in a comparative study of imagery in relationship to the number of sex chromosomes in three groups of males, one with the regular count of 46,XY, and two with supernumerary chromosomes, either 47,XXY or 47,XYY.

Still another explanation might pertain to a comparative study of bisexual imagery in both boys and girls with and without a prenatal history of an above-normal level of male hormone absorbed by brain cells in the sex-regulating regions of the brain.

For the respondent, these topic-by-topic explanations continue the initial phase of defining the interview as a whole so as to make it reasonable and sensible. They also take the interview down from the doctor-knows-best pedestal of authoritarian condescension and superiority, and allow it to become an enterprise that is more genuinely collaborative.

Catch-22 Technique

A Catch-22 question is one of the meanest questions on earth, and it may be introduced as such. It puts the listener in a damned-if-you-do, damned if you don't dilemma. Have you stopped raping your son or your daughter? is a Catch-22. So also is: If you keep having sex with your partner, you'll get HIV infected and die with AIDS. If you quit having sex, your partner will commit suicide. Which alternative do you justify?

A Catch-22 question may be used as a device of open-ended inquiry insofar as it invites examination of the implications of a dilemma at one remove from actually being caught in the dilemma. Like a joke, a Catch-22 question breaches a topic that is stigmatizing and censored. Especially among teenagers, personal homosexual history qualifies as such a topic. The skyscraper test is the Catch-22 that breaches it. The sex and pronouns of the protagonists and the proposed sexual activity are adapted to suit variable requirements. One version for male respondents is: You are at the top of the Empire State Building. A crazed sex terrorist is on the loose with a handgun. He entraps you on the parapet and demands, "Suck my dick or you go over." Which would you do? One of the utilities of this particular Catch-22 is that it paves the way for further inquiry based on the difference between homosexuality defined as an act and as an orientation—in other words, the difference between homosexual fellatio and homosexual gender identity. With this differentiation in place, an informant may be enabled to give a more accurate sexual biography.

As-If Technique

Unlike Catch-22s, as-if questions are quite benign. They allow a respondent to speculate without having to guard against censure or ridicule. "Spin the calendar ahead ten years," one says to a child of ten who is underachieving in school. "You are twenty. What are you doing with your life?"

This is a *fast-forward question*. It is modifiable to suit age, sex, and individual circumstance. Sometimes the answers are surprisingly disarming, as when a twenty-year-old prostitute, a dropout from rehabilitation, says that in a year she will be back in the life again, picking up rough men whose sadism will give her orgasms of maximum masochistic ecstasy, becoming pregnant again, and then making sure that social service will not be taking this baby away from her and forcing it into adoption.

Children from as young as age eight, in some cases, are able to fastforward to teenage and the onset of their dating life, sex life, and married life, projecting in detail the imagery and ideation of their subjectively formed "lovemap."

Fast-forward applies also to the closing end of the life-span: "You're sitting in your rocking chair, retired, and looking back over the glories and regrets of your life. Tell me what they might be."

As-if questions of a different species are *destiny questions*. They have to do with fate and the chance of either good luck or catastrophe. Good luck, for instance, is that "you have just won the lottery for $13 million. What does that do to your life?" And catastrophe: "Two months ago, you had a regular health check-up, and now the blood-test results show you are HIV positive. What difference might that make in your life?"

Other destiny questions pertain to being overdue in making both a will and a living will; or to having parents both in the eighties and no plans for yourself when they die; or to engaging in illegal sexual activity, or illegal commerce, and not having the name and phone number of an attorney to call should you be arrested. The list of destiny questions goes on and on, with different questions for different people.

As-if questions of yet another species are those that pertain to *as-if words* and their as-if meanings. As-if words sound as though they should be in the dictionary, but they are not. One set of as-if words resembles words built on the stem "sense," but their stem word is sex. Sense, sensual, and sensuality are actual words, and so are sex, sexual, and sexuality. But the following sex words are as-if words: sexuous, sexitive, sexitize, sexory, sexualism, sexualist, sexualistic, sextience, sextient, sextiment, and sextimental, to which may be added, for good measure, sexcitement.

Guessing meanings for these as-if words can become a parlor game. In a more serious vein, however, their guessed meanings become a vehicle for open-ended exploration of the combined interoceptive experience and exteroceptive expression of one's own intimate sexuality which, all too often, is limited through lack of conceptual terminology with which to analyze it.

Parable Technique

The secret monster in one's life is not always simply unspeakable but also, in some instances, "unwordable." The words of self-information have not yet been put into sequence. For example, in one sentence, a man retrieves his boyhood history of intense personal conflict over the feasibility of sex-reassignment as a solution to his own disability of congenital micropenis. In the second sentence, forty years later, he tells of the miraculous calm that the sight of blood produces when he mercilessly mutilates his own legs. He does not relate the second sentence to the first. An impasse has been reached.

Having reached an impasse in a thematic interview, the interviewer may resort to the technique of telling a parable. The parable in this case is derived from the man's own biography. It is a parable about a boy who forfeited the idea of sex reassignment to live as a girl after having ascertained that surgery could not provide the girl with a uterus, so that she would be sterile. As an alter ego she did not vanish but, in teenage, retaliated against a pubertally virilizing body with a micropenis by nearly disposing of it in suicide. After twenty years in absentia, she struck again, first in a wave of terrifying panic attacks, and next in a sabotage mission of mutilation that threatened to end in throat-slitting suicide.

For many people, professionals included, suicide is an unspeakable monster. The handbook of old wives' tales teaches the philosophy of the social contagion of evil. This is the philosophy of the proverbial three monkeys who hear, see, and speak no evil. It is still a popular and influential philosophy especially in its application to matters of sex and death. It prevents even professionals from inquiring about the details of suicidal imagery, even with a respondent for whom the imagery of suicide is a mental videotape played daily. Hence the applicability of the parable technique, as in the parable of the student whose suicide was foiled by a snowfall (Chapter 4).

Sex and death are unspeakable topics that need a parable to allow them to be spoken about. There is such a parable. It is drawn from the case of a young man, dependent since early childhood on a daily dose of cortisol to prevent death from irreversible adrenocortical hormonal deficiency. He resented both his illness and those who took care of it. He had a long history of failure to keep follow-up appointments. After an interval of years, he telephoned long-distance, greatly agitated in the midst of a crisis that required urgent attention, but he could not disclose its nature. Matters of such urgency, he was told, are usually sex and death; if death, suicide or homicide; if sex, human or animal, self or other, homosexual or heterosexual. That released the erstwhile unspeakable: "It's the gawdam dawg!" In drunken despair at having alienated his wife, he came home to an empty house, had tried to have sex with his pet, and would have killed both himself and the bitch had the phone call not saved him.

Instead of sex and death, sex and the checkbook may be the issue. The appropriate parable is brief. Drawn from pooled data, it is actuarial in nature, as follows: In the course of the past year, quite a few couples like yourselves came here with marital discord like your own. In at least four out of five cases they discovered that the grievances and complaints they first presented were really a cover-up for more basic issues of sex and money, or both. So, you two may make the same discovery.

A parable is a narrative sequence. Its events exist in time, not in causality. Thus, whereas one can construct a parable for the phenomenon of alter ego as an occurrence in time, like dual and multiple personality, there is no parable of its cause. Similarly, there is no scientific, causal parable of the gender-transposition phenomenon manifested as sex-reassignment transexualism.

A parable is not an explanation that is either true or false, right or wrong. It does not require the respondent's agreement or disagreement, but simply his/her consideration. The parable technique is a technique of open-ended inquiry designed to introduce a different viewpoint, and release new information that may have practical and applied significance in case management, or in data on long-term outcome.

A parable may be derived from one particular case, or from a composite of cases, provided it has the ring of authenticity. It may be tailored specifically to match what is suspected, though not yet apparent in the biography of a particular respondent. Alternatively, one particular parable may be routinely included in a batch of thematic interviews with a view to obtaining prevalence data for statistical enumeration.

Paleodigms

A parable may be derived conjointly from sources in folk wisdom and clinical wisdom—for example, that of the dwarf who needed only "a good, old-fashioned Victorian rest cure" in order to begin catching up in growth. This is a parable for parents and relatives of a child whose extreme form of dwarfism is diagnostically suspected, but needs to be confirmed as being domicile specific and secondary to secret but extremely abusive neglect and cruelty at home (Chapter 2). The promise of a rest cure as a solution, unlike the threat of having the child "taken away," does not evoke litigious retaliation. In the long run, it may permit the parents to disclose their pathological history of abuse, and to bring it to an end.

Yet another source from which a parable may be derived is literature. The older and more widely diffused the literature, the more likely is it to have spawned paleodigms (Greek, *paleo*, old, + *deiknynai*, to show), that is, very ancient bits of venerated wisdom known to all (Chapter 5). From the Bible, for instance, one derives a parable of the father Abraham abusing his son Isaac by tying him up and getting ready to kill him as a sacrifice for the remission of the sins of the father. This is a parable for the murderously abusive parent, father or mother, whose own child may quite literally die as a sacrifice and atonement for the parent's own sin. The parable technique may allow the parent to bring forth a connection between his/her own sin and sacrifice. The sin itself may have been hitherto unspeakable, like the mother's own birth as a product of father-daughter incest, for instance.

Another paleodigm from which is derived a parable of widespread modern significance is that fasting purifies the spirit. The parable of the fasting virgin applies to anorexia nervosa, the fasting disorder that purifies the spirit from the sins of the flesh, even at the cost of the annihilation of the flesh in death.

Free-Association Exercise

It is inherent in the very idea of open-ended inquiry that, except for the announced topic, there are no instructions or rules that put constraints on what the informant has to say by way of response. Thus the response may be characterized as free association to a topic. Completely free association lacks even the constraint of an announced topic. For children it may be likened to switching on one's own mental radio, and listening to the talk that comes out.

For some people the interrogatory checklist or inventory serves as a memory aid that maximizes the disclosure of personal and sensitive information. Confronted with the associative method of recall, they become tongue-tied. Conversely, there are some for whom interrogatories are incompatible with their predominant style of mentalization which is associative. These are people for whom an exercise in free association is eminently suited to the recall and disclosure of personal and sensitive information. As one association leads to another, it evokes information that would have escaped a more formal inquiry. Strategically placed in the course of a thematic interview, an exercise in free association allows the respondent free reign to review information already given, to recall additional memories, to make projections into the future, and to formulate new concepts and propositions.

Metaphorically, an exercise in free association may be regarded as the projection of imagery and ideation onto an empty surface in space, or into an empty period in time. Using the same metaphor, the parable technique may be regarded as a projection of imagery and ideation into space and time that is not empty, but confined within the boundaries set by the parable. The parable technique is a technique of contained association.

Projective Tests

Other techniques of contained association involve imagery and ideation projected within the confines not of a parable but some other stimulus. In the well-known Thematic Apperception Test, for example, each stimulus is a black-and-white drawing depicting a potentially dramatic theme. Into each picture, the respondent projects a story that may or may not be biographical. It may also be assigned a score on various rating scales.

Like story telling, sentence completion also involves the projection of verbal imagery and ideation. The constraints are tight, as they are determined by the first half of each unfinished sentence which is hand-picked to produce information on a topic deemed to be important—for example, the relationship to mother, father, or siblings. Sentences can be completed in writing or by dictation. Information is obtained on twenty-five topics with four sentences apiece. The yield of information is high relative to the time expended. In addition, each unusual response may be flagged and used as the stimulus to further inquiry.

In the well-known Rorschach ink-blot test, the respondent projects visual imagery and ideation onto each of ten printed ink blots. Whatever is reported as having been seen in each blot is relatively inconsequential as compared with the scoring category to which it is assigned. From the sumtotal of scores a personality profile is constructed, using concepts and terminology too diffuse to be either confirmed or disconfirmed, pragmatically. Rorschach readings are, alas, not too far removed from horoscope readings. This opinion is not, however, endorsed by members of the Rorschach-testing fraternity.

Based on the observation that the quality of children's drawing is age-dependent, human-figure drawing was initially devised as a test to measure mental age. The content of a drawing is also a projection of the respondent's imagery and ideation onto a surface. Thus drawing the human figure, singly or severally, evolved into a projective test on the basis of the premise that what is projected will incorporate prominent features of the body image of the person doing the drawing. For example, when the first instruction is to draw a person, the majority of people draw a person of their own sex. Not to do so is possibly, though not invariably, an indication of a gender-identity ambiguity.

A high-yield series of drawings comprises a person; a person of the other sex; yourself; yourself and friend; your family. Inquiry about body parts that are omitted, elaborated, or distorted gives contextual meaning to those parts and their significance for the self, as well as for whomever other than the self is depicted.

When two or more people are drawn on a page, inquiry may uncover a narrative or drama epitomized by their locations, activities, sizes, and graphic quality relative to one another. In family drawings, the same applies to the omission of self or another family member. Erasures, false starts, and superimpositions have their own significance. Thus, to preserve what might otherwise be erased, a felt-tip pen is better than a pencil.

Human-figure drawing may be looked upon as a nonverbal mode of open-ended inquiry. It allows the leaking out of information that may be exponible in words only after having first been pictorialized. Whereas some people are predominantly audile, others are predominantly visile.

Sportscaster Technique

"Doctor, let me ask you one thing." Unfurl the red flag of danger ahead as soon as you hear an entrapment request of this type. By giving consent, the listener is in the trap of being obliged to submit to a request without knowing how outrageous it might be. The request might be for a personal favor (Could you lend me fifty dollars until payday?); a request hinting at future intimacy (Are you married yourself?); or a request to take sides (Was I right or was I wrong? What would you have done if it had been your own child?).

The response that circumvents being entrapped by a red-flag question is: "I don't answer true/false questions, but you can spell out what it is you want to know."

In these instances when the red-flag question is the opening gambit of a ploy to lure the doctor or other health-care person into the role of a mercenary in an ongoing dispute, it is followed by a self-justifying account of the dispute. The account omits substantiating detail and achieves plausibility, if at all, by being cast in propositions that are abstruse, overinclusive, and overgeneralized. It falls into the metaphorical category of "high altitude cloud talk." The sportscaster technique is a way of coming down from the clouds.

As its name implies, the sportscaster technique is patterned after the play-by-play account of a game broadcast on radio. The sportscaster must convey the details of visible, three-dimensional action in words. Without the details of time, place, person, and action, the listener cannot follow the game. Similarly, in the absence of such detail, the health-care interviewer lacks the data from which to reconstruct, as accurately as possible, a dispute or other event as it actually occurred.

If each participant and observer of an event gives his/her version of what took place, the accuracy of its reconstruction is increased, and its significance may be quite differently construed. Individual participants or observers do not construe the same event or happening in identically the same way, but in ways that are idiosyncratic and mutually incompatible.

Data produced by the sportscaster technique allow the interviewer to escape entrapment as a mercenary. They also eliminate the role of mercenary by allowing the dispute to be reconstructed in propositions that permit its resolution. Such a change is exemplified in the case of a depressed person who has become a grievance collector, living in the role of self-perpetuating victimization. Application of the sportscaster technique to analyze, play-by-play, and person-to-person build-up of a particular grievance is, metaphorically, a "behavioral autopsy." The pathological finding is the tyranny of illness. That is to say, the victim of illness recognizes only his own victimization, and not that victimization in turn becomes the tyranny of illness for the caretakers. Threats of suicide tyrannize the caretakers, for example, whereas for the victim of depression they are a terminal symptom. Their tyranny alienates the caretakers and, in turn, perpetuates the cycle of victimization. Recognition of the cycle, and then arresting it, is a possible outcome of the sportscaster technique.

· 8 ·

Interview:
Sexological Redaction

Registration-Desk Inquiry

Part of the registration form is designed for over-all institutional usage, and part to meet the particular requirements of a particular project. Take nothing for granted, not even name and sex which, in the case of new born hermaphrodite babies, may not have been settled. Keep a record of a.k.a. (also known as), which applies to change of name with marriage or adoption, and to pseudonym, professional names, imposture names, and, in cases of transexualism, sex-change names. Extend the record of names, birth dates, and ages to include those of next of kin, parents, siblings, spouses or cohabitants, and offspring in particular. Include step-parents as well as natal parents, with dates of birth and marriage. List the ordinal position of the proband and his/her siblings by date of birth. Do the same for the proband's own offspring. Include miscarriages, abortions, and deaths. Include also siblings and offspring by adoption, fostering, step-parenthood, or nonmarital parenthood. List names and addresses of kin or friends who are prominent in the proband's life and who may be important in locating the proband for future follow-up.

Record the name, profession, and location data of the person or person's responsible for the proband's referral. If self-referral, explain how it came about.

Identify the various educational, vocational, social service, hospital, laboratory, clinical, military, and correctional agencies from which already existent records may be obtained. Record the Social Security number or other I.D. number, and details of health-insurance or other financial arrangements, as applicable.

It may be feasible for registration personnel to fill out supplementary sheets covering such additional information as composition of the household, household income, parental occupations, ethnic genealogy, residential history, travel history, manifestation of possible genetic traits or illnesses in the family pedigree, and so on. The pregnancy and birth history are often overlooked in psychological and social research, but should not be.

After the form has been filled out, date it, classify it by name, for example the name of the program or project in which it will be filed, identify the informant, and identify yourself by name and function as the person who filled it out.

Probative Tests

Probative means serving to test, try, or prove. Probative tests are those that require the subject being tested to try doing the task on which he is being tested on the spot, here and now, so as to prove whether or not he can succeed. Memorization and recall tests are probative tests, and so are tests for their impairment, manifested as aphasia and agnosia following brain injury. Tests of reaction time in responding to a stimulus, discriminating paired stimuli, or in finding or recognizing word associations also are probative, and so are dichotic (left-right) listening and discrimination tests. Intelligence tests are like academic and vocational achievement tests in being also of the probative type.

One of the defining characteristics of a probative test is that the person taking the test follows an instruction and produces a response which is scored by someone else, usually the person administering the test, who must follow standardized scoring instructions.

Intelligence tests are the most widely used of the probative tests in psychology. They are used to keep a record of mental age in relation to chronological age from which the IQ is calculated ($MA/CA \times 100 = IQ$). Since no instrument or machine exists with which to measure the actual amount of mental growth per annum, there is no guarantee that the amount is identical every year. Thus it is not known whether mental growth spurts at puberty like height does. Consequently, there is no way of guaranteeing that the IQ will be the same from year to year instead of fluctuating. Thus IQ should be regarded in the same way as blood pressure, and retested from time to time, so that changes can be recognized. In sexology, for example, it would be silly as well as unjustifiable to assume that children with pubertas precox who undergo the onset of puberty with extremely rapid physical growth from as early as age three, or even younger, will have an IQ that is fixed from then until teenage.

Cost alone may prohibit testing for IQ in every sexological research project. However, much remains to be ascertained about the relationship between sexological and intellectual development. The inclusion of intelligence testing is therefore recommended as part of a complete workup.

An IQ is obtained from an intelligence test on the basis of standardized norms calculated from the scores of a random probability sample of individuals culled from a much larger census population. There are no probative sexological tests for which similarly standardized norms exist. At best, an individual's test score can be compared with the average score of a specially selected small comparison or control group. For example, in a toy-play test of gender-identity/role (G-I/R), one records a juvenile proband's spontaneous use of toys stereotyped as masculine or feminine. A masculinity/femininity rating or score is then calculated from the record and compared with the average for a group of children who are either similar or different according to a particular criterion standard—a boy's score is compared with that of boys and girls of his own age, for example, and correspondingly for a girl.

Probative tests that are sexological and specific to genital function are few and far between. Tests that measure penis size during spontaneous nocturnal penile tumescence (NPT) fall into this category. In cases of copulatory erectile failure, NPT tests are alleged to differentiate so-called organic impotence, associated with diabetes mellitus, for instance, from so-called psychogenic impotence associated with a mental blockage. False positives and false negatives are so sufficiently frequent, however, that it is safer to use the NPT test for either group comparison studies, or for a before-and-after study of the same individual and never as the exclusive criterion for a diagnosis.

The same caution is needed with respect to tests of sexuoerotical arousal in response to auditory or visual arousal. Like NPT tests, these also use devices or gages attached to the penis to measure its erectile response. In women they measure changes in blood flow to the vulva or wall of the vagina. Especially in men, such tests have achieved undue professional and commercial prominence as would-be diagnostic tests for the legal offenses of rape and child molestation.

It would be sexologically feasible to design a probative test of successful and unsuccessful copulatory endeavor. Despite the potential diagnostic significance of such a test for couples afflicted with copulatory failure or incompetence, the sexual squeamishness of our era vetoes it. Moral prudery formerly vetoed the medical examination of an unclothed woman, irrespective of its life-and-death urgency, as it still does in some parts of the world.

Reportage Tests

Reportage means that which reports or gives an account of something. Reportage tests are often in the form of checklists or inventories. They require the proband being tested to report or declare a type of behavior or mental state, image, or idea that has already been manifested, that presently exists, or that is projected into the future. Reportage testing typically requires responses to an inventory of true/false or multiple-choice questions, or to an inventory of items to be rank-ordered or given a numerical rating, usually a three to seven-point rating scale. Responses may be given orally, graphically, or by card-sort. Reportage tests require self-report or a report on someone else, for example, one's child, one's parent, or one's spouse.

Reportage tests have the virtue of uniformity. The printout of the test question and the answer sheet are identical for each person to whom the test is administered, and so is the set of instructions. Many can be administered, either singly or to a large group, by a trained clerk, and then machine-tabulated and scored on the basis of standardized statistical norms. Uniformity is not the same as objectivity, however. What reportage tests gain in uniformity they lose in the subjective and individually variable criterion standards that each individual brings to the test (see Chapter 6). Reportage tests that are also forced-answer leave no room for individual provisos and qualifications, not to mention partial illiteracy in reading the test items. Therefore, no test score should be accepted as absolute. Especially for diagnostic purposes, upon which a person's very career may hinge, item analysis is a must. In an item analysis, responses that earned negative credits are identified and pursued further in open-ended inquiry so as to gain supplemental information regarding their significance. Negative, idiosyncratic, or bizarre responses very often may turn out to be of crucial diagnostic significance. A symptom check list like the Cornell Index, or some form of health inventory is very useful in this respect (Weider et al., 1948).

Some people are more adept at revealing embarrassingly intimate personal information first by making a mark on a checklist then by initiating a disclosure in open-ended dialogue. A parallel exists here with very young children some of whom are able to answer test questions with brief answers only, but fail to tell fantasy stories on request. The latter, however, may emerge at length in fantasy play.

Well-known reportage tests, like the self-reporting Minnesota Multiphasic Personality Inventory, are of minor relevance to sexology insofar as they lack sexological items of sufficient detail and discrimination (Hathaway et al., 1990). They also lack sexological scoring standards. Those concerned with diagnosis of psychopathology do not include sexological diagnoses. In consequence, they erroneously superimpose nonsexological diagnoses on sexological patients—misrepresenting paraphilia, for example, as borderline personality disorder.

Sexology is an impoverished science with few reportage tests of its own, and none with norms based on a national or other large-scale probability sample. This lack is explained by the success of the political and religious New Right in suppressing the funding of a national sexological survey, which is especially needed in the era of AIDS.

It is easy to assemble a list of questions and name it a test or scale. The value of such a scale, even though not fully standardized, is contingent on its epistemological foundations, and, in turn, on its veridicality relative to the phenomenon it purposes to assess. Defective epistemology and veridicality constitute a seriously neglected problem in sexological test construction. Much sexological research is thereby marred. One recent exception, and one of outstandingly good quality, was devised by Coxon and coauthors for the investigation of sexual behavior in relation to HIV transmission (Coxon et al., 1992). It has an excellent system for the reduction of raw data to code symbols.

Projective Tests

In its specifically psychological sense, projective means serving to externalize or objectify that which is primarily mental and subjective, as by analogy in transmitting a cinematographic image from a film onto a screen. A projective test is not an examination with right or wrong answers, but rather a formalized procedure designed to present a stimulus and to elicit a response that might uncover information not otherwise forthcoming.

Ideally, projective tests uncover information that is idiosyncratic and, therefore, does not lend itself to the establishment of norms. When formal scoring is attempted, as in the Rorschach inkblot test, its interpretation is more in the nature of an elusive prophesy than an actuarial prediction.

In sexology, projective tests are not diagnostic tests, although they may provide information contributory to a diagnosis. By and large, they are best defined not as tests but as procedures used to augment an open-ended interview—which is why they are dealt with in Chapter 6 above.

Inventory of Oblique Inquiries

An oblique inquiry is one in which a particular question, remark, or locution is used as a stimulus to evoke associated imagery and ideation. The parable technique (Chapter 6) is an example of oblique inquiry. Like the parable technique, all oblique inquiry is open-ended. It is the converse of orthogonal or direct inquiry or interrogation.

Unlike the published versions of projective tests, which also are oblique methods of inquiry, there are no commercially produced inventories of oblique inquiries. The following inventory of oblique topics can be adapted to the circumstances of the interview and the age of the informant. Each topic can be introduced as the title of a story to be narrated and recorded for a listener or an audience.

- My three greatest wishes
- What I would do with a million dollars
- The one crew member I would take with me on a long space voyage for two

- When I can be invisible for a day
- Supposing I can be born again
- Supposing I can change sex
- If I had only ten more years to live
- The animal I would most like to be
- The one thing that I really want to change about myself
- The earliest thing I can remember
- My other early memories
- Self-profile: For a pen pal
- Myself ten years from now
- My life in review in old age
- My obituary: By me
- My advice to parents
- I teach my student doctor about myself
- If I were the doctor, and you were the patient
- Mirror, mirror on the wall, how would I look if I were perfect?
- My idea of a good personality
- Pygmalion teaches his statue the meanings of six human emotions, one by one
- My idea of a psychiatrist (or other health care specialist)
- The first thing that comes into my mind, right now

Some individuals are adept at dealing with oblique inquiry, some not. In some cases the inventory will prove to be noncontributory, whereas in others it will lead to the disclosure of extensive biographical information, that may not otherwise be elicited. There is no formal or standardized scoring system.

Alter Ego Inquiry

Most of us have had the experience of talking to a person whom we know very well and feeling that we are talking to a stranger. One explanation is that people are not utterly consistent from minute to minute, day to day, and month to month. In fact, on a daily basis, everyone alters from being a person asleep and possibly dreaming, to being a person awake and processing a greater magnitude of information than when asleep. In some people the state of waking consciousness changes episodically. These are people who undergo an altered state of consciousness as, for example, from an abusive rage attack to affectionate tenderness.

Others have an alter ego, or dual personality, or maybe a multiple personality, each of which is likely to have its own name or nickname. An indisputable albeit extreme example of an alter ego is encountered in the cross-dressed, cross-gendered transvestophile who is Henry, the macho male at work, and Lisetta, the pampered ingenue when clothed as a female at home or at a party.

The Henry/Lisetta extreme highlights much lesser degrees of duality as, for example, in the formal personality that goes with one's title as Mr., Mrs., or Miss versus the informal personality that goes with one's first name. A first name and a nickname may similarly signify different personalities. Bobbie, for example, may be a bit of a rogue, but as Robert he is more conventional and highly productive as an artist.

A change of name may signify a change of personality which may happen, to a greater or lesser degree, when a woman changes from Miss to Mrs., or when either a man or a woman is invested with a title (Chapter 2). Greater significance, however, attaches to an elective name change when one discards with one's name something of the personality that went with it, and begins anew, either licitly or illicitly, with an alias.

Names, nicknames, and aliases, hating or being proud of one's given name, all carry enough personal significance to make the **Names Inquiry Technique** an open-ended inquiry into the self. Its counterpart is the **Age Inquiry Technique** of open-ended inquiry.

It is a byword that a woman's admitted age is a lie. Likewise a man's admitted age does not necessarily agree with his birthday age. In neither instance does the admitted age necessarily correspond with one's subjectively experienced age which may be either younger or older than the birthday age. Subjective age is the steering wheel that hauls much of the freight of the personality behind it. The pedophile's subjective age is juvenile. The adolescent's subjective age claims full-grown maturity. The man or woman in mid-life with a late adolescent or early-twenties subjective age becomes restless in marriage and leaves in search of a partner who matches his/her subjective age. Some grandparents reach the age of grandparenthood prematurely and stagnate. Others, never reaching it, search in vain for rejuvenation. Identify your subjective age and the circumstances of its advancement or standing still, and you reveal yourself anew.

With or without its own name or age, an alter ego may have its own privately recognized body image—that is to say, an image of the organs and parts of the body and of its morphological appearance as it ought to be ideally, and not as it is recognized and characterized by other people. It may actually happen, in some instances, that even the mirror reflects the privately recognized body image of the alter ego.

It is in pursuit of the privately recognized body image that millions of Americans pay millions of dollars to participate in weight reduction and exercise fitness programs. Hundreds of thousands pay millions more in support of the plastic-surgical industry to alter the morphology and appearance of the body in facial reconstruction, breast and pectoral implants, buttock reshaping, fat removal, and scalp hair implants. If the surgical outcome were more satisfactory, men would spend millions more for penis enlargements and foreskin restoration.

Tattoo and scarification gives visible evidence of the idealized body image, and has done so transculturally and apparently since time immemorial. Perfection of the idealized body image may be achieved also by the attachment of jewelry through holes pierced in the ear lobes, nostrils, lips, nipples, genitalia, and tongue. The human body is sexually dimorphic. So also is the body image, as is dramatically illustrated when the sexual morphology of the body image is discordant with the morphology of the natal sex, namely, in cases of transexualism. In these cases, the idealized body image is approximated by hormonal and surgical sex reassignment.

There are many aspects of the body image that people are able to talk about or depict in drawings upon request. Other aspects are more inchoate. They may disclose themselves more surreptitiously in the course of oblique inquiry.

Health Inquiry

The health inquiry is not a substitute for, but a supplement to the pediatric or adult medical chart and all that it contains from the physical examination, laboratory findings, specialty-clinic consultations and procedures, surgical, radiological, and pharmacologic treatments, and so on. The health-biography interview does require, however, that the interviewer be conversant with the etiology, diagnosis, prognosis, and treatment of the proband's syndrome and all the syndromes with which he works as an interview specialist.

Irrespective of what is in the written medical chart, it is always the proband's and/or the kinsfolk's own version of the history of health and illness from prenatal life onward that is sought for in the health-inquiry interview. The meaning and significance of a diagnosis is not necessarily the same for the expert, the proband, and the kinsfolk. In fact, the disparity may be remarkable. To illustrate: in one case (Money, 1991a, Ch.10) the meaning of a very young boy's symptoms was, for the experts, subsumed under the diagnosis of congenital virilizing adrenal hyperplasia (CVAH), a genetically recessive hereditary condition. For the mother the disorder signified God's punishment of her for having conceived the child in sibling incest. For the boy the significance of his disorder was that it made him the victim of capricious but extreme maternal child abuse which included noncompliance in the treatment program. Obviously, no one version of a person's health history should be taken as exclusively and absolutely correct. The different versions need to be considered together and consolidated into a unity.

Contributory factors from the prenatal, natal, and neonatal health biography are overlooked with sufficient frequency that inquiry about them requires special vigilance. Factors that may have affected the fetus include medications and other pharmacologic substances transported through the placenta. Conversely, nutritional substances may have been lacking.

From birth to death, at any time during the life span, the health history may be influenced by pharmacologic products. They may be inhaled, ingested, injected, or absorbed through the skin. Some are toxic, some not. Toxins may be absorbed accidentally, as in the case of lead-based, indoor paint chips, and of contaminants in the atmosphere, the drinking water, or food products. Some toxic substances may be obtained illicitly. Some do not need a prescription. Some prescribed drugs do have adverse side-effects of which the patient is not forewarned, as for example the hyposexual effects of antihypertensive drugs and of some psychotropic drugs. Since only prescription drugs will be on record in the medical chart, the only informant of nonprescription drug effects will be the person who has taken the drugs. Hence the importance of being nonjudgmental. Otherwise this often-neglected data in the health-history interview may remain unascertained.

Behavioral and mental manifestations or symptoms are a concomitant of many and diverse syndromes. They may be a derivative overlay, superimposed on the main symptoms, or they may themselves be primary. Regardless of origin, their expression is manifested ultimately by way of central and/or peripheral nervous-system function and its behavioral and mental synchronies and conjunctions. Some of these expressions are prodromal, and may lead to an early diagnosis—for example, the overactivity and distractibility that, in school, are early signs of the onset of juvenile hyperthyroidism; and conversely the lethargy and tardiness that herald the onset of juvenile hypothyroidism. Prodromal signs of this type are popularly construed as disobedience, laziness, or bad habits—quite erroneously, of course.

Giggling or chuckling to oneself may seem harmlessly trivial. With some embarrassment, a mother inquired about it in her son, a boy of six with extremely advanced idiopathic precocious puberty. It was, in fact, a symptom of gelastic (laughing) epilepsy, and the first sign that a tumor, a hamartoma, adjacent to the posterior pituitary gland, near the tuber cinereum, was responsible for the early onset of puberty, as well as laughing epilepsy (Money and Hosta, 1967; Niedemeyer, 1972).

Signs and symptoms of the foregoing type constitute a category of behavior for which, in the dictionary, no generic name exists. Specimens of behavior that are represented in this innominate category and that are pursued in the health inquiry are inventoried as follows.

- Motoric tics, twitches, spasms, posturings, and choreiform movements
- Behavioral reflexes like yawning, hiccuping, coughing

- Skin reactions as in shivering, sweating, itching, burning sensations, turning white, blushing, and being blue with cold or bruises
- Complex self-pacifying actions like thumb-sucking, rocking, head-banging, hair-twisting
- Complex self-mutilatory actions like nail-biting, scratching, self-cutting or burning, and chewing or plucking at parts of one's own body
- Unusual odors from the body or its excreta, some of which are syndrome specific
- Vocalizations, vocal tics, stammering and stuttering, crying, laughing, and raging
- Idiosyncratic behavior related to diet, eating, drinking, food-hoarding, regurgitation, and vomiting
- Idiosyncratic behavior related to elimination, feces-smearing, hoarding excrement, soiling household furniture and clothing (encopresis), and enuresis
- Behavior that is temporally dysregulated by being either too rapid, urgent, and hyperkinetic, or too slow, lethargic, and hypokinetic
- Behavior that is dysrhythmic, as in irregularity of breathing, heart rate, sleep-wake cyclicity, and hunger satiation cyclicity
- Unorthodox behavior secondary to sensory deficit such as congenital absence of the sense of pain, congenital anosmia, tone deafness, and color blindness
- Unorthodox behavior secondary to eidetic imagery in dreams, nightmares, fantasies, and hallucinations
- Eccentrically ritualistic behavior as in phobias, obsessions, addictions, and paraphilias

If the foregoing inventory were not of specimens of behavior, but of languages, then it would be possible to speak of a system subdivisible into letters, words, phrases, sentences, and paragraphs, with grammar, syntax, and idiom. There is no parallel set of names for the subdivision of the system of behavior from the top down to the basic bits and pieces from which it is built.

The irreducible bits and pieces that constitute the basic building blocks of paragraphs or large segments of behavior belong to us as members of the human species. They are part not of our individual or ontogenetic heritage, but of our species or phylogenetic heritage. The behavioral edifice that is constructed from them is the work of our individuality, whereas in and of themselves they are shared by all of us.

What are they, these elemental particles of behavior that are unlearned and phylogenetically shared? I rejected the term "phylogenetic mechanisms," as being too machine like and settled on the short word **phylism** (Money, 1983b; 1986b) which is defined as follows (Money, 1988a, p.218).

phylism: a newly coined term used to refer to an element or unit of response or behavior of an organism that belongs to an individual through its phylogenetic heritage as a member of its species (from Greek, *phylon*, tribe or race).

Some phylisms have everyday vernacular names, such as breathing, coughing, sneezing, hiccupping, drinking, swallowing, biting, chewing, pissing, shitting, fucking, laughing, crying, walking, grasping, holding, sweating, touching, hurting, tasting, smelling, hearing, and seeing. The complete list has not been counted. Other phylisms have Latinate names, like thermoregulation, salt regulation, and immunoregulation. Still others exist that have yet to be named, or that have been named only recently, for example, pairbonding and troopbonding (Money, 1990c, p.446).

Feierman (1990, p.458), taking a critical look at the concept of phylism from the viewpoint of ethology as applied to psychiatry wrote as follows.

A "phylism" also is compatible with the ethological definition, "a unit of adaptive functioning." This definition would make the relationship of a phylism to function similar to the relationship of a fixed-action pattern to (behavioral) structure. Fixed-action patterns change in function phylogenetically but maintain structural integrity, whereas phylisms change in structure phylogenetically but maintain functional integrity. Although it is likely that fixed-action patterns are under the control of the same or similar DNA on homologous chromosomes in closely related species, this mechanism is unknown and unlikely for phylisms. The mechanism of genetic transmission through phylogeny for a trait that is defined on the basis of function is yet to be fully understood. Nevertheless, the concept of a phylism seems to fill a certain need at this time inasmuch as there is no other term that means the same thing.

A phylism is not per se a symptom, but it becomes incorporated into a symptom which, in turn, becomes incorporated into a syndrome. At the present time, it is the responsibility of the diagnostician to know all of the syndromes in which a particular symptom and its constituent phylisms might appear. Should a computerized lexicon and thesaurus of phylisms and symptoms ever be constructed, it would increase every interviewer's diagnostic acumen.

Developmental Ages

It becomes evident from children who have either extreme retardation or extreme acceleration of growth and/or pubertal maturation that everyone has three ages: chronological or birthday age, physique or statural age, and social or behavioral age. Most people develop with the three ages in synchrony, but some do not. Either the physique age or the social age, or both, may be ahead of or behind the birthday age. The origins of discrepancies, when they develop, are manifold, ranging from errors of the genome to parental abuse and neglect. The ramifications of such discrepancies are individually and societally extensive in magnitude.

Developmental age data obtained directly from a proband are augmented with data, including test data, obtainable from kinsfolk, school teachers, and other outside sources. Retrospective data are, to a large extent, obtainable only from other people and documentary records.

Physique age is, for most purposes, equated with **height age**. Standardized tables of height age are routinely used in pediatrics. There are also tables for **bone age**, read from X-ray films of the bones of the hand. Physique is more than height and bone maturation, but its complexities, as in being overweight or underweight, for example, are too great to permit it to be standardized according to age. The changes of development at puberty introduce another complexity, especially since the chronological age at the onset of puberty is variable. There are, however, standards for the five stages of puberty regardless of age of onset (Tanner, 1975). It is considered within normal range if the onset of puberty is between the ages of 9 and 13 in girls, and 11 and 15 in boys. At the extremes, the onset of puberty may be as early as age 18 months, and as late as age 19 years.

Social age is not a monolithic unit, but rather a unity composed of modules that can be subdivided, rearranged, or consolidated as need be. The modules include mental age, scholastic age, sartorial age, recreational age, and vocational age.

In infancy, social age is subsumed under the over-all rubric of developmental age, which is appraised on the basis of the so-called milestones of development, namely, sequential achievements of sensorimotor coordination as in visual tracking, vocalization, lifting head or limbs, sitting, creeping, standing, walking, saying words, holding a cup, eating with a spoon, and so on.

For two-year-olds, there are tests and norms for developmental age. Some are renamed as tests for **mental age**, and some as tests for **social age** or social maturity. The latter comprise such items as self-feeding, self-dressing, buttoning a coat, tying laces, and so on. In the juvenile years, there are no formal tests of social age, insofar as social interaction with people of all ages rapidly becomes too complex to test in a formal way. By contrast, there are formal tests of mental age for all ages through adulthood.

In addition to mental age, **scholastic age** is the most tested component of social age. The tests are age-graded tests of achievement at school. Achievement tests are geared to the school curriculum so that their applicability is limited to schools that have the same curriculum.

Intelligence tests, by contrast, are predicated on a more widely dispersed pool of common knowledge, and so can be translated into foreign languages. Some modifications are needed along with new scoring norms in conformity with local customs and standards. Intelligence tests are not culture-free but culture-bound. Misunderstanding of this principle leads to systematic errors in the attribution of mental age to the members of cul-

tures other than those of the culture in which the test was originally standardized. The Wechsler Intelligence Scales, for example, were standardized
primarily on white middle-class and working-class Americans. They do not
tell the truth about the mental ages of Aboriginal Australians in Arnhem
Land on the north-central coast of Australia, nor of members of the black-
ghetto underclass culture in America.

Regardless of being "politically correct" or not, it would be foolish to
exclude the data of achievement tests and intelligence tests from the social
biography on the basis of the criticism that the norms of the tests are not
absolute, but are relative to time and place. When allowance is made for
their relativity and mutability, these scores are often of great value in revealing a discrepancy between birthday age and either scholastic age or
mental age, or both. The discrepancy may extend also to physique age.
Knowledge of a discrepancy opens the door to its possible rectification.

A discrepancy between birthday age and mental age may represent either
an elevated mental age or a retarded mental age either in toto or in part. It
is not uncommon to find specific superiorities or specific deficits in mental
functioning associated with specific syndromes, for example, syndromes
characterized by a chromosomal error. Girls with Turner (45,X) syndrome
are at risk for a specific disability for the logic of rotation of shapes in space.
It is a disability that has an adverse effect on map reading and direction
sense, and on mathematics and other primarily nonverbal forms of learning, but not on linguistic learning. By contrast, boys with Klinefelter
(47,XXY) syndrome are at risk for a specific disability for the logic of sequential arrangement in time. It has an adverse effect on language learning
and reading, insofar as spoken and written speech unfolds sequentially over
time. Praxic learning, that is, of spatial and three-dimensional skill, is not
affected in Klinefelter syndrome.

It was formerly an article of faith in the doctrine of intelligence testing
that the rate of intelligence growth does not fluctuate, and that mental age
increases in perfect synchrony with birthday age. Longitudinal follow-up
with repeated retesting of the same individuals shows this not to be so.
Change in IQ that reflects fluctuation, up or down, in the rate of intellectual
growth are characteristic not only of some children, but also of some syndromes, for example, the Kaspar Hauser syndrome of psychosocial (child-
abuse induced) dwarfism (Chapter 2).

A big fluctuation, up or down, in the role of intellectual growth is likely
to be paralleled by a fluctuation in the rate of scholastic growth. Scholastic
growth, however, is subject to its own fluctuations. Under favorable conditions, it may accelerate. Under unfavorable conditions it may not only de-
celerate, but come to a standstill. The catalogue of unfavorable conditions
is manifold and ranges from brain disease to psychopathology among close
kin and disciplinary abuse within the classroom.

Whereas the concept of **sartorial age** (Latin, *sartorius*, tailor) is widely
applied in the children's clothing industry, the term itself is not in common

usage. From the cradle to adolescence children's wear is age-graded not only according to size but also to style. Stylistically, the grading is not by annual increments, but more loosely by stages of development. Thus clothing style, to which may be added hair style, cosmetics, and adornments, may be used as an informal sartorial index of social age. Age-graded school uniforms are a more formal index.

The sartorial index may be used to advantage in cases in which the physique age and the pubertal age are out of step with the birthday age. The boy or girl of small stature and delayed onset of puberty, for example, may upgrade his/her sartorial age, which for a girl may include wearing a padded bra, so that it is closer to that of age-mates than to those of the same physique age. Correspondingly, in cases of advanced physique age and precocious onset of puberty, downgrading the sartorial age toward the birthday age enables the child not to appear older in social age than is, in fact, the case.

Children whose physique age and sartorial age are both in arrears are infantilized or juvenilized by age-mates and adults, so that their social age becomes arrested. The converse holds for children whose physique age and sartorial age are both precocious. They are "adolescentized" by others and penalized for not being adolescent in social age.

Sartorial precocity is consistent with misrepresentation of legal age which, in the event of a sexual relationship with an older partner, may have catastrophic legal repercussions for both parties on charges of sexual abuse of a minor.

Sartorial age is sex differential. Gender cross-dressing may be a fad, but it may also be an indicator of crossed gender.

Just as there are no formal tests of sartorial age, so also are there none for **recreational age**. Recreational age is not subdivided into annual increments, but loosely and informally into stages of development. There are age-graded toys and sit-down games and hobbies for children, as well as age-graded play groups, clubs, organizations, and sports teams. In the age-hierarchy of institutions like Boy Scouts and Girl Guides, growing up can be marked by graduation from one level to the next.

In an impressionist way, children do get rated by other children as well as adults, usually with disapproval if they engage too much or exclusively in recreations out of synchrony with their chronological age. A recreational age that is too low is, in general, more strongly disapproved than one that is too high, and more likely to be rated as an indication of something that has gone developmentally awry. Maintaining a recreational age in synchrony with birthday age is virtually insurmountable for children whose physique age is greatly retarded, and problematic for those whose physique age is precocious. They are advised to take up sports which put a premium on individual skill, not team cooperation, for example, gymnastics, skating, horseback-riding, skiing, scuba-diving, motorcycling, and the like.

During school years, the selectivity of team sports works to the advantage of those who qualify, and to the disadvantage of others. Compulsory sports for those who by temperament or physique do not qualify may be a disaster. For example, children with a birth defect of the genitalia, or with any deformity, may suffer the torture of the damned if forced to undress in public in the sports locker room. The repercussions may be extreme, for example, in lowering the scholastic age to the level of failure, and they may be very long-lasting, even throughout adulthood.

Play in infancy and childhood, especially inventive and creative play, involves a great deal of rehearsing the roles and activities of adulthood, including the vocations of adulthood.

Recreational age, together with scholastic age, blends imperceptively into **vocational age** for those whose academic career is extended into vocational or professional training. By contrast, in the absence of advanced training, there is an abrupt break between scholastic age and vocational age. An abrupt break, more so than a gradual transition, entails the risk that vocational growth will become prematurely arrested and vocational age retarded. The risk is greatest in a society in which the rate of total population expansion exceeds the rate of total occupational expansion. Under these conditions, vocational growth and increase in vocational age becomes the privilege of a segment of the society. In the nonprivileged segment, vocational growth is thwarted and vocational age retarded. When vocational growth is thwarted, the outcome is either resignation or rebellion, each of which may become societally epidemic, with manifold symptoms. One of the symptoms of resignation, for instance, is the perfection of resignation and the promise of better things to come under the pharmacologic influence of mind-altering drugs.

By contrast, one of the symptoms of rebellion is capricious criminality, targeted not against the privileged, but against the least powerful of one's own segment of society, including one's own kinsfolk and friends. Among the victims is the self, for this system is self-sabotaging and self-destructive. It leads to vengeance and imprisonment, or death.

In the segment of the society for which the gateway to vocational growth is open, some individuals achieve not only a high level of growth, but extraordinary feats of accomplishments as well. Some are the most brilliant accomplishments of civilization. Others, like the Inquisition and the Holocaust, are the most dismal black holes of civilization. Growth, per se, is growth. It may be healthy or cancerous and, dependent on one's criterion, good or bad, moral or immoral.

Kith and Kin Inquiry

Kith is defined in *Webster's New World Dictionary* as familiar friends, neighbors, or relatives, respectively; and kin is defined as one's relatives, collectively, or one's kindred. Thus kith and kin is a convenient and idiomatic term for those people who constitute what is, in the ethological sense, one's personal primate troop, namely, one's closest associates and family. These are the people among whom one grows up and under whose influence one's social identity is established.

When the proband is in the pediatric age group, it is taken for granted that the chief informants will be the parents or guardians. Somewhat naively, it is also taken for granted that they are paragons of accuracy and truth, so that too much reliance is put on what they declare, errors, memory lapses, and deceptions included. It is equally naive to put exclusive reliance on what the proband, whether juvenile, adolescent, or adult, has to say about interactions with parents, spouse, offspring, or other kindred or friends. For each informant, the same platitude applies, namely, that we all see the world, and the world of our human relationships, through our own eyes, sometimes in consensus with others and sometimes not. The kith and kin inquiry should, therefore, include more than one informant, each of whom will be protected with the guarantee of confidentiality. Mostly, only one person, the proband, will be considered the primary informant, but there may be two or more probands, as in cases involving sexological issues between a couple, or distributions of power and autonomy within a family.

One of the defining characteristics of a human kith and kin troop is that its members are typecast according to two criteria: sexual morphology and age morphology. Superimposed on these two criteria is the principle of role complementarity. The roles of men and women complement each other at a minimum on the criterion of procreation. The role of older and younger complement one another at a minimum on the criterion of responsibility and dependency.

Despite the morphological ambiguity of the sex organs that occurs in congenital intersexuality or hermaphroditism, babies with this birth defect are not typecast as intersex with a pronoun of their own, but as male or female, he or she. The challenge of growing up to be a person is, throughout the world, inseparable from the challenge of growing up masculine or feminine, or failing that, in-between. Developmentally, children meet the masculine/feminine challenge on the basis of the principle of gender complementarity and its counterpart, gender identification. Gender complementarity means reciprocation of one's own role with that of others whose sexual body morphology is not the same as one's own. Gender identification means conformation of one's own role in accord with that of others whose sexual body morphology is the same as one's own.

With respect to the criterion of age morphology, there is no way of beginning life as a mammal except as an infant utterly dependent on being nourished and otherwise protected by someone older and larger. The infant is born already equipped with phylisms prerequisite to establishing complementarity of pairbonding between helpless baby and providing mother. If these phylisms are absent or thwarted, of if they are not reciprocated by the mother, or surrogate mother, then pairbonding fails and the baby perishes.

On the criterion of age morphology, the challenge of growing up is one of progressive autonomy and independence from the authority of older and bigger people, including parents. The transition from one age stage to the next is not abruptly demarcated. Even the transition from juvenile through puberty to adolescence is gradual, albeit dramatic in its effect. Nonetheless, there are different and distinct roles for the infant, the toddler, the pre-schooler, the juvenile, the pubescent, the adolescent, the young adult, the young parent, the mid-life adult, and the grandparent. At each stage, the principle of age complementarity between oneself and people at each of the other morphological stages is at work; and so also is the principle of identification with others whose morphological stage is the same as one's own.

The principles of gender and age complementarity and identification are culture blind, but the contents of gender roles and age roles are not. On the contrary, the contents of these different roles are proportionately very much a product of time and place, but in combination with phyletic deter-minants also. The cultural content of roles is absorbed, assimilated, and incorporated into the individual members of the culture through the bi-ology of learning in the brain.

The cultural and historical dictates of gender and age roles vary from stereotypically strict to unstereotypically lax. Within the kith and kin troop, as well as within the larger society, there may be either consensus and conformity to the roles as set. Or there may be dissent and discord between the occupants of the two gender roles, or between two or more of the age roles.

So it is that dissension erupts into power struggles that may be vicious, even deadly, between males and females, husbands and wives, brothers and sisters, and other kith and kin. The issue is fairness and unfairness in the distribution of power and independence, and autonomy with respect not only to love and lust in the sexual encounter, but all the other implications of power in gender-differentiated roles.

The strategies and tactics of feuding include, on the one side, verbal abuse, humiliation, killing, brutal assault, sexual coercion, sexual molesta-tion, incest, financial deprivation, social confinement, starvation, abandon-ment, and divorce.

On the other side, the strategy and tactics of feuding include chronic proneness to aches, pains, bodily dysfunctions, and disease; accident prone-ness, addiction to abuse, abuse provocation, sexuoerotical aversion, false accusations of incest and sexual child abuse, pharmacologic dependency, depression and suicide.

When nongender dissension erupts between juveniles and adults or other age groups of the kith and kin, especially between parents and offspring, the same feuding tactics are in evidence. Age feuds like gender feuds revolve around issues of fairness and unfairness in the distribution of power, independence, and autonomy.

Power struggles between parents and minor children wreak havoc within families insofar as parents have more brute strength, more wealth, and more legal power than do their offspring. They also have the moral and religious support of a society that still largely endorses abusive discipline and deprivation in its philosophy of child-rearing.

As the relatively powerless underdogs, children have power over their parents only deviously. Armed with matches they burn things up. With knives and scissors they cut things. They steal and destroy things. They become sick, or suicidal. They become gender-dysphoric. They become school failures and dropouts. They attack siblings and friends. They join gangs. They take drugs. They become pregnant. The self-sabotaging litany goes on. For both the parents and the children it becomes a no-win situation, and continues in mutual agony and ambivalence into adulthood until the tables are eventually turned when old age progressively deprives parents of their erstwhile power.

Feuding within the network of the kith and kin troop may be countermanded by the necessity of an alliance against an enemy. Feuding factions within the troop then do not separate, but compromise and stay together, attached by the love/hate glue of ambivalence. Thus is the destructive force of unresolved power distribution passed on from one generation to the next, a slow-spreading epidemic that contaminates an ever increasing community with its ugly pathology.

The reverse holds true with respect to kith and kin troops that exist in harmony. Being healthy they mostly keep away from hospitals where pathology is the specialty, and away from criminology, the specialty of courts. They receive no specialty attention, and have no specialists to write about them.

An inquiry that focuses on the entire network of individuals in a kith and kin troop is a sociological task of a magnitude too great for a clinical workup of one proband, or perhaps a pair. Therefore, the focus is on the proband, so as to untangle, as much as is feasible, his/her alignments with key people in each generation of individuals in the network of those who are his/her allies and adversaries, or sometimes one, sometimes the other. Inquiry should identify the key people by the name they are known by, and by relationship to the proband as kin or kith. In addition, the inquiry should be oriented toward the history of the relationship with each person.

Aggression Inquiry

The circumstances of a particular person or study may indicate the inclusion of a detailed inquiry focused on a particular issue in the developmental history, such as the experience of pain, anxiety, fear, grief, depression, obsession, trance, euphoria, love-smittenness (limerence), or aggression— the topic of this section. Why focus here on aggression? The explanation is historical.

In the 1960s, it became a special topic of inquiry in the study of a newly discovered chromosomal anomaly, namely, the supernumerary Y or 47,XYY syndrome in males. Most of the early cases were identified in the course of a chromosomal survey of blood samples drawn from inmates of a maximum-security prison (Jacobs et al., 1968). Whereas it eventually transpired that the offenses of the 47,XYY men were predominantly offenses against property, not persons, the first and premature assumption was that males with the extra Y chromosome were dangerously aggressive and prone to crimes of violence, including sadistic rape and serial lust murder (Court Brown et al., 1968).

This assumption was not upheld when, in a study of a group of men and boys with the supernumerary Y syndrome, an aggression inquiry was included. It was found that they were loners not all of whom had a history of aggressive conduct, whereas all did have a history of capricious impulsiveness, variously manifested as impulsive acts of generosity, kindness, love, lust, theft, weeping, and suicide as well as of destructiveness and aggression (Money, Gaskin and Hull, 1970). The regulatory mechanism that translates foresight and forewarning into caution and restraint was out of order.

The inventory of topics in the aggression inquiry includes the following.

- History of temper tantrums or rage attacks from infancy onward
- History of sibling rivalry in infancy and childhood
- History of being a loner, outside the hierarchical pecking order of childhood
- History of team membership and body-contact sports
- History of juvenile and adolescent gang membership
- History of delinquent violence, destructiveness, and stealing
- History of cruelty to animals
- History of fascination with violent and warlike games in fantasy or enactment
- History of spectator cruelty
- History of personal participation in fights
- History of military experiences and activities
- History of arrests and charges
- History of nonviolent rivalry and competitiveness
- History of acquisitiveness and possessiveness
- History of gambling
- History of sex offending and paraphilia
- History of sexual jealousy and possessiveness

- History of depersonalization experiences and déjà vu
- History of alcohol, drugs, and medications
- History and significance of tattoos, if any
- History of body piercings, if any

Lovemap Inquiry

Sex. The word itself means your civil status as male or female quite independently of whether you have had sex or not, and if you have had sex, whether it was with a male or female, or possibly with yourself alone. One word with manifold meanings creates semantic chaos. Hence the title of this section is not sex inquiry, but lovemap inquiry. Lovemap is a new term (Money, 1983c) defined in the book *Lovemaps* as follows (Money, 1986a).

> lovemap: a developmental representation or template synchronously in the mind and in the brain depicting the idealized lover, the idealized love affair, and the idealized program of sexuoerotic activity projected in imagery or actually engaged in with that lover.

In subprimate species, the lovemap is manifested as a preliminary courtship ritual, comprised variously of invitational display, gesturing, and vocalization, followed by an act, or multiple acts of copulation. The coding of the lovemap in these species is differentiated as masculine or feminine in the nuclei and pathways of the sexual brain, under the direction of sex hormones during, for the most part, prenatal or perinatal life (Sitsen, 1988). Under contrived experimentation, however, including sex-segregated rearing, the subprimate lovemap is subject to alteration so that its expression is thwarted or distorted. The primate lovemap is, to an even greater degree, subject to postnatal intervention. The evidence in subhuman primates is experimental. In humans it is clinical, and it demonstrates that only the primordium of the lovemap is under the direction of brain hormonalization in prenatal life. Its coding is completed postnatally and is contingent on input that reaches the sexual brain through the senses—predominantly through the skin senses, perhaps augmented by smell and taste, and through the eyes and ears. The process is assimilative and unnoticed as well as apperceptive and explicitly learned.

The postnatal phase of lovemap formation begins in earliest infancy and is mediated through the skin senses. Nuzzling and sucking at the nipple is obviously life-sustaining. So also, though less well known, is stroking, petting, and rubbing of the skin surface, as it triggers the release of growth hormone from the pituitary gland (Money, 1992b, Ch.10). In boys the visibility of an erect penis while breast-feeding leaves no doubt that the close infant-mother skin contact has a sensuous, genital effect, and reciprocally the not uncommon maternal report of orgasm while breast-feeding leaves no doubt of an effect that for the mother is not only sensuous but also explicitly sexuoerotical.

The infant's early bond with the mother through breast-feeding and over-all skin stimulation is not only life-sustaining, but also a rehearsal for what will subsequently be recapitulated or replayed as proceptive loveplay or foreplay, preliminary to the reciprocal acceptance or union of the genitalia. This rehearsal/recapitulation phenomenon is not unique to lovemap formation. It is found also in the play of young animals and children as, for example, when kittens play at stalking and pouncing at a small moving object as though it were a mouse or a bird. The principle of recapitulation in the context of evolution is summed up in Ernst Haeckel's nineteenth-century dictum that ontogeny recapitulates phylogeny. Using this terminology, proceptive loveplay corresponds to ontogeny, and the infant-mother body-contact bond to phylogeny.

In the lovemap inquiry, the amount of retrievable information regarding the early infantile phase of lovemap formation is dependent on the availability of informants. There are, for example, some data from a follow-up study of young adults with a history of the syndrome of child-abuse dwarfism (Money, Annecillo and Lobato, 1990). These data indicate that deficient input from the mother-infant bond into the lovemap correlates with subsequent defective or impaired output in subsequent lover-lover proceptive loveplay. There are, as yet, no correlation data for the population at large.

What is needed from the lovemap inquiry is a body of data from which the developmental history of lovemap formation can be construed. The earliest data will be observational and provided by others, especially parents. In addition, the earliest data will include the proband's own policies, preconceptions, knowledge, and responses regarding the sexuality and eroticism of infancy and childhood. Topics of inquiry that pertain to lovemap development from infancy through prepuberty are as follows.

- History of genital self-exploration and genital self-play digitally or by rubbing or rocking
- History of early childhood rehearsal or gender-differential flirtatiousness in complementarity to an older person of the other sex, as in daddy's little girl, and mommy's little escort
- History of incongruous differentiation of gender identity
- History of kindergarten romance and affectionate attachment
- History of becoming aware of boy-girl genital difference and show-me demonstrations
- History of becoming aware of man-woman genital differences, and of child-adult differences in body morphology
- History of genital investigation play, as in playing doctor, or playing pregnancy and delivery

- History of dreams and fantasies of pregnancy and parenthood
- History of knowing where babies come from, and watching the birth of animals
- History of knowing about sexual intercourse
- History of dreams and fantasies of romance, weddings, and sexual intercourse
- History of boy-boy, girl-girl, and boy-girl sexual rehearsal play of the type normal among primate species, including simulated or penetrative genital intercourse
- History of animal sexual contacts
- History of sexual and reproductive information transmitted informally by age-mates or others, or formally in sex-educational instruction
- History of any untoward experiences rightly or wrongly construed as sexual molestation or abuse
- History of any experiences suspected of adversely affecting lovemap formation, such as abusive prohibition or discipline of childhood sexual curiosity or behavior, deprivation of normal sexual learning, the destruction of a childhood romance by separation or death, or the loss of a parent in divorce or death
- History of sleeping arrangements
- History of knowing about the meaning of homosexual, lesbian, and gay
- History of being teased or taunted as sissy, gay, lessie, or butch
- History of knowing about sexually transmitted diseases including HIV/AIDS
- History of knowledge of contraception
- Knowledge of pregnancies among teenaged friends
- Knowledge of sexual topics in the public domain, for example, abortion rights, teenaged pregnancy, etc.
- Age of onset, or prospective onset of personal sex life

Perhaps as early as age three, a child may be able to communicate fragments of information in a lovemap inquiry, but even by age five the information sought is difficult for children to process upon request. They already know that sexual knowledge is forbidden fruit plucked from the tree of the knowledge of good and evil, and that whatever they might have done sexually is prohibited in public, if not in private. Mostly they have received no help in translating vaguely comprehensible hearsay knowledge into its clearly comprehensible three-dimensional representation, and they have been given no clear guidelines as to what is rational and factual, and what is irrational and fictional. They inconsistently mix history with pseudologia fantastica. Under pressure, they guess and manufacture answers if answering per se promises to bring the moment of escape nearer.

Thus the current dogma of victimologists that from children they always obtain the truth about sex and sexual abuse is itself not true (Chapter 3). Nonetheless, what children do say about sex, although it may be valueless as courtroom testimony, is not valueless in terms of the lovemap and its developmental formation or malformation.

In lovemap histories obtained in the sexological clinic, developmental experiences centered on age eight keep turning up as having special significance for lovemap formation and malformation. Eight is the earliest age of the onset of a genuinely limerent love affair that goes on through adolescence into adulthood. Eight is also the age from which a paraphilic adult may date the first awareness of ideation and imagery pertaining to his/her paraphilia. It is the age when the still fragile lovemap is vulnerable to being impaired by either chronic or acute trauma that is either nonspecific or specifically genital, sexual, or erotic. The type of impairment may be either hypophilic, hyperphilic, or paraphilic—hypophilic more often in girls than boys, according to today's evidence, paraphilic more often in boys than girls, and hyperphilic perhaps equally in both.

Eight is the age when children's dreams become more complex and lengthy, as they will be throughout maturity (Foulkes, 1982; Foulkes et al., 1991). Cognitively, it is the age of being able to appreciate the conceptual ambiguity of jokes, riddles, and double entendres. Eight-year-olds are able to appreciate the conceptual ambivalence of their kith and kin, especially their parents, as well as of the entire society in which they are growing up, toward juvenile sexuality and eroticism. This ambivalence entraps a juvenile in the Catch-22 of being damned for being sexual and erotic, and damned for not being so. The damnation continues through puberty and adolescence. It demands the separation within the lovemap of love and affection, which is not damned, from lust and carnality, which is. Damned lust becomes confined in the dungeons of hypophilia, lost in the labyrinths of paraphilia, or else uncaged as hyperphilia.

In the later juvenile years or prepuberty, some children are able to contribute information to a lovemap inquiry, and some are not. In some the information may be vetoed, except for talk with age-mates, and in some it may be in a state of dormancy not available for disclosure until a later age.

The hormones of puberty activate the lovemap, but they do not create it. They do their work of activating what is already there by changing thresholds. They lower the threshold and thereby increase the sensitivity of the lovemap to the recognition of sexuoerotical imagery that matches its own and is transmitted to it by way of the senses. The hormones of puberty also lower the level of impedance at the threshold across which the lovemap spontaneously releases its sexuoerotical imagery and ideation to be manifested in dreams and fantasies. In addition, the hormones of puberty also lower the threshold for the transmission of sexuoerotical signals to the genitalia. In the vernacular, the outcome is to be more horny. In traditional psychological and psychoanalytic vocabulary, it is to have a sexual drive or to experience sexual desire or libido.

The hormones of puberty probably have another threshold effect, at least indirectly, namely, in lowering the threshold for being limerent, in other words for being love-smitten or, in the case of partially or wholly unrequited love, sick with the debilitating syndrome of lovesickness.

Both before and after puberty, there are religious, political, legal, societal, and individual constraints on the range of topics that may be covered in a lovemap inquiry. Other topics are relevant at one developmental age but not another. The following inventory of topics may, therefore, need to be abridged and adapted according to the circumstances and person at hand. An unusual circumstance, by way of illustration, would be that of a ten-year-old already postpubertal or, conversely, a nineteen-year-old still prepubertal. The inventory is as follows.

- Personal version of the onset and developmental milestones of puberty including, in females, menstrual history
- History of success or ineptitude in courtship, dating, and petting
- History of love-smittenness (limerence) and lovesickness
- History of sexuoerotic dreams and fantasies, with or without orgasm
- Visual versus tactual and other sensory channels of optimal sexuoerotic arousal for a) the self, and b) the partner(s)
- Personal experience of characterization of orgasm
- Erotic zones or regions relative to induction and locus of orgasm
- History of problems of attaining or timing of orgasm
- History of problems of erection, lubrication, or penovaginal penetration phobia
- Autoerotic history
- History of participation in specific erotosexual acts with partner of a) other sex, b) same sex as self
- Self-definition as gay or straight; homosexual, heterosexual, or bisexual; transvestite or transexual
- History of personal sex life and types of partnership
- Marital or cohabitational history
- History of parenthood
- Contraceptive history
- STD (sexually transmitted disease) history, and risk of exposure to HIV/AIDS
- History of use of aphrodisiacs, sexual drugs, or sexual toys
- History of exposure and response to explicit depictions of sex in narrative, pictorials, movies, and videotapes
- Knowledge of varieties of sex known as kinky, perverted, or paraphilic
- Personal experience with kinky, perverted, or paraphilic sex

- Personal sexuoerotical aversion
- Personal experience of sexual apathy and inertia (hyposexuality) versus hypersexuality
- Actual body measurements, morphology, and appearance as compared with idealized body-image
- Personal experience of genital mutilations, or of genital piercing and tattoo
- Personally recognized sexuoerotical changes associated with age, and in women before, during, and following the menopause
- History of acquisition of knowledge of sexual function, male and female

Diary-of-a-Day Inquiry

There is no inventory of topics of inquiry that can be so constructed as to divine, in advance, everything of significance that every respondent might have to disclose. Switching the organization of the inquiry from concepts to chronology allows miscellaneous information to emerge, whereas it might otherwise be missed. In the diary-of-a-day inquiry, the informant is requested to use the sportscaster technique to give a detail-by-detail account of what happened on a particular day of a specified date, from wake-up time to going to sleep. The details include not only acts that might be observed, but also thought ideas, and imaginations, as well as bodily sensations, feelings, and functions.

The diary-of-a-day may be narrated or written in retrospect one day later, or entries may be noted during the course of the actual day. Various items it contains may subsequently need further explanation or augmentation, and what did not happen may turn out to be as significant as what did.

A one-day diary of bodily sensations, feelings, and functions may be extended for a week or two, so as to capture diurnal and other rhythms and changes within.

Transcendence Inquiry

There are rules, ideals, allegiances, doctrines, and dogmas conformity to which is transcendent in people's lives. Transcendencies may be rational to you, and irrational to me, or vice versa. That is beside the point. Omission of the transcendence inquiry may lead to failure to recognize a principle of coherence in otherwise chaotic-appearing data from other inquiries. The inventory of the transcendence inquiry includes the following.

- History of religious upbringing, present adherence and degree of devotion

- History of membership in secular organizations dedicated to suprapersonal causes
- History of the clique one runs with, in school or elsewhere, and of gang membership
- History of heroes and hero-worship in childhood, adolescence, and later
- History of supernatural or uncanny experiences
- Belief in reincarnation
- History of depersonalization or déjà vu
- Belief in spiritual healing
- Personal philosophy of life and death

Flexibility of the Schedule of Inquiry

The same schedule of inquiry is used for each member of a particular cohort of individuals under evaluation or study, although the schedule itself is subject to revision or abbreviation so as to accommodate the requirement and objective of different programs and projects. The sequence in which topics are presented is flexible so as to accommodate the dialogue to the idiosyncrasies of each individual's biography and to allow it to proceed without becoming stilted. Administration of the schedule is additionally flexible in being transferrable from one staff person to another, each of whom complete separate sections, checking each topic as it has been covered. The schedule can also be adapted for telephone or mail inquires in projects involving long-term followup by establishing an inventory of significant questions or topics.

For patients in long-term followup, it is an advantage to be acquainted with several interviewers, as this makes for personalized continuity of care despite staff absences or changes, and also in the event of emergency. For the same reasons it is an advantage to have one or more trainees audit an interview. Having a staff mixed for age, race, and sex is advantageous, especially for those children who relate more readily to male or female, young or old, black or white.

· 9 ·

Clinical Biography

Case Management: The Prepositor

Prepositor (Latin, *praepositus*, placed before, a chief) is the title given to the person who is assigned to be the coordinator and manager of a case workup. The prepositor's job specification is to arrange a timetable for the tests and interviews conducted with the proband and other informants, to assign staff to do the tests and interviews, to keep track of test records and tape transcripts, and to obtain copies of other documents needed to complete the proband's consolidated record. Other documents include, variously, reports of pediatric, medical, and other clinical evaluations and treatments, laboratory data, admission and discharge summaries, operative notes, social service reports, school reports, records of hospitalization or institutionalization elsewhere, and, if applicable, court and prison records. The prepositor also monitors the distribution of outgoing documents related to the case. It is also a responsibility of the prepositor to monitor the format of the report.

Formatting the Report

The report is subdivided into sections, each with its own differentiating characteristics. The printout of the **first section**, and all copies thereof, is on letterhead, and dated so that its source of origin is evident. It names the prepositor. It lists all the information necessary to identify the proband by name, registration number, date of birth, address, phone number, and other details as needed. Then follows a list, in sequence, of the testing and interview sessions, and the names of the staff persons, including auditors, and subjects in each individual session and in the final joint session.

Section two contains referral information: the name and address of the referring person or agency, or the source of information for a self-referral. In addition, this section contains an explicit statement of the reason for referral, and the question for which an answer is requested. If the request lacks a boundary, then the response will be equally lacking and the report will be vague and diffuse like a phrenology reading, which, alas, is all too often the case in psychology and sexology. By contrast, an on-target question gets an on-target answer, even if it is to the effect that no definite answer, positive or negative, could be ascertained.

A referral without an on-target question is, in health-care practice, to be suspected as a deceptive way of "unloading" a nonpaying patient, or one with a complaint for which no adequate diagnosis has been made, and no satisfactory treatment has been found.

In **section three** there is a record of observational and descriptive data not of what the proband said, but of the method of delivery; the gestures and postures of body language; anomalies of muscular and motor movement; etiquette and demeanor; clothing style and visible appearance relative to age and gender status; any incidental observations worthy of note in proband-kin interactions; peculiarities of behavior while being tested and interviewed; and whatever else may seem pertinent to put on record.

The main body of the report begins with **section four**, the reporting of psychological testing. Each test is written up separately, with its own heading, and commences with a tabulation of actual scores and, for those tests that have them, normative ratings. Then follows specific mention of within-test peculiarities between subtests or in the responses to specific items. Examples may be reproduced, either in writing, or in xerox copies, for example of drawings. The possible diagnostic interpretations of ratings or within-test anomalies are noted, but in reference to the test record only, excluding in the meantime any reference whatsoever to the individual taking the test, or to that individual's diagnosis. The person doing the test write-up is as if blind to whom the write-up is about; and each test is written up without reference to the other tests or to the interviews. Comparisons come later.

Information from the interviews is reported in **section five**. In some cases a copy of the transcript of an interview or excerpts from an interview may be attached as an appendix. Mostly, however, only a conceptual abstract is called for, with the bulk of the transcripts filed and available to those authorized to see them. Topic headings typed into the transcripts of interviews (Chapter 6) expedite the indexing of the interviews thematically, which in turn expedites the composition of the abstract, and guards against omissions. The abstract is a record of what transpired, not an opinion as to what it signifies. It is phenomenological and descriptive, not interpretive.

Interpretation is reserved for **section six**. This is the section where the first-person singular pronoun may freely be used for the first time, accurately attributing inferences, conjectures, speculations, opinions, judgments, hypotheses, and theories as to their source of origin. One avoids at all costs the cagey evasiveness of hedging one's bets by using the passive voice without identifying the agent of action; by imposing provisos and conditionals (perhaps, probably, maybe, if, might, would be, should be, could be, it is interesting to note that, and such like); and by using terms that signify amorphous and ill-definable psychological states (inner life, instinctual drives, dependency needs, massive resistance, and other such intrapsychic homunculi who can be multiplied ad infinitum by adding -ivity or -uality to any stem).

Instead of being evasive, one makes a list of alternative possibilities or hypotheses similar to a list of differential diagnoses. Then the pros and cons of each alternative are considered. Missing information that might be obtained is called for. Then one alternative is given priority, or else priority cannot be assigned and uncertainty is not resolved. It is better to claim uncertainty than to guess and be wrong. Ignorance is not shameful when admitted, but to claim certitude falsely is imposture. To make an honest mistake is a source of mortification. It is to avoid mistakes that one undergoes advanced specialty training and, above all, consults with colleagues for a second opinion when in doubt. Not to do so is to commit the sin of hubris!

Medicine and justice both earn a living from what has gone wrong. Medicine searches for pathology, the judicial system for crime. The preponderance of their statements about health and behavior are, metaphorically, that the tank is half-empty, not half-full. This metaphor can be applied to the writing of a report. For example, one may tell a girl with congenital absence of ovaries that she is sterile and will not bear children, or that she will have children perhaps by embryo implantation, or by adoption, or by marrying an instant family.

Some of the half-empty statements that are the mainstay of psychological medicine are derogatory and objectionable in the ears of those to whom they apply. Thus to tell a person that he is lazy and unmotivated is quite different from saying that he undergoes periods of apathetic inertia, though the symptoms are the same. The one lays the responsibility on him; the other recognizes him as debilitated by an unidentified agent.

All reports should be written with the tank half-full, not half-empty. The litmus test is that the writer must read the report aloud to the person about whom it is written, and must defend it sentence by sentence as if in a courtroom where he is on trial for libelous statements. Half-full reports become therapeutic documents (and so do half-full interviews), whereas half-empty ones are injuriously traumatizing and offensive.

A report concludes with **section seven**, headed Recommendations. No airy-fairy here—everything must be very practicable. The rule of thumb is: make only recommendations the implementation of which you yourself will be able to oversee and be responsible for. This is a maddening restriction, especially when the ideal recommendation is unattainable through, say, lack of financial resources. Nonetheless, facing up to it may allow a lesser alternative not to be overlooked; or it may possibly contribute ultimately to an improvement in the availability of resources.

Illustrative Example I

This first illustrative example, together with the second which it precedes, are real-life documents. In each instance, the report was written for the benefit of the propositus who read it and gave permission for its publication, as did also the parents in the case of the boy. The boy's evaluation was made independently of the subsequent plan to submit the report for publication under the title, "Medicoscientific nonjudgmentalism incompatible with legal judgmentalism: A model case report—kleptomania" (Money, 1983a). The report is presented in two sections, A and B.

Prologue

Science belongs in one metaphysical universe of discourse, whereas law belongs in another. The ultimate propositions of science are principles of cause and effect formulated as experimental and statistical truths. The ultimate propositions of law are principles of good and bad formulated as established and ideological truths.

In law, free will and voluntary choice constitute the metaphysical foundation of the doctrine of personal responsibility for good and bad conduct. In the natural sciences, the concepts of free will and voluntary choice are alien to the concept of causality. In fact the more general concept of teleology is alien to the physical sciences; and its anachronistic retention in some versions of evolutionary theory in biology are the covert source of the creationist controversy. It is in the social sciences, however, that teleological theory, far from being alien or anachronistic, is still fashionable, particularly under the banner of humanistic science. In psychology and psychiatry, teleology exists as motivation theory, still the prevailing theory of purpose and causality in human behavior, despite the divergent theories of behavior modification, biological psychiatry, and neuroscience.

Motivation theory lays claim to being scientific. Because it deals with motives, it creates the illusion that it has the power to provide a scientific explanation of why a person does what he/she does, whether consciously or unconsciously, voluntarily or involuntarily. A motivational, that is, a teleological explanation, is not a scientific one, however. It is an explanation of causal purpose, whereas a scientific explanation is one of causal mechanism. Only the latter leads to prediction, prevention, and, ultimately, to control or regulation.

In the courtroom, a psychologist or psychiatrist as an expert witness is expected to be both scientific and teleological. Thus he is expected to be able to make a scientific statement about both motivation and a defendant's competence to stand trial on the basis of his voluntary competence and ability to know right from wrong at the time of the alleged crime.

The fact of the matter is that no psychologist or psychiatrist can make such a statement scientifically, for it is not a scientific but a judgmental one.

That is why law, on the one hand, and psychology/psychiatry on the other, are forever at loggerheads regarding criminal responsibility. It is the proper business of psychology/psychiatry, when it is being scientific, to be impartial and nonjudgmental. Judgmentalism is the business of the law. The law should not expect psychologists/psychiatrists to be judicial experts by profession, and they in turn should not become extensions of the judicial system.

The role of the psychologist/psychiatrist as an expert witness is to give information impartially and nonjudgmentally. For better or worse, lawyers, judge, and jury must bear the responsibility of making judgments of guilt or innocence, responsibility or incompetence. Legislators must bear responsibility of either updating laws to keep them abreast of science, or of failing to do so.

The following case report is written as a model of an impartial and nonjudgmental way of reporting the facts of the case. It is formulated without utilizing motivational theory. Instead, biographical relationships are established temporally.

Section A: Psychologic Test Report

Name: Anonymous
Chronologic Age: 13 years, 6 months
Date of Testing: July 29, 1982
Examiners: Gregory K. Lehne, Ph.D., Charles Annecillo, Sc.D.
Report Preparation: John Money, Ph.D.

Wechsler Intelligence Scale
for Children Revised (WISC-R)

Verbal IQ:	117
Performance IQ:	118
Full Scale IQ:	120

Subtested Scaled Scores

Verbal		Performance	
Information	10	Coding	13
Comprehension	19	Picture Completion	18
Arithmetic	11	Block Design	9
Similarities	11	Picture Arrangement	14
Digit Span	10	Object Assembly	9
Vocabulary	13	Mazes	9

Specific Factor Quotients (IQ Equivalents)

Verbal Reasoning (Info. + Comp. + Sim. + Voc.)	119
Numerical Reasoning (Arith. + Digit Span)	102
Praxic Reasoning (Block Des. + Obj. Assem.)	92

According to Wechsler, IQs between 120 and 129 are classified as Superior, 92nd to 98th percentile. IQs of 110–119 are classified as High Average, 75th to 91st percentile. IQs of 90–109 are Average, and are obtained by the middle 50 percent of the population.

The Verbal and Performance IQs do not differ significantly. However, the IQ Equivalent for Verbal Reasoning is more than 15 points higher than the IQ Equivalent for Numerical Reasoning and Praxic Reasoning, which is atypical, except in people gifted in social intelligence and ability to influence people.

The range of subtest scores is within acceptable limits except for very superior scores on Comprehension (19) and Picture Completion (18).

Individual item responses on the subtests are of good quality. For most of the subtests a regular pattern of successes is followed by failures on the most difficult items. On the Information and Vocabulary subtests, a scattering of successes on more difficult items is followed by failure on easier items. A lack of familiarity with the American cultural content of the failed items probably contributes to this pattern, but does not wholly explain it. On two subtests, Comprehension and Picture Completion, the maximum score for age was obtained, and there was not a single error.

Discussion: IQ

Today's testing was done to provide information for educational planning and placement. The boy was very cooperative and attentive during testing. The test results may be a few points too low, as is usually expected when a foreign boy takes an American test instead of a foreign revision. In addition, as above noted, he may have achieved a higher score on two tests had there been more difficult items.

There is no basis on which to make a statement regarding IQ constancy, except that it would be very rare to find a genuine lowering of IQ in the future.

Verbal reasoning is indicative of the ability for a high level of academic achievement, particularly in an academic program without too much emphasis on mathematics, mechanics, physics, and chemistry. Actual achievement, however, is a product not only of high IQ but also of other more elusive factors, commonly referred to as emotional. This boy is fortunate in being able to receive expert attention to problems of this nature which he is encountering in his development as a thirteen-year-old (see Psychohormonal Clinic Report, below).

Cornell Inventory

Index 21
Stop Questions 0

An index score of more than 13 is indicative of health problems, including psychopathy. A stop-question score of 0 indicates that none of the problems is incapacitating in the usual sense in which illness is said to be incapacitating.

In this case, the main problems are self-admitted fears and inadequacies (eight items), some symptoms of depression (three items) and some troublesome difficulties with anger and impulsive behavior (four items).

When interviewed about the test responses, the boy changed four answers from Yes to No, which lowered the Index Score on the test from 25 to 21, as analyzed above.

Sacks Sentence Completion Test

Rating	Frequency
2	2
1	1
0	12

There are fifteen subtests of four items each. On each subtest, a rating of 2, and to a lesser extent 1, indicates problematic relationships or concerns which may require therapeutic intervention. A rating of 0 indicates that all four completions were either bland or benign.

The ratings of 2 derive from completions indicating negative self-worth, for example:
My greatest mistake was being born.
The worst thing I ever did was steal.
My greatest weakness is work and life.
When luck turns against me I turn against myself.

Draw-A-Person Test (Harris Scoring)

	Male	Female
Raw Score	M-9	W-8
Standard Score	121	117
Percentile Rank	92	87

The first drawing, "a person," is of a male face. He said he began intending to draw "Doc," but could not draw him "so well," so he completed it as "just anyone, out of my head—devil from outer space, mad professor."

To draw a male first is typical of boys, although most often a full figure is drawn.

The "other sex" drawing is of a full figure, front view, a woman with the word "help" printed as being screamed by her—"She has just been attacked by someone trying to take her bag." This drawing "was going to be an old lady with a cigarette hanging out of her mouth," he said, but I "didn't know how to do that." The "draw yourself" figure is a full-fronted view with legs spread wide apart, elbows bent, hands in the pocket of a long jacket, and wearing a necktie, running spikes, and socks. The hair is dark and curly, and the mouth exaggerated and toothy (as in the other two drawings).

The "draw your family" picture depicts the six family members, including his older sister's baby, and the three cats; but, like a photographer, he did not put himself in the family. The figures, including the faces, are less detailed and more hurriedly drawn than in the first three drawings.

The centile rating of drawings is acceptable and is in line with Performance IQ.

Even though the drawings reflect lack of graphic training, this lack alone does not explain the grotesque appearance of the faces in the first three drawings. They are really masks with big, toothy mouths. The appearance of the face as an emblem of racial difference may be a major issue in this boy's personality.

Section B: Psychohormonal Clinic Report
Supplemental Data from Behavior Observed or on Record

The following catalogue of information is derived from parental report and my own observation of the boy.

He has a childhood history of avoiding television shows with black entertainers, dismissing them as rubbish; and of not mentioning himself as black.

From a Boy Scout, father-son weekend, he adopted a nickname for his father and often continues to use it instead of addressing him as dad. Though he has no corresponding name for his mother, it is seldom that one hears him address her as mum. In the course of narrative conversation, however, he does refer to his parents as my dad and my mother.

He does not have a history of having been quarrelsome, rebellious, defiant, or nonconforming in the home, either as a child or currently.

He has a history of living his own joys and sorrows rather autonomously, and not easily confiding them to others. He has made few close friendships.

Currently, one may at times interpret him as being subclinically depressed; or as emotionally inert and indifferent; or as antagonistic and resentful at being intruded upon; or as overtaken by elective mutism that prevents certain "unspeakable" personal issues or events (being adopted, illegitimate, and black) from being mentioned or even recognized for what they are. In adolescents, it is very difficult to differentiate these four clinical states from one another. The only term the boy himself could supply for them, subjectively, was being bored.

He is able to supervise his own sleep-wake cycle reasonably, and in conformity with daytime demands. His circadian sleep time, if he is undisturbed, is as long as ten hours. When he wakes up, he gets up. When he gets into bed, he goes to sleep readily and sleeps very soundly.

He likes to follow a self-demand meal schedule, and does not get hungry or thirsty for long periods of time. When he does eat, the amount is small. He often omits breakfast, or has a small bowl of cornflakes and milk, and often does not get hungry until midafternoon. Some days he eats only once a day—eating too soon, or too much, he said, makes his stomach feel bad.

He could eat excessive amounts of sweets, and distrusts his ability not to. Therefore, he said, he would rather avoid buying a large quantity, even to use as a gift.

His preferred menu is very restricted in range and excludes most fruits and vegetables. It also excludes beer, wine, and any alcoholic beverage. Additionally, there is no use of tobacco, medications, or drugs.

Though his total food intake is atypically low for a teenager as fully adolescent as he is at age thirteen and a half, he is healthy and has a good muscular physique.

He is self-scheduled with respect to personal hygiene. He sometimes likes to soak in a long hot bath. Otherwise he showers daily.

He is meticulous about wearing clean clothes. When it is necessary to take personal responsibility for his own laundry, he does so regularly, without fail. By contrast, it does not bother him to have clothing unfolded, and lying about where it was taken off.

He takes a proper share of responsibility in household tasks. For example, he does not need to be asked to do such tasks as mowing the grass, vacuuming and cleaning the swimming pool, or, in the kitchen, loading the dishwasher, but does these things as he sees that they need to be done.

He has a high degree of autonomy, capability, and confidence in traveling alone, either internationally with adult supervision through customs and passport control, or domestically by train or bus without any prior adult supervision or assistance in planning.

He likes living away from home, and wants to go away to boarding school again. He has no explanation other than that he likes it, just as he likes returning home for holidays.

He would like to go to school in the U.S. where he could be among other black students. Being with black people, he said, was more exciting. He was very positive in his enjoyment of living in a black urban area, despite the clutter, crowding, and untidiness outdoors, which he discounted by saying that it was very comfortable inside.

He did not find any appeal in the urban drug and crime scene, and gravitated toward young people who were like-minded.

He has no history of being into neighborhood delinquency or being a member of a delinquent group. There is only the recent history of becoming the partner of a same-aged delinquent (thieving) youth, with whom he joined in breaking and entering.

He has been in trouble at boarding school with complaints of bullying other students, stealing money, and subsequently lying about it. He cannot accept his status as having been expelled from school, witness the several long-distance returns he has made, completely on his own decision, in a vain attempt to be reinstated, and the regularity with which he wears his school sweatshirt.

At home, attending the local day school, he has been in trouble for stealing, and for being disruptive in the French class in which he is below grade level as a consequence of having been transferred from boarding school.

The history of school stealing, since it involved money (except once for sweets from the "tuck shop"), has the appearance of ordinary larceny, all the more so if under the aegis of a larcenous partner. But it is not ordinary larceny. The stealing at home and from relatives reveals that all of the boy's stealing has been the typical irrational stealing of kleptomania. That is to say, the excitement of the automatism of the stealing itself, of disposing of the loot without being discovered, and lying one's way through the denial of having done it, is the primary determinant. The loot itself was always inconsequential, and a white elephant once in his possession. Even the money was not needed or fully spent. If really needed it could have been obtained by the simple expedient of asking for it at home, which the boy readily admits to.

There is no way for the boy to find an explanation for his stealing, except to say that he does not know why—which is quite correct. He knows that he does it and, like an addict, cannot prevent its happening again.

If pressurized under questioning about stealing, his reaction is to hang his head and say nothing, in the typical fashion of elective mutism. This reaction occurs regardless of guilt or innocence, as was proved on one important occasion when he was under accusation that subsequently proved to be completely in error. He then had no technique for entering into a rational dialogue in his own defense. It was as if he did not know, when something was missing, whether he was responsible or not. He looked bewildered and confused. His answers were made in desperation, as if he were already defeated and never able to win. There was no retaliation, and no anger, just hopelessness in confrontation with a fate over which he had no control.

In addition to kleptomania, there is a history of being a prankster—for example, disappearing briefly from a companion as if lost; startling a companion from behind a curtain or doorway; deceptively touching a companion as if a third party had done it; and making the equivalent of April Fool's jokes and deceptions.

Some prankish incidents have had serious repercussions because of their being construed as sexual in import. One was to hide in a closet in the guest room at home and startle a longtime family friend as she prepared for bed. Another occurred after he had watched a TV horror movie with his sister and her visiting girlfriends who slept over. He disturbed the girls by trying to get into the bed with them. A third more recent incident occurred with a boyfriend when the two of them teased local girls by trying to touch their breasts. Subsequently, when alone, he tried the same tactic on a stranger (a Southern girl visiting overseas from the U.S.) who panicked and reported an attempted rape. Because of his advanced physical development, she could not judge his correct age of thirteen, despite his diminutive stature.

His knowledge of reproduction was utilitarian, but not scientifically and sexologically complete. The most important missing factor was the usual one, namely, that the realities of sexual intercourse could be legitimized as a topic of personal reference that he could discuss on an equal footing with adults. He categorized such information, as he did much else as well, as rubbish. Nonetheless, he did sit through a formal session of explicit films on coital technique, contraception, and childbirth used in the instruction of medical students and of parents and their adolescents with a sexological diagnosis. He had difficulty with the concept that his parents would rather help him to establish a contracepted sexual life with the consent of a partner (and the partner's parents) than have him in legal trouble for touching a stranger's breasts.

With respect to establishing a sexual life with a partner, the evidence is quite overt that he is not yet ready for sexual intercourse. Because he is physically mature enough to pass for sixteen years old, he was accepted as such when visiting in a black urban neighborhood in the U.S. There he had ample opportunity to meet partners of either sex. Whereas he showed no erotic interest in any boy, he was responsive to a sixteen-year-old girl's explicitly declared romantic interest in him. He visited in her home, but restricted the relationship to one of talking and socializing only, with no touching, kissing, or other body contact. He was not able to cope with overt, consensual sexual intimacy.

The other side of the coin of phobic avoidancy is addiction. In addiction, a person acts as a reckless daredevil, as it were, irrationally defiant of anxiety, fear, and consequences, as in the present history of stealing and alleged rape. In phobia, there is irrational anxiety, fear, or panic over consequences that to other people are trivial or even nonexistent. Phobia and addiction are polar opposites. Where one exists, the other may also lurk. There is in this case a history also of phobia. The boy has an extreme phobia of heights, and cannot look down from a window three or more floors up. He is incapacitated on tourist lookouts on tall buildings. He has also an extreme phobia of crawling, flying, and hopping insects, and of reptiles.

It is a commonplace of conventional folk wisdom and of theatrical art that chewing one's fingernails symbolically conveys apprehension. It may also mask apprehension, so that the person cannibalizes his nails instead of actually experiencing apprehension about something. Symbolism notwithstanding, it is very common for people who are addicted to some form of behavior that is punishable as antisocial to be nail chewers. In this boy's case it is a veritable compulsion. He has no nails or cuticles. Even though he looks absurd in public, at times of tension he cannot tolerate to be interrupted from having half his fist in his mouth, as he chews around his nails. He would like to quit this compulsion, and inquired about painting his fingers bitter as an aid to doing so.

Sometimes, though not always, it is possible to relate the boy's nail-chewing tension in some way to the issue of stealing. For example, upon his first entering a place, it is likely to occur as a respite from an initial agitated visual surveying and searching, together with restless opening of things to inspect their contents. It is though something is lost, the holy grail, so to speak, that could be in the room, and retrieved, if only he could locate it.

This peculiar type of agitation may actually spill over into sleep walking. On the first night of one visit away from home, the boy wandered into an adjacent bedroom and awakened one of the two women asleep there. It was 3 a.m., at which time he would normally have been too deeply asleep to be roused. Always modest about wearing pajamas, he had gone to sleep with them on, but now was naked. Questioned, he mumbled something about looking for the room he had gone to sleep in and returned there. Five hours later he was still sound asleep. Subsequently, he could not account for what he was told had happened.

Five Life Issues Delineated

Anyone who is in some way divergent from a criterion standard, no matter what the criterion, has no alternative except to come to terms with being divergent. This principle applies irrespective of whether or not the person can formulate the divergency as a personal issue. The greater the degree to which it remains unformulated, the more it becomes an unspeakable monster dissociated from the strategy for coping with it.

In this boy's case, I have been able to specify, and to discuss with him, five ways in which he is divergent.

First, he is the only adopted child in his household. The two younger sisters are offspring of the father and mother who are his adoptive parents, whereas the older sister and brother have the same mother but a different father.

Second, he is the only black member of an all-white family.

Third, he lives in a provincial town with a very small black population, and belongs to an even smaller affluent, middle-class black minority.

Fourth, he had an early onset of puberty by age twelve and completed the first four of the five stages of puberty by age thirteen and a half, whereas many of his contemporaries have not yet experienced the onset of puberty.

Fifth, his bone age, which is decreed by the hormones of puberty, formerly advanced him staturally over his age mates, but now will rapidly level off, leaving him short, at an estimated height as an adult of under one hundred and sixty-seven centimeters (five and a half feet).

It is very common, if not universal, among adopted children that the issue of their origins has a profound influence on them. For example, the very terminology of natural and biological parents implies that adoptive parents are unnatural and unbiological, which by further implication may mean that they are freaks of some sort. For this reason, the terminology I always use is birth parents, or natal parents.

In the present instance, the boy has not ever been denied information, such as is known, about his birth parents. When he was younger, he categorized the information as rubbish and did not talk about it. Recently, he listened to it again. His birth parents were studying abroad. Their home island was located for him on a map. His birth mother was a nurse, and his birth father a medical student. A cousin of the latter, a man of some position back home, was the man whom the birth mother planned to marry. This man came and married her with the idea of accepting the baby, but found himself unable to do so. The woman had to choose between him and the baby, and so gave the baby up for adoption.

The adopting parents had decided to extend their parenthood to include one adopted child. The possibility of adopting a black child, when they were informed of it, though totally unexpected, fitted in with their philosophy of sharing the hospitality of parenthood and the good fortune of affluence with a child who would otherwise be lacking them.

These few facts alone do not necessarily answer all the questions that may have occupied the imagination of this boy as to what manner of people his birth parents were, and how and why the pregnancy occurred. His imagination, like that of any child, adopted or otherwise, might have conjured up a theory to substitute for the official account of his parentage—for example, that the mother who had ostensibly adopted him had, in fact, given birth to him as a love child conceived illegitimately with a black man; or that his father had conceived him in adultery with a black girlfriend and then legitimized him as an adoptive son. Either alternative would allow additional fantasy conjectures as to the identity of the missing parent, and whether that person still existed. Similar conjectures are applicable to both of the natal parents if they did actually give up their child into adoption. The fantasy of untraced parentage is often a fantasy of lost grandeur. A hint of this was exposed in the present instance when the boy, practicing on the typewriter, wrote a playful note in which he assigned to himself the status of nobility.

Eventually, I think, he will need to track down his natal parents in order to demythologize them, and in order to evaluate at first hand whether he is more at peace in the island locale of his mythical home, where nearly everyone is black, or in his actual home in the town where he resides and where he has the possibility of becoming a celebrity because he stands out as a black person of the privileged class.

I do not know how soon this pilgrimage to his ancestral island should be scheduled, if at all. Nor does he. A determining factor will be his success in becoming relieved of his symptoms, particularly of kleptomania. The more successful, the less urgent the pilgrimage.

In family life, it is a well-established principle, universalized in Hans Anderson's story of the ugly duckling, that the sibling who is conspicuously different from the others is subject to different pressures of socialization. If benign, the difference is one of ascription, but if not, then of stigmatization. Either way, the difference is there, and must be dealt with by the child in daily life. One difference which is well exemplified in black American family life is divergence with respect to lightness and darkness of skin color— it is more prestigious to be light. This same prestige is accorded not only in the family, but in the neighborhood, school, and wider community. It is subtle and insidious in its influence.

There is no doubt whatsoever that such subtle and insidious influences have, in the present instance, affected this boy's life in ways many of which are too inchoate for him to put into words.

To illustrate, being black and adopted into a white family means being exposed to constant though covert doubt, suspicion, or curiosity when he is with white relatives if he refers to them as his siblings, parents, grandparents, cousins, aunts, and uncles. To be believed he must explain that he is adopted.

His being adopted means also the possible insinuation of being an illegitimate half-brother, born of his white mother and an unidentified black father, or of his white father and an unidentified black mother. In the schoolyard, such an insinuation can be made very explicit as an insult— and not be reported. And, of course, any adopted child is a target for being insulted as a bastard.

Being a member of a middle-class family as well as being black is the source of a special interracial issue, namely, that there is a paucity of middle-class black age-mates with whom to socialize and establish companionships. To be on an equal footing with friends of a lower socioeconomic class requires, almost inevitably, espousing some of their cultural values and relinquishing some of one's own.

To be precocious or delayed in the onset of puberty puts one's physique age out of synchrony with that of chronological age-mates. The gap between physique age and chronological age puts a strain on social age which is anchored to neither. In the present instance, the boy's physique age is somewhat precociously postpubertal (Stage IV on Tanner's five-stage scale) which is typically attained at age fifteen or sixteen, not at age thirteen and a half years. His social age is more advanced than that of prepubertal boys aged thirteen to fourteen, but not as advanced as that of postpubertal boys aged fifteen to sixteen. The same applies to pedagogical age.

Eventually the discrepancy between the three ages—physique, social, and chronological—will iron itself out. In the meantime, however, it puts special demands on the boy. At school, for example, he is not fully integrated with either his own chronological age group nor his own physique age group. Academically, his placement is related to chronological age, which means that his schoolmates look and act too immature for him. For them and for his teachers, he looks so much older than his chronological age that they expect more maturity than his years permit. The insidious consequence, particularly among adults, is that they fall into the trap of misconstruing him as a middle teenager who does not measure up mentally, emotionally, and behaviorally. The insidiousness of this error is pervasive, and is extraordinarily difficult to counteract.

The effects of early puberty are further compounded by the rapid increase in height during the pubertal growth spurt which gives a boy statural superiority over his age-mates. Soon, however, with epiphyseal fusion, the growing tips of the bones cement over, and one's final adult height becomes fixed. In the present instance, the boy's personal expectancy was for continued growth in height, so that he could be a tall athlete. There may be some further gain, but not enough to fulfill his ideal expectations. It is not easy for a boy to have to revise his ideal, and settle for something less.

Kleptomania: A Solution That Does Not Work

According to my appraisal, it is being an adopted, black minority of one amidst a white family and a predominantly white community that has overtaxed this boy's ability to cope. Early onset of puberty has increased the overload.

In human development, an overloaded system reacts in three ways or modes. One is to become mentally deranged and thought-disordered. One is to succumb to internal suffering, neurosis, and incapacitation. The third is to become externally directed toward doing something, however futile or antisocial. Usually one of the three predominates.

In the present state of knowledge, there is no theory to explain how or why any of these reactions will take place in any given individual. They are certainly not a matter of free will or voluntary choice. Nor can they be controlled by punishment or discipline.

In the present case, the boy's phobias belong in the second mode; but kleptomania, which predominates, belongs in the third mode, so also does paraphilic sexual assault which threatened to develop but did not.

Kleptomania, as already mentioned, is stealing that does not make sense in terms of the utility of what is stolen. Judged by the standards of professional larceny, it is very unprofessional and inept. It is impulsive rather than planned, and usually found out, even by way of self-incrimination. There is excitement in the stealing, in disposing of, or concealing the evidence, and in lying and alibiing, if accused.

The kleptomaniac cannot give a rational explanation of his stealing, nor of why a particular item was stolen. Kleptomania, by its very definition, is irrational. The thing stolen is a token, emblem, or symbol of something more valuable than it could ever be—a sort of holy grail embodying special power.

The holy grail, in this boy's case, can be defined as his birthright. It cannot be bestowed by the family and kin of his adoption, who in a sense took it away from him. Stealing is an act of desperation and futility, one may say, in an attempt to retrieve it. But it is not conceptualized in that way by the boy himself, for his birthright is the key to his identity, and it requires a high degree of sophistication in existential philosophy to put that into words.

The key to his discovering his identity, at this present phase of his existence, lies with black people, not white, for he himself is black. Thus it makes sense that he said he likes to go away from home to boarding school—for he cannot find his identity at home right now. It makes further sense that he felt very much at home among the black people of urban Baltimore; and that he said he would like to go to school in Baltimore and would be returning "sooner than you think." In a way, he has partly worked out the formula of his own salvation.

In some cases, kleptomania has erotic and sexual significance and is then called kleptophilia. That does not apply here. The sexual element in the case, namely, the forbiddeness of touching breasts, may be viewed as most likely a segment of the human courtship and foreplay ritual, misapplied and out of context. Its link with kleptomania may be formulated as another component of an identity search, namely, whether he will evolve erotosexually as the lover and partner of a white woman or a black one.

It is possible that these issues may already be resolved as a result of the combined effect of his experience with explicit sex education and with a black girlfriend during his stay in the U.S.

The pathology of kleptomania may already be going into remission, but the boy will not be able to consider himself safe from another attack until he is secure in his identity as a black person who has already been culturally whitened.

One of the worst things that could have happened to him did happen, namely, that the authorities in the boarding school where he felt that he belonged, reacting like his parents of birth, disinherited him for the second time—this time by expelling him. It could not have been more ill-timed—right at the time of coping with puberty. When he needed help the most, his trust was betrayed. He was given every reason to distrust the white establishment; and also what he must construe as the hypocrisy of academic democracy; and the hypocrisy of retaining fees for education which he did not receive because he was expelled as a thief! In addition, he was given an unspoken lesson in racism.

Of course he was a victim of nineteenth century penal philosophy which automatically classifies kleptomania as a crime or delinquency, and not as an illness. The one bright spot, and the hope for his future, is that his parents did not replicate the error. Because he is so young, and because it is still possible to treat him in the medicoscientific and not the penal mode, he can be rescued. Punishment and the penal system reinforces kleptomania by intensifying the excitement of risk. Thus the law achieves exactly the opposite of what it sets out to do.

Recommendations

Kleptomanic stealing shares some phenomenological features with psychomotor epileptic seizures, especially insofar as it repeats itself despite the patient's valiant effort never to do it again. The more it persists, therefore, the wiser it is to get a brainwave (EEG) workup. It is remotely possible that an antiepileptic medication or tranquilizer may help to bring the problem under control, if it persists. However, I prefer to be conservative with respect to medications, all the more so in teenage with its problems of compliancy.

In persistent cases, a period of hospitalization may be considered. The hospital must be one with a strong program specifically for teenagers. Few hospitals offer such a program.

Individual talking therapy of the nondirective or free-associative type does not work in a case like this one, for the problem expresses itself in action, not in talking about it.

The key to treatment lies in first of all figuring what to do and then, in consultation with the boy himself, arranging its implementation. He has independently arrived at the decision that he should go away to school, but he cannot specify what type of school, other than like the one he was expelled from.

My recommendation is for a school that has a very enlightened policy for teenagers—not traditional in either curriculum or discipline, and not paramilitary; but at the same time structuring and supervising the utilization of time with plenty of things to do. In this type of environment, the opportunities for kleptomania to reassert itself will be minimized. Then, as often happens in the pathologies of teenage, time may prove to be on his side and the disorder will go into remission as he resolves the issues of his birthright and his identity as an acculturated black citizen in a white, economically privileged culture.

It will be ideal if there is a boarding school for him that caters to black as well as white students in equal proportions, so that he will not be cast in the role of a minority student. There may be an international school that is racially integrated, pitched at a suitably high level academically, and able to help children who are struggling with personal behavioral problems.

Many a successful career, including those of great and famous people, has been built on the basis of turning trauma into triumph—or weakness into strength, debit into asset. Thus, in this boy's case, he could capitalize on his propensity for locating and stealing things by taking up a career as a private detective, or as an international espionage agent.

In all cases of behavioral pathology that constitutes a legal offense, a grave difficulty for the offender is that he gets cast into an adversarial relationship with just about everyone except those of his own spiritual kin, that is, those who do the same things as he does. What he lacks most are people who, being neither vindictive punishers nor permissive pushovers, are impartial and nonjudgmental toward the person, but not toward the pathological behavior and its consequences. That is a difficult role for one and the same person to adhere to—especially for a parent who feels the full weight of responsibility. All too often it is easier to be either accusatory and angered, or to pussyfoot around mentioning the taboo topic. Neither extreme works. There are times when a proverbial spade needs to be called a spade. It can be done in a nonjudgmental way, just as when one sometimes must talk to an epileptic relative about the further occurrence of seizures and their implications.

In this boy's case, it is to his benefit to have important people, like his parents, able to talk with him nonjudgmentally about black minority experiences, adoption, about finding his birth parents, the recurrence of stealing spells, psychosexual status, and sex life—neither too often, nor too seldom. Sometimes an opportune moment arrives unplanned. Otherwise there can be a regularly scheduled family conference time in which feelings can be aired and reactions expressed all round, as they are in family therapy.

Do-it-yourself family therapy is not easy to direct. If it should turn out that there are family tensions needing to be aired because of their bearing on the boy's future progress, then supervised family sessions should be arranged. It could happen, for instance, that if stealing has served as a safety valve, then without it the boy could go through a period of subsurface rage with his family for having had the issues of being black in a white household glossed over for years. This is not a prediction, but simply an example of what may or may not come up.

This report will serve as a good source of information to be shared between parents and child, and opened for discussion as need be. Therefore, I would like the boy himself to read it.

It can, of course, serve also as a document for use by such professionals and agencies as try to provide help for the boy and his family.

Epilogue

The style of this report belongs to the impartial and nonjudgmental scientific universe of discourse. It searches for the interconnectedness of things, as does all science. In this instance, the interconnectedness is between components of the biography in all of its aspects in both bodily and mental development. Interconnectedness is established more as a temporal than a causal relationship, because authentic causality cannot be proved on the basis of one case alone, but only when there is a larger population all manifesting the same phenomenon.

The impartiality and nonjudgmentalism of finding the connectedness of the biography is achieved by eschewing teleological or purposive explanations which, in psychology are manifested as explanations in terms of instincts, drives, needs, and motives. As a class, these are motivational explanations. They are, in fact, not explanations at all, but simply paraphrases of recorded observations.

Even though free will and voluntary choice may be expressly disavowed, motivational explanations nonetheless always imply personal responsibility for the conduct or misconduct involved. In an insidious way, this implication of personal responsibility enters into the majority of psychologic or psychiatric reports. Thus when a report is read by the person about whom it is written, it sounds accusatory and deprecatory. It also sounds stigmatizing and offensive since, by definition, the subject matter of a clinical report is pathology, not health. The effect of such a report on the person to whom it refers is traumatizing, not therapeutic.

By contrast, a report that is written impartially and nonjudgmentally does not carry overtones of personal blame. Instead of being traumatic, it may be given to the person concerned as a therapeutic document. It is not a license for unlimited permissiveness, as is popularly misconstrued by those who confuse scientific impartiality and professional nonjudgmentalism with permissiveness.

An impartial and nonjudgmental report does not project onto the person the blame that should be reserved for the pathology of the disease or disorder. It protects the person from the opprobrium, fear, and vengeance that rightfully should be directed to pathology. Even more importantly, it casts the person in the role of an ally in the fight against the pathology, not as an offender because of his/her being a victim of it. The patient is not the pathology.

A simple but telling illustration is that of a person with syphilis: one may punish the person for self-exposure to the infection, and in turn for exposing others to it; or one may break the chain of contagion by intervention with antibiotics. The patient is then cast in the role of an ally against the infection, and not as an offender against society. The patient is not his infection, but the victim of it.

In the case of kleptomania, and in fact of the majority of the behavioral diseases, there is as yet no equivalent of the spirochete onto which blame for the condition can be directed. It is therefore perilously easy to project blame and responsibility onto the person, so that he/she becomes equated with the disease, and the recipient of opprobrium, fear, and vengeance directed toward it. Once cast into the role of a disease, instead of the agent or victim of it, a person has no escape, except into the company and nonjudgmentalism of fellow sufferers. Pathology feasts upon itself. Progressive debilitation robs rehabilitation of its potential. Repeated punishment breeds recidivism for, as in all types of abuse, a person becomes addicted to being punished or abused. Like any addict, he/she cannot live without another fix.

Scientific impartiality and scientific nonjudgmentalism are as much concerned with bringing about change as is punitive judgmentalism. The latter system, through centuries of torture, Inquisition, and penal colonies has proved itself ineffectual. In the scientific system of medicine, the search is for interventions that will deconnect negative outcomes of biographical experience and reinforce positive ones. Biographical experience is unity of bodymind, so that interventions may be primarily through either body or the mind, or both.

The legal, which is also the pedagogical way of treatment is punitive and debilitative. The medicoscientific way of treatment is curative and rehabilitative. As the present case report illustrates, medicine and the law are at cross-purposes. Society does not yet know how to reconcile them.

Addendum, Ten Year Outcome: What might have become a sexological problem did not materialize. Perhaps as a legacy of his own adoption as a black infant into a white family, the man adopted a black infant son of the white woman whom he married, and subsequently they had a son of their own. With both of the boys the father established a very strong paternal bond. For eight years, the syndrome of kleptomania failed to go into long-term remission, but it may have done so after the young father found employment as a security officer, policing in other people the behavior that formerly he could not police in himself.

Illustrative Example II

This is an example of a case report (Money, 1990a) prepared specifically as a forensic document submitted to the county court by the attorney for a defendant who, as a serial lust murderer and rapist, was on trial for one of a series of murders and two of a series of rapes, namely, those that had been committed within the county in which the trial was held. The format of this report departs from the usual in having no section specifically for test and interview data, for which the explanation is that the defendant was seen in person only once, during a visit to the county jail where he was held on trial. The bulk of the copious data that he personally supplied beforehand had been in correspondence over the course of two years.

Although it runs contrary to the policy of this book, the language of causality was used in the report as a concession to the jury and others in the judicial system accustomed to the idiom of personal motivation and free will as the cause of criminal behavior. The defendant did not deny his crime. The issue on trial was whether or not it could have been self-prevented.

Prologue

Forensic sexology is a specialty in its own right, but its place in the courtroom is usually taken by forensic psychiatry and forensic psychology, the practitioners of which generally lack a specialty training in the sexology of paraphilic criminality. Criminal sex offenders seldom meet the diagnostic criteria of being psychotically schizophrenic, manic-depressive, or degeneratively brain diseased. Forensic argument usually centers therefore around the pros and cons of antisocial or so-called psychopathic personality disorder. Such arguments prove to be judicially irrelevant insofar as there is no precedent for either diagnosis to absolve a criminal sex offender from being legally responsible for his or her sexual conduct.

Legally, as well as on the criterion of community standards, a criminal sex-offense is antisocial. A sex offense is not, however, a symptom of a diffuse disease of antisocialism, but of a specific sexological disease of the type classified in DSM-III-R (Diagnostic and Statistical Manual of the American Psychiatric Association, Third Edition, Revised, 1987) as paraphilia. There are at least forty named paraphilias (Money, 1986a), not all of them criminally sex offending, most of which belong in DSM-III-R under entry #309.90, Paraphilia Not Otherwise Specified. One of the eight paraphilias listed by name in DSM-III-R is #302.84, Sexual Sadism, which encompasses paraphilic rape and lust murder.

Paraphilia (from the Greek, para-, beyond, amiss or altered +-philia, love) is a biomedical term. First used by I. F. Krauss, it was adopted by Wilhelm Stekel, whose pupil Benjamin Karpman, introduced it to American psychiatry in 1934 (Money and Lamacz, 1989). Its first official use was as a replacement for the legal term, "perversion," in DSM-III in 1980.

Raptophilia is derived from Latin rapere, to seize +-philia, and biastophilia from Greek biastes, rape or forced violation +-philia. These synonyms are names for rape as a paraphilic syndrome or disease, which is different from rape as coercive copulation imposed on, say, captives of war by marauding soldiers. Erotophonophilia is derived from Greek, *eros*, love + *phonein*, to murder, +-philia.

The judicial system has not yet caught up with contemporary forensic sexological medical science regarding the paraphilias that qualify legally as sex-offending. Judical and public sentiment alike favor the death sentence for the eradication of criminal sex offenders. The cause of their behavior, and the prevention of its incipient development in today's generation of boys and girls as they grow into puberty, adolescence, and adulthood, is not considered a public-health concern.

The following testimony is precedent setting in the State of Florida, and perhaps in all the other states as well. It recognizes the qualification of a sexologist as an expert in a sex-offender trial. Thus it serves notice to all sexologists nationwide as to where their future forensic responsibility lies.

In Florida, crimes that carry the death penalty require two jury trials, the first to decide guilt, and the second to decide sentencing. In the present instance, the defendant was on trial for sentencing with respect to three of his crimes, namely, two paraphilic rapes and one paraphilic lust murder. The jury members were selected on the basis of their not knowing that he had a history of multiple other offenses in both categories in a neighboring county.

Causality of Sexual Sadism

In *DSM-III-R* there are no separate categories for raptophilia and erotophonophilia, hence the defendant's diagnosis is classified under the "Sexual Disorders" as "Paraphilia 302.84, Sexual Sadism." In sexual sadism, an obsessive and compelling repetition of sexual thoughts, dreams, or fantasies may translate into acts in which the mental or physical suffering or a victim is intensely sexually arousing. Sexual sadism may involve restraining, blindfolding, or gagging as well as torturing by means of whipping, pinching, burning, electrical shock, cutting, stabbing, mutilating, raping, strangulating, and killing. In some instances the victim is a consenting masochist, and in others a non-consenting stranger who has been abducted or kidnapped.

Like other paraphilias, sexual sadism is a brain disease. The disease affects the centers and pathways in the brain that are responsible for sexual arousal, mating behavior, and reproduction of the species. The main part of the brain affected is known as the limbic system or paleocortex, which includes the amygdala, the hippocampus, and the hypothalamus (Maclean, 1962). The limbic region of the brain is responsible also for predation and attack in defense of both the self and the species. In the disease of sexual sadism, the brain becomes pathologically activated to transmit messages of attack simultaneously with messages of sexual arousal and mating behavior.

This pathological mix-up of messages in the brain is brought into being by faulty functioning of the brain's own chemistry. Faulty functioning may be triggered by something as grossly identifiable as brain damage resulting from the growth of a tumor, or from an open or closed head injury. Alternatively, the trigger may be submicroscopic and too subtle to be identified on the basis of current brain-scanning technology.

In either case, the faulty functioning is not continuous, but paroxysmal or episodic, in a manner similar to the seizure episodes of epilepsy. There is, in fact, a parallel between the episodic seizures of sexual sadism and epileptic seizures of the nonconvulsive type known as psychomotor or temporal lobe seizures. Psychomotor seizures take place in the temporal lobe, within the limbic region of the brain. As in other paraphilias, sexual sadism and epilepsy do, in some patients, coexist as a double diagnosis.

Whereas in any given case one contributory cause alone might not itself be sufficient to produce sexual sadism, the condition might occur as the aftermath of more than one contributory cause. Five categories of contributory causes are listed, as follows.

—Hereditary Predisposition: It may be in the family tree. Alternatively, it may be unique to the genes and chromosomes of the individual concerned. It might reveal itself as an inborn temperament or predisposition toward, for example, emotional instability and/or impulsiveness.

—Hormonal Functioning: It may be impaired, not only from puberty onward, but also in prenatal and neonatal life when hormones influence the sexual formation of the brain.

—Pathological Relationships: They may exist between child and parents, or child and other members of the household during the formative years.

—Sexual Abuse: If there is a history of childhood sexual abuse, it may not be retrievable. The less the chance of escape or rescue from sexual child abuse, the more traumatic the impact, and the less likely that it will be uncovered at a later date.

—Syndrome Overlap: There may be a predisposition toward another syndrome, which may or may not be hereditary. Temporal-lobe epilepsy has already been mentioned. Others include: bipolar (manic-depressive) disorder; schizoid preoccupations and obsessions; antisocialism and delinquency; and dissociative personality disorder. One form of dissociative disorder is dual or multiple personality (the so-called Three Faces of Eve or Dr. Jekyll and Mr. Hyde phenomena). Another form of dissociation is the fugue state (fugue is Latin for flight), meaning a flight into another self or personality (as in dual personality).

Contributory Causes in the Etiology of the Defendant's Sexual Sadism

—Hereditary Predisposition: The contributory causes include the possibility of hereditary predisposition on both the paternal and maternal side. Genes for the sexual behavior-type might have been transmitted by the father, insofar as it is said of him by his wife that when she was fourteen or fifteen, he raped her and threatened to kill her if she would not marry him (which she did).

Genes for emotional instability could very well have been transmitted from the mother. In addition, at the invisible level of the genes, there may be a hereditary error affecting hormonal function, insofar as there is a male cousin, son of a maternal aunt, who grew breasts at puberty, as did the defendant. The condition, known as gynecomastia, required surgical removal of the defendant's breasts at age fifteen.

The test for the defendant's own chromosome count showed that he does not have any extra or missing chromosomes. This does not indicate whether or not there are any errors among the genes of each chromosome.

—Hormonal Functioning: The history of adolescent gynecomastia is an indication of the failure of the defendant's own body to respond to its own male hormone in the normal male way. Another indication is the sparseness of body hair, the growth of which is dependent on male hormone. In addition, the blood level of the male hormone testosterone (tested on 13 May 1989) was reported at 283 ng/dl, whereas the mean is 627 ng/dl and the range is between 350 to 1030 ng/dl for the normal male. The pituitary hormones (the gonadotropins FSH and LH) that stimulate testicles to produce testosterone were normal, so they were not at fault. Though it seems contrary to common sense that a sexual sadist would have a deficient level of male hormone, such an occurrence is far from unique. It is congruent with the theory, presently under investigation, that a long-term deficiency in the supply of male hormone to a male's brain cells, first prenatally, and then after puberty, may have a demasculinizing effect and, indirectly, may be a contributory cause of abnormal masculine sexuality manifested as sexual sadism.

—Pathological Relationships: To the extent that pathological relationships within the family and household may be a contributory cause, they were certainly present in abundance during the defendant's juvenile years.

—Sexual Abuse: In the biography, as presently retrieved from the defendant, there was no childhood history of explicit sexual abuse. However, the living conditions required the defendant to share a bed with his mother until an advanced age of childhood, which can be very sexually disturbing to a growing boy. His mother would bring home a new male friend on many occasions, thus requiring her son to move from his bed to a sofa in the living room.

—Syndrome Overlap, Bipolar Disorder: There may be an overlap with manic-depressive bipolar disorder insofar as the defendant has a history of episodic insomnia, agitation, and not eating, with monomanic fixation, in fantasy and/or actual performance, on sexually sadistic rape or rape-murder. There was no ensuing state of overt depression, but a return to nonsadistic normality after prolonged sleep lasting fourteen hours or longer.

—Syndrome Overlap, Schizoid Disorder: The overlap with schizoid dis-

order does not, in this case, pertain to ruminative and obsessional intro-
spection, but to a paranoidal self-justifying rationalization that women
secretly entertain a fantasy of being coercively raped. This rationalization
does not extend to lust murder, for the performance of which the defendant
has absolutely no self-defense. His self-image does not include being a
killer.

—Syndrome Overlap, Antisocial Personality Disorder: The overlap with
antisocial personality disorder is, in effect, a semantic artifact, for sexual
sadism is, by definition, antisocial. The defendant had a juvenile and adolescent history of being in a network of age-mates who were on the wild
side. Their escapades were, however, insufficient to explain his becoming a
sexual sadist. Moreover, he prided himself on not having had sex with girls
who were already attached to boys whom he considered his special companions, opportunity notwithstanding.

—Syndrome Overlap, Epilepsy: In the present instance the overlap of
paraphilia with epilepsy was not manifested, as it is in some cases, as a
double diagnosis of paraphilia and epilepsy. The defendant does not have a
history of EEG-verified epileptic seizures either of the grand-mal convulsive
type, or of the temporal-lobe type, also known as psychomotor seizures.
He does, however, have a history of paraphilic attacks which resemble psychomotor seizures. Temporal-lobe or psychomotor seizures are characterized by an altered state of consciousness. They are not accompanied by
convulsions or loss of consciousness. While being in an altered state of
consciousness during a prolonged psychomotor seizure, a person may engage in activities that appear to be purposeful and voluntary, whereas they
are actually robotic and involuntary. Behavior that appears to be purposeful and voluntary is also characteristic of the altered state of consciousness
for which the technical term is paraphilic fugue state. For the duration of
the paraphilic fugue, there is, as the Latin etymology indicates, a flight from
the normal into the altered state of consciousness.

—Syndrome Overlap, Multiple Personality Disorder: The closest degree
of overlap between paraphilia and other diagnoses pertains to the dissociative disorder of multiple personality, in this case dual personality. The two
personalities are known by the defendant as Good Bobby and Bad Bobby.
When Good Bobby is in the ascendant, the handwriting of his letters from
prison differs from that in the letters from Bad Bobby. Both writers are of
high IQ and literate, but their letters differ in content and logic. Good
Bobby's letters are rational and realistic, even with respect to the pros and
cons of his fate on death row, and they do not evade self-incriminating
disclosures. Bad Bobby's letters are irrational, hostile, intolerant, and self-
sabotaging. It is in them that sexual sadism reemerges.

Precipitating Cause: Head Injury

—Childhood Head Injuries: Accident prone in childhood, the defendant
had five head injuries between ages three and nine. In the accident at age

seven, he was hit by an automobile and required hospitalization for facial and head wounds. The possibility of closed-brain impact injury is not on record; nor is there any record of whether or not there was a post-traumatic behavioral change.

—Adult Head Injury: Fifteen years ago there was another head injury at age twenty, as the consequence of being thrown from a motorcycle in a collision with an automobile. The head and facial impact was on the left, leaving him unconscious and in need of hospitalization. Again the medical record at the time is silent, one way or the other, regarding the possibility of either intracranial injury or behavioral changes. The collision produced identifiable, long-term trauma to the retina of the left eye, to the left facial nerves, and to the left inner-ear (vestibular) organs of balance.

The long-term outcome of the trauma to the retina is that it is evident in the course of an eye examination, but it is not subjectively bothersome. Injury to the facial nerves has left a feeling of tingling and numbness on the left side of the face. Damage to the organs of balance in the left inner ear has left a residual impairment of the sense of balance such that the walls of a room seem to be constantly moving, as if in an illusion or hallucination of motion.

The significance of the left-sided injury is that when brain injury is identifiable in sex offenders, it is more prevalent on the left than the right. In the present instance, the extent of possible residual brain injury was not revealed on a CAT scan. An EEG revealed a possible abnormality in the brain's limbic region, the region most likely to be damaged in sexual sadism. A battery of neurocognitional tests showed a deficit in the defendant's ability to classify and to perform tasks based on tactile discrimination, but did not localize the deficit.

There is no reference in the medical record at the time of the accident to any type of change in sexual behavior, thoughts, or fantasies—which is to be expected, insofar as in customary medical and hospital practice the sexological examination is routinely omitted. According to the defendant's own recall, however, and according to the recall of his ex-wife, he became hypersexual. Prior to the accident, the frequency of sexual intercourse was approximately three-four times a week, and of solo masturbation four-five times a week, which added up to a weekly total of eight or nine sexual orgasms, each with ejaculation. After the accident, the daily total became four or five, which adds up to a weekly average of thirty-two sexual orgasms per week, each with ejaculation. This high frequency is so abnormal that it is defined as hyperorgasmia or hypersexuality. It is never found in normal males, but it is typical in those with a diagnosis of paraphilia. It has also been recorded in some men following unsuccessful brain surgery for temporal-lobe epilepsy. It may also occur as the result of a brain lesion caused by a tumor or by a penetrating head wound.

Over and beyond the onset of hypersexuality following the head injury accident at age twenty, there was another change in sexuality. This was the onset of a progressive series of episodes in which the defendant loses possession of himself and becomes possessed by mental imagery, thoughts, and ideas of sexual sadism. He calls these episodes "one of my moods." During the course of one, he has the feeling of being "wired," and of being on "automatic pilot," and he pays no attention to eating and other everyday routines. He is fixated, like a dreamer having a nightmare, on a sexually sadistic fantasy. In former times, he might have held these "moods" temporarily at bay by means of daily periods of intense athletic activity to the point of exhaustion, followed by prolonged sleep. However, the "moods" could be neither started nor stopped by voluntary decision. Nowadays, in prison, they are suppressed by the medication Sinequan (doxepin hydrochloride), according to subjective report.

The technical term for what the defendant names a "mood" is, as stated above, a paraphilic fugue state, also known as a paraphilic attack. While having a paraphilic attack he undergoes an altered state of consciousness. In the altered state, he may actually have switched to the alternate personality, that is, from Good Bobby to Bad Bobby. It is in the fantasying and sleep dreaming of the altered state that crimes of rape and rape-murder may appear, after which they may be actually carried out, as in the case of the crimes for which the defendant was arrested and imprisoned five years ago, and for which he is presently on trial.

In conformity with the sum-total of evidence, there can be no doubt that the defendant was in an altered state of consciousness when he committed his crimes. In other words, he had taken flight from his rational self and had become irrationally possessed as a paraphilic sexual sadist.

Diagnostic Resources and Social Comment

As in all cases of paraphilia, the basis of the above conclusion regarding the etiology and diagnosis of the defendant's disorder is the clinical sexological workup which includes evidence from self-disclosure, behavioral and observational data, substantiating evidence from independent informants, and relevant documents and records.

Ideally, the defendant's sexological workup would have included the state-of-the-art brain investigations of the type that are done not routinely, but only at a few major research laboratories. For example, diagnostic Brain Electrical Activity Mapping (BEAM) monitors changes in brain activity over several hours or days. It has been used successfully by Pontius (1984, 1988) to demonstrate bilateral frontotemporal brain dysfunction in an atypical case of paraphilia.

There could have been more detailed brain-imaging with the CAT scan, PET scan, and MRI (Magnetic Resonance Imaging). According to Professor S. S. Cole, at the University of Michigan (personal communication, July 13, 1989), brain-imaging pictures hold the promise of demonstrating an association between brain injury and paraphilic behavioral change as they do for other types of behavioral change. With further investigation, a cryptic brain anomaly might be found in all paraphiles. The ideal would be to do the brain imaging while the paraphile is actually undergoing a paraphilic attack, and is in a paraphilically altered state of consciousness.

The complete sexological workup for sexual sadism and other paraphilias includes a pharmacological suppression test with a medication known to control paraphilic attacks. In the present instance the defendant has been taking the medication Sinequan, which does have the desired effect, thus confirming the diagnosis.

In North America the first use of a pharmacologic suppression test in a case of paraphilia was by Money, Migeon, and Rivarola in 1966 (Money 1970, 1987) using the antiandrogenic hormone medoxyprogesterone acetate (Depo-Provera®). In addition to its antiandrogenic effect, this hormone also has a direct brain effect, for it binds to cells in the anterior hypothalamus (Rees et al., 1986).

Another hormonal suppression test utilizes the antiandrogenic hormone, cyproterone acetate (Androcur®). This test is popular in Europe, but is not used in the U.S. as the hormone has not been cleared by the Food and Drug Administration.

With the gradual awakening of professional interest in paraphilic pharmacology in the recent past, other pharmacologic products have been shown to have a paraphilic suppression effect (Goldberg and Buongiorno, 1982–83; Fedoroff, 1988; Cesnik and Coleman, 1989). These include carbamazepine (Tegretol), buspirone hydrochloride (BuSpar), and lithium carbonate. The suppressive efficacy of the different medications is not the same for all paraphilias. Thus the efficacy of each one needs to be tested empirically for each individual.

According to a recent informal estimate by practicing trial attorneys, the cost of putting a criminal offender to death in the electric chair in Florida is $2,500,000. At that cost society relieves itself of one sexually sadistic, paraphilic rapist and murderer, but not of future occurrences of the same disease.

The folly of trying to eradicate disease by killing those who have it is that society deprives itself and its biomedical scientists of the chance to discover the cause of that disease. As in the case of the AIDS epidemic, knowing the cause of a disease is a first step toward discovering the method of preventing its recurrence. A paraphilic criminal may (or may not) have a vested interest in staying alive to volunteer for studies of the cause and prevention of paraphilic criminality in society. Society in its own self-interest can ill afford not to allow the paraphile to remain alive. Its atavistic alternative is to spend a king's ransom to guarantee the continuation of ignorance, which is not exactly the mark of being either civilized or scientific.

Summary

Forensic sexology is not synonymous with either forensic psychiatry or forensic psychology. It is a specialty in its own right, and is needed in the courtroom. Paraphilic sex offenders on trial are misrepresented as being, by their own choice, psychopathic or sociopathic deviates. They are unable to explain their paraphilic criminality to either themselves or society. In the case of serial rape and serial lust murder here presented, the contributory causes are examined and differentiated as hereditary predisposition, hormonal functioning, pathological relationships, sexual abuse, and syndrome overlap with bipolar disorder, schizoid disorder, antisocial personality disorder, epilepsy, and multiple-personality disorder. The precipitating causes were differentiated as childhood head injuries, and adult head injury at age twenty. The full range of diagnostic resources was not available for a prisoner on death row. Capital punishment has not prevented the reemergence in each new generation of serial rape and serial lust murder as an epidemiological public health problem. Punishment is an ineffectual substitute for epidemiological research into cause, effect, and prevention.

Addendum

Five years later, in preparation for a retrial in 1993, the defendant was given a PET scan. "It shows clearly," he wrote, "that there is an abnormality on the left side (the side fractured in 1974), and a clear difference in the function of the left and right sides."

Supplemental Resources

Vandalized Lovemaps (Money and Lamacz, 1989) contains seven clinical biographies which document paraphilic outcome of sexological development in seven cases originally referred to pediatric psychoendocrinology not with a paraphilia, but some other infantile or juvenile syndrome.

Biographies of Gender and Hermaphroditism in Paired Comparisons (Money, 1991a), subtitled *Clinical Supplement to the Handbook of Sexology*, contains twenty-four clinical biographies in twelve matched pairs. Each case in a pair serves as a comparison or contrast to the other on the basis of being in part similar and in part divergent. For example, two siblings are born with the same syndrome of male hermaphroditism. Both are officially assigned as girls. In adulthood, one lives as a man, the other as a woman.

· 10 ·

Sexology: Temporal vs. Causal Explanations, I

Temporal and Causal Sequences

There are two kinds of predictions in science. One is temporal. The other is causal. Temporal predictions tell you what will happen next as a sequel to what has already happened. For example, if daylight dawns, then the darkness of night will ensue later. But as everyone knows, daylight does not cause darkness. The causal explanation of predictable regularity is different. Ever since long before Aristotle, with his separation of causality into necessary and sufficient, causal explanations have had great intellectual prestige. Even when they are wrong they promise a guarantee of sublime predictability. Temporal sequences, however, when they occur with unerring regularity, guarantee as much predictive power as do causal sequences. They are also much more foolproof, for they survive the life and death of all explanations of what causes them as, for example, the regularities of the heavenly bodies have survived changes in cosmological explanations of their motion from astrology to spacecraft astronomy.

Some causal explanations are dismissed as the delusions of crackpots, some are venerated as the doctrines of believers, and some are renowned as the principles of science. Delusions, doctrines, and principles, despite their differences, have their historical origin in an axiom or postulate that can be neither proved nor disproved, but simply espoused or not espoused. Hence the profound and homicidal disputes that arise over differences in causal explanation as, for example, the dispute over creationism as a religious doctrine, and evolutionism as a scientific principle. Within its own confines, science has witnessed some monumental disputes over principles of causality, as for instance the eighteenth-century geological dispute over neptunism and plutonism as causal explanations of rock stratification.

In today's behavioral science, there is dispute over causal explanations dichotomized as nature versus nurture, biological versus nonbiological, essentialism versus social constructionism, mechanism versus teleology, and organic versus psychogenic.

Although these five dichotomies are almost synonymous for one another, the one that today permeates the theory and practice of sexology is organic versus psychogenic. By and large, persons with a training in medical and biological sciences gravitate toward and earn a living from biological causal explanations, whereas those with a training in behavioral and humanistic sciences gravitate toward and earn a living from psychogenic, including sociogenic causal explanations.

Psychogenic explanations attract, on the fringes, explanations in terms of spiritual values, and they also attract explanations framed in terms of personal moral responsibility and cognitive choice. In addition, psychogenic explanations of causality belong to yet another dichotomy, namely, that between behaviorism and behavior modification theory on the one hand, and motivationism and psychodynamic theory, heavily indebted to Freudian and neo-Freudian doctrines, on the other.

There is some overlap between behaviorism and motivationism of the type in which drives are not wholly instinctual but partly acquired, namely, in their shared attraction to causal explanations based on learning. Learning according to the principle of operant conditioning is the mainstay of behaviorism. Applied to therapy as behavior modification, behaviorism like motivationism postulates that whatever has been learned can be unlearned—a postulation that is quite incompatible with the permanence of some learning characterized in ethological theory as imprinting.

Behaviorism and motivationism are equally at a loss to explain original creativity and genius. Both are also at a loss to accommodate the concepts of behavior genetics, and the role of chromosomes, genes, or the genome with respect to specific capabilities or impairments. Behavior genetics is ostensibly too organic! Paradoxically, learning is not too organic, even though there is a substantial and expanding body of knowledge in experimental neuroscience and neurochemistry on the biology of learning and remembering in the brain. Formulations of causality that disregard this body of knowledge are already anachronistic, and on the way to becoming cultish doctrines.

For the person who must find order in the chaos of the raw data of a clinical biography, a prior allegiance to an explanatory doctrine that is exclusively either organic or psychogenic may lead to disastrous errors of diagnosis and treatment. The way of escape is to formulate temporal sequences which may or may not graduate to the status of causal sequences only after they have been tested in the fiery crucibles of science and earned the right to enter causality's hall of fame. In all of psychology, there are few causal explanations, whether organic or psychogenic, that have earned this right.

There is always a temptation to jump on the back of the first causal explanation that presents itself and to ride it to death, unmindful of the other contenders in the field. Hence the ensuing inventory of alternative contenders. It applies specifically to disorders and malfunctions of a sexological nature, but exemplifies general principles that apply to every case workup.

Errors of Genetic Coding

At this early stage of the history of the mapping and sequencing of the human genome, genetic coding for sexual differentiation of the early embryo has been traced to the testis-determining factor (TDF) of the short arm of the Y chromosome within which is encoded the gene named SRY for sex-determining region of the Y chromosome (Berta et al., 1990; Koopman et al., 1991). From the SRY issues a long and complex developmental sequence responsible for male versus female morphological differentiation.

There are no known genes that code specifically for sexological functions or dysfunctions, whether or not there are, within every one of the cells of the body, the expected number of 46 chromosomes (46,XX for females; 46,XY for males) to each of which a part of the genome in its entirety is appointed.

In the general population, there has been no census of the incidence and prevalence of chromosomal errors of various types. There are chromosome breakages, isochromosomal separations, translocations, ring formations, knobs (as in the fragile-X chromosome), mosaics (as in the 45X,46XY combination), lost X or Y chromosomes (45,X), supernumerary X or Y chromosomes, as in 47,XXX (trisomy-X syndrome), 47,XXY (Klinefelter syndrome), or 47,XYY (supernumerary-Y syndrome), and supernumerary autosomal chromosomes as in trisomy-21 (Down syndrome). In all of these errors, the magnitude of the genome is diminished, increased, or otherwise altered. The effect on sexological function and dysfunction, if any, is not discrete, but global and individually variable. Thus in adult males and females with trisomy-21, cuddly affection is overt, as expressed by a young infant or even by a beloved pet, without necessarily being explicitly genital. In 47,XYY males there is an increased potential incidence of paraphilia and bisexuality, as well as of infertility (Money et al., 1974). In 47,XXY males, infertility is pathognomonic, partial sexuoerotical inertia is common, and major gender-identity anomalies may be somewhat above the mean. In 45,X women, fertility is pathognomonic, romantic and parental bonding are not diminished, and genital sexuoeroticality is often diminished (Money, 1975).

Cytogenetic screening of the newborn has revealed the following incidence figures: 45,X (Turner syndrome) 1:10000 morphologic females; 47,XXY (Klinefelter syndrome) 1:1000 morphologic males; and 47,XYY (supernumerary-Y syndrome) 1:1000 morphologic males (Grumbach and

Conte, 1985). These figures pertain to the pool from which individuals are drawn for a sexological referral. Thus the concentration of cytogenetic anomalies among referrals is sufficiently great that their existence must be considered in sexological research as well as clinical service.

Contemporary advances in gene mapping have made it possible to go beyond anomalies that involve an entire chromosome and to search the arms of a single chromosome for a genetic marker of a particular inherited trait or function. One search is under way for the genetics of sexual orientation as homosexual or heterosexual. Hamer and co-workers (1993) did a DNA analysis of forty families in which there were two gay brothers whose other gay male relatives, if any, were on the maternal side only. They found linkage markers on region Xq28 of the long arm of the X chromosome. These markers were found, if at all, in approximately two-thirds of the gay males, and in some instances their mothers. The next step will be to search for the responsible gene or genes within region Xq28 that plays a role in sexual orientation, and then to identify exactly what role it plays, if any.

Birth Defects of the Sex Organs

In the sequence of male/female embryonic differentiation, the cluster of cells that will become the gonads become testes if the SRY gene is present, and ovaries if it is not. The testes take the leadership in male/female differentiation according to the principal of Eve first, then Adam, and they do so by secreting hormones, testosterone (T), the masculinizing hormone, and antimullerian hormone (AMH) which suppresses the formation of a uterus and fallopian tubes (the mullerian organs). Testosterone or one of its derivatives promotes the formation of first the internal accessory organs of the male reproductive tract, and then of the external organs, the penis and scrotum. In the absence of T and AMH, the internal and external organs of reproduction form as female.

The formative period is in two stages: from the sixth to the twelfth week for the internal organs, and up to the sixteenth week for the external organs. Errors of sexual differentiation that take place during this early formative period are not self-correcting, so that the baby is born with a birth defect of the sex organs. For some of these defects, no adequate explanation has yet been discovered. The most adequate explanations presently available are for defects that are the outcome of hormonal error. There are three major types of hormonal error. Insufficiency of AMH in a male fetus allows the uterus and fallopian tubes to form. Insufficiency of hormonal masculinizing, especially with respect to the external genitalia, is synonymous with feminizing. Excess of hormonal masculinizing in a female fetus, no matter where the hormone comes from, has a masculinizing effect on the external genitalia.

In the extreme cases of demasculinization of the male fetus, the formation of the external genitalia may be the same as for a female. Conversely, in extreme masculinization of the female fetus, the formation of the external genitalia may be the same as for a male with undescended testes. In less extreme cases, in both the male and the female fetus, the formation of the external genitalia is unfinished and ambiguous so that the sex of the baby cannot be announced at birth on the basis of genital inspection alone.

A prenatal hormonal error may be self-generated within the fetus itself, on the basis of a specific gene defect; or it may be transmitted to the fetus through the placenta from the maternal blood stream. The mother's own circulating hormone level may have been altered by a hormonal disease, by medications like barbiturates that change hormonal levels, or by hormone injections or pills like synthetic progestin and DES (diethylstilbestrol) that half a century ago were prescribed to hundreds of thousands of pregnant women on the assumption, now disproved, that they would prevent miscarriage.

Birth defects of the sex organs not known to be hormone-related in prenatal life include micropenis in boys. This condition may be so extreme that the penis is no more than twice or three times the size of a clitoris. Hypospadias, also in boys, is the condition in which the urinary opening is wrongly placed anywhere from near the tip of the penis to the base of the penis where it joins the scrotum. In girls there is atresia of the vagina, a birth defect in which the vagina is formed as a shallow pouch, or maybe a dimple, with no cervix, and a cord-like structure for a uterus. In both sexes, epispadias is an extensive malformation of the pelvic region involving a failure of midline fusion of the bladder and genitalia.

The major birth defects of the sex organs are, with varying degrees of success, subject to corrective surgical intervention. Irrespective of the degree of surgical success, there is a high probability of a secondary overlay of stigmatization and self-devaluation from childhood into adulthood, with a deleterious effect on sexuoerotical functioning. In addition, there are likely to be residual, postsurgical defects and imperfections that directly impede genital sexual function, and erotical sensory feeling, including orgasm.

Minor birth defects of the sex organs may, through lack of sufficiently detailed examination, readily be overlooked. Even if they are not, their significance with respect to sexuoerotical function may be discounted, through lack of substantiating statistical evidence. Sexuoerotical function may also be adversely affected derivatively, if a birth defect, minor or major, is associated with major menstrual disability, pregnancy failure, or, in males as well as females, sterility.

Prenatal Brain Hormonalization

After the pelvic genitalia have differentiated as either female or male, the brain follows suit. The principle is the same: Eve first, then Adam. Feminization of the regions and pathways that mediate the use of the pelvic genitalia in mammalian mating and breeding takes precedence over masculinization. Brain feminization requires simply the absence of masculinizing sex hormone, whereas brain masculinization requires its presence, irrespective of whether they come from the baby itself or the mother.

Developmentally, the timing of male/female brain differentiation varies according to species. It may be completed either prior to or following birth. In the human species, even its onset as well as the completion may be postnatal. The supporting evidence is hormonal: postnatally, between the ages of two and ten weeks, approximately, boys and girls are hormonally different. In boys, the testicles secrete masculinizing hormone into the bloodstream in a surge that reaches the level of puberty and then subsides for the remainder of childhood. There is no corresponding phenomenon in baby girls.

Ample experimental animal evidence, summarized in many reference books, has demonstrated a male/female difference or dimorphism in the size and cell number of selected nuclei in the anterior hypothalamic region and elsewhere in the brain (Sitsen, 1988; Money, 1988a). Male/female hypothalamic dimorphism is contingent on whether or not the anterior hypothalamus underwent hormonal masculinization in prenatal or neonatal life. Male/female dimorphism of mating behavior is, in turn, contingent on anterior hypothalamic dimorphism working in concert with posterior hypothalamic governance of the pituitary gland and its hormones of reproduction.

In laboratory mammals, the outcome of hypothalamic masculinization of a female fetus or neonate is masculinization or defeminization of mating behavior. Correspondingly, the outcome of hypothalamic demasculinization of a male fetus or neonate is demasculinization of mating behavior. The substantiating evidence from animals is experimental, and from human beings clinical. The human clinical evidence is derived from cases of hermaphroditism in which there is a known history of prenatal and neonatal hormonal anomaly, and a known history of some degree of homosexual/heterosexual transposition in the sexuoerotical orientation of adulthood (Money et al., 1984). Nothing has yet been ascertained, however, regarding hypothalamic neuroanatomical dimorphism in these cases of hermaphroditism.

The possibility of a correlation in nonhermaphroditic people between sexuoerotical orientation as homosexual or heterosexual and neuroanatomical structures in or near the region of the hypothalamus has not been settled one way or the other. There are only three studies reporting data from autopsies performed on a small sample of brains bequeathed to research by gay males before they died from AIDS. Swaab and Hofman reported an increase in the magnitude of the suprachiasmic nucleus in the brains of the test sample as compared with the control sample (Swaab and Hofman, 1990). LeVay reported a diminution in the magnitude of the

INAH 3, the third interstitial nucleus of the anterior hypothalamus, in the test brains versus the control brains (LeVay, 1991). Allen and Gorski (1992) reported that the midsaggital plane of the anterior commissure in homo-sexual males was 34 percent larger than in control males. The anterior commissure is a tract of axons that primarily connects the right and left neocortex of the middle and inferior temporal lobes.

Whether or not these new data will prove to have explanatory or diag-nostic significance remains to be seen. Meantime, they sound a warning alert, namely, that with or without reference to the brain it is unsafe to attribute final and absolute truth to any theory of the origin, diagnosis, and prognosis of homo-/hetero-/ or bi-sexuoerotical orientation or of any other aspect of sexuoeroticality, in childhood, adolescence, or adulthood.

Pubertal Target-Organ Hormonalization

In the years of middle childhood before the onset of puberty, the gonads are not sex-hormonally completely inert as popularly believed, nor is the gonadal-pituitary feedback effect. In boys, the earliest sign that the biologi-cal clock of puberty has turned on is usually palpable enlargement of the testicles, beginning on average, within the age range of nine and a half to thirteen and a half years, at age twelve. In girls, the earliest sign usually is palpable breast budding, on the average within the age range of eight and a half and twelve and a half years, at age eleven.

The brain location of the biological clock of puberty has not yet been discovered. It is presumed to be in the region of the hypothalamus where it governs the secretion of hypothalamic-releasing hormone (RH) which, in turn, governs the secretion of hormones from the nearby pituitary gland. LHRH governs the secretion of luteinizing hormone (LH) and of follicle-stimulating hormone (FSH). LHRH release must be pulsatile or episodic, not continuous; otherwise puberty is suppressed. LH and FSH govern the release of sex hormones—estrogen and progestin from the ovaries, and an-drogen from the testicles. The sex hormones send feedback signals that keep the production of LHRH, LH, and FSH in balance.

This reciprocal balancing system, referred to as the hypothalamic-pituitary-gonadal axis, exemplifies the general principle of hormones of puberty, namely, that they are activators, not creators. They activate target cells that are ready and waiting to bind them, molecule by molecule, and to be roused from dormancy to activity. This principle of activation applies to the functioning of cells responsible for the sexuoeroticality of puberty as well as to the growth of cells responsible for the secondary sexual signs and morphological development of puberty. Erectility of the penis is an example par excellence.

The penis's erectile capability is present even before birth and has been demonstrated in ultrasound imaging of the fetus in utero. The manifestation of erection continues spontaneously in the newborn period, infancy, and childhood. Nocturnal penile tumescence (NPT) is associated especially with REM (rapid eye movement) phases of sleep and dreaming. Episodes of NPT average three per night. The final episode may merge with morning awakening. The total NPT time averages between two and three hours. NPT continues through adulthood and lessens in advanced age. With the onset of hormonal puberty NPT reaches its peak of frequency and duration. It is at this stage of development that NPT becomes associated with spontaneous ejaculation while asleep, or while awakening to the accompaniment of sexuoerotical dream imagery (the so-called wet dream).

Ejaculation, spontaneous or otherwise, together with the subjective experience of orgasm, is contingent on pubertal hormonal maturation of the liquid-producing internal genitalia which synchronizes with the maturation of the penis to adult size. The wet dream is contingent on brain and spinal cord processes that respond to pubertal sex hormones in ways not yet understood.

Even before puberty, the waking brain is able to initiate erection in response to sexuoerotical stimuli, but only if the spinal cord is intact. By contrast, tactile stimulation of the external genitalia is able to initiate erection reflexively, by way of the lower spinal cord, even if the brain is disconnected from the lower cord.

Erectility progressively declines as age advances. So also does the blood level of the sex hormone testosterone. Increasing the testosterone level by means of hormone injections does not however, increase erectility.

In females, tumescence of the clitoris and vulva is, in comparison with tumescence of the penis in the male, relatively inaccessible to observation and far more difficult to measure. Female tumescence is also subject to different pubertal hormonalization and, subsequently, to hormonal function that cycles in synchrony with the menstrual cycle, except for the interruptions of pregnancy, and after menopause. Differences notwithstanding, male and female share the same principle of the hypothalamic-pituitary-gonadal hormones of puberty, namely, that they are activators of what is already in place, not creators of something entirely new.

Pubertal Hormonal Timing Discrepancies

Discrepancies of timing are those in which the age of pubertal onset is either too early or too late relative to chronological age. In pubertas precox, the onset of puberty is earlier than age eight and a half years in girls, and nine and a half years in boys. In the rare, extreme case pubertal onset may be as early as the first weeks of life. In pubertal delay, the onset of puberty is later than age fourteen in girls and age fifteen in boys. In cases of total hormonal failure, pubertal onset is permanently delayed unless hormonal substitution therapy is provided.

Discrepancies of timing are etiologically and prognostically diverse. Endocrine interventions to correct them are correspondingly diverse. Interventions to correct idiopathic precocious puberty are ameliorative and fall short of being ideal, whereas other forms of precocity, for example CVAH (congenital virilizing adrenal hyperplasia) precocity, are more amenable to treatment.

Timing when to begin hormonal intervention, with either gonadal steroid or pituitary gonadotropin or both, is the main issue in the correction of pubertal delay. The outcome of corrective intervention is fair to excellent, except in boys with a syndrome of insensitivity to androgen whose failure to masculinize creates a lifetime of trouble. Androgen-insensitive men look too juvenile and too androgynous, and are often mistaken for teenaged youths.

Discrepancies of timing demonstrate that the pubertal hormonalization of the body is not automatically accompanied by a corresponding pubertal hormonalization of the mind. The sexuoerotical age of children with pubertas precox is geared less to their pubertal stage than to their stage of social maturation and experience. Some advance more rapidly than others. Conversely, in children with pubertal delay, some are more socially and sexuoerotically retarded than are others during the teenaged years prior to the onset of hormone-substitution treatment. Those few who, although prepubertally delayed, keep more or less in step with their pubertal agemates demonstrate the principle that sexuoerotical development is not rigidly tied to hormonal development. Hypersexuality, as manifested in some children with a history of normal pubertal timing and premature prepubertal exposure to age-discrepant sexual practices, demonstrates another version of the same principle.

In the years of adulthood, the aftermath of pubertal hormonal-timing discrepancies may be either short-lived and insignificant, or long-lived and pathological. A pathological outcome may be secondary to the timing discrepancy, or it may be primary, and a continuing manifestation of the original syndrome. One syndrome for which this may well be the case is Kallmann syndrome of hypogonadotropic hypogonadism associated with partial or complete congenital absence of the sense of smell (anosmia).

Kallmann syndrome occurs more often in males than females. It is explained sequentially as beginning with an intragenic deletion of the KALIG-1 gene on the distal end of the short arm of the X chromosome (Bick et al., 1992). This, in turn, prevents the migration of embryonic brain cells from the olfactory placode to their destinations in the olfactory lobe to govern smell acuity, and in the hypothalamus to govern the secretion of gonadotropin-releasing hormone (GnRH). The missing neurones impair both the sense of smell and the biological clock of puberty. The latter impairs the secretion of luteinizing releasing hormone (LHRH), which in turn impairs the secretion of pituitary gonadotropins, which impairs the release of gonadal hormones, which impairs puberty and allows the body to grow tall and eunuchoid in its proportions. In an unknown proportion of cases, the brain component of Kallmann syndrome impairs the capacity of pair-bonding and falling in love. The individual grows up as a loner, often very highly achieved, and often with peculiar premises underlying otherwise logical thought processes that, in the vernacular, qualify as being "spaced out" (Money and Sollod, 1978; Bobrow et al., 1971).

Kallmann syndrome serves as a paradigm for a peculiarity of brain and mental function in association with a peculiarity of genital function. There are sporadic occurrences of this conjunction in other syndromes, including the supernumerary Y syndrome (47,XYY); Klinefelter syndrome (47,XXY), the C.H.A.R.G.E. syndrome of micropenis (Money and Norman, 1988), and some types of male hermaphroditism.

Of a completely different order, there is another peculiarity of brain and mental function associated with puberty, namely, the so-called periodic psychosis of puberty in females. In this case, the pubertal association is hormonal. The symptoms of psychosis which qualify in the vernacular as "stark raving mad" are cyclic, more or less in synchrony with the menstrual cycle, and are apparently associated with an elevated blood level of estrogen. They are made worse by the administration of estrogen, whereas they are relieved by the administration of progesterone or a progestinic steroid (Berlin et al., 1982). Between attacks of psychosis are intervals of complete lucidity. The syndrome, being subject to misdiagnosis, is likely to be improperly treated.

Pubertal Hormonal Morphological Discrepancies

Morphological discrepancies are those in which there is a discrepancy between, on the one hand, pubertal hormonalization of the morphology as either masculine or feminine and, on the other hand, the natal sex, the sex announced at birth on the basis of the genital morphology.

A morphological discrepancy may be the outcome of a hormonal error. One example is that of a girl who does not receive corrected hormonal treatment with cortisone for the syndrome of congenital virilizing adrenal hyperplasia (CVAH). In such a case, pubertal masculinization begins precociously early and is total. Another example is that of a girl who develops masculine body and facial hair, a deep voice, menstrual failure, and breast shrinkage under the influence of a masculinizing hormone secreted into the blood stream possibly from an ovarian or adrenocortical tumor or other hormone secreting anomaly. The statistically predictable reaction in such cases is that the signs of masculinization will be experienced subjectively as an unwelcome curse, and not as welcome harbingers of a change of sex.

Instead of being the outcome of a hormonal error, a morphological discrepancy may be the outcome of faulty processing and utilization of sex hormone within the cells of the target organ. An example is adolescent gynecomastia, excessive enlargement of the breasts in boys. Gynecomastia is attributed to undue sensitivity of the glandular cells beneath the nipples to the feminizing hormone estrogen, which normal testicles secrete in addition to the masculinizing hormone testosterone. Alternatively, the cells may be unduly resistant to testosterone.

Whereas minor and transient gynecomastia is common in pubertal boys, female-sized and persistent gynecomastia is rare. Breast enlargement is more common in boys with Klinefelter (47,XXY) syndrome than in chromosomally normal (46,XY) boys. Together with over-all deficiency of pubertal masculinization, breast enlargement is a defining characteristic of puberty in boys with a history of hermaphroditic ambiguity of the sex organs attributable to the syndrome of partial androgen insensitivity. Androgen dependent cells throughout their bodies are androgen resistant, but responsive to testicular estrogen.

Almost all boys with adolescent gynecomastia, irrespective of its etiology, are mortified by the feminine appearance of the chest. Intellectually, they may question whether or not their bodies are changing sex, but their innermost conviction, with few exceptions, is that their breasts should be gotten rid of, not that they are a welcome confirmation of a chance to become a girl.

A third type of morphologic discrepancy is attributable neither to a hormone error nor to a faulty utilization of hormone in target cells. This is the transexual discrepancy in which the entire pubertal hormonal morphology as either masculine or feminine, respectively, is at variance with the idealized body image. Anima muliebris virili corpore inclusa (the mind of a woman entrapped within the body of a man) is the maxim, borrowed from Ulrichs (1864), that male-to-female transexuals have adopted as their own. It is appropriately modified by female-to-male transexuals. How the woman's mind gets into the man's body, or conversely the man's mind into the woman's body, is a problem as yet unsolved.

All three of the foregoing types of morphologic discrepancy illustrate the same principle, namely, that the hormones of masculinization and feminization of the body from puberty onward do not automatically serve also to masculinize or feminize the sexuoeroticality of the mind.

Pharmacologic Side-Effects

The relationship between sex and drugs has an extremely ancient lineage which began, according to the records of Indian Ayurvedic and Chinese traditional medicine, as a quest for aphrodisiacs. It is a quest that has never been satisfied. Consumers' demands are for four varieties of aphrodisiac:

activators, rejuvenators, sustentators, and amplifiers (Money et al., 1988). Activators are love potions, charms, or spells that will render oneself irresistible as a potential sexual partner, and attract or disinhibit an inattentive or reluctant partner. They exist only in the realm of magic. Rejuvenators are elixirs that will recapture the sexual vigor of youth and arrest the decline of aging. Hormones, most recently growth hormone, have been cast in this role, but in fact there are no authentic rejuvenators. Amplifiers are pharmacologic substances, derived chiefly from plants, that promise to heighten and enhance the subjective experience of ecstasy leading up to and culminating in orgasm. Whereas the efficacy of amplifiers is modest at best, and not universal, claims on their behalf tend to be either exaggerated or denied. Sustentators are concoctions that promise to restore impaired sexual performance, prolong its duration, or shorten the refractory period or recovery interval between performances. When the blood level of sex hormones is deficient, replacement hormones are effective. Other concoctions, like those that include powdered rhinoceros horn or stag antler as ingredients, are not. Nor are various pharmacologically active products marketed as aphrodisiac sustentators. However, a select few α-adrenergic blockers, along with other smooth muscle relaxants, have proved to be intermittently effective in correcting chronic loss or partial loss of erectility, but only when injected directly into the corpora cavernosa of the penis. Irrespective of thoughts and imagery, the penis then erects in response to the injection. Papaverine hydrochloride is widely used, alone or in combination with phentolamine mesylate (Regitine). It has very recently been discovered that drugs which act as smooth muscle relaxants in the corpora cavernosa do so by stimulating the release of nitric oxide (NO) from neurons that regulate the arterial inflow of blood (Ignarro, 1992; Burnett et al., 1992). Blood fills the minute spaces of the spongy corpora and inflates them so as to create an erection.

Paradoxically, the sustentation effect of some α-adrenergics in promoting erectility of the penis may in some, but not all males, be suppressed as a side-effect of various other α-adrenergic blocking agents. Some, like phenoxybenzamine hydrochloride, are prescribed for the suppression of high blood pressure. Others, such as phenothiazines like chlorpromazine and haloperidol, are prescribed for the suppression of psychotic symptoms. As antiaphrodisiacs, α-adrenergic blockers alter the availability and utilization of biogenic amines, namely, epinephrine and norepinephrine (alternatively named adrenalin and noradrenalin), serotonin, dopamine, and acetylcholine.

The impairments which aphrodisiac sustentators promise to correct have, in both popular and medical tradition, been imprecisely attributed to deficits in such amorphous entities as libido, sexual desire, sexual drive, potency, sustaining power, and virility. Femininity is conspicuous by its absence in aphrodisiology, and has been ever since, in ancient times, the dogma of the sexual and erotic primacy of the male first came into being. According to this dogma, it is the role of the woman to serve as an aphrodisiac for man, not the other way round.

Neglect of woman's sexuoeroticality has persisted into the present and is evident not only in aphrodisiology but also its obverse, the antiaphrodisic effects or side-effects of various pharmacologic substances, either officially prescribed or self-prescribed. Although there is less neglect of the antiaphrodisic side-effects of prescription drugs on males than females, neglect is nonetheless extensive. Data are ascertained and reported anecdotally and casually, not systematically and statistically. Methodology is not exclusively the problem, however, insofar as the antiaphrodisic side-effects of drugs are inconsistent, individually variable, dose-responsive, and tolerance-related. In the case of alcohol, for example, it is well known that one or two drinks may be sexuoerotically disinhibiting, whereas more induce a stuporose condition. Chronic alcoholic disease chronically suppresses genitosexual function.

The sexological problems most frequently mentioned as pharmacologic side-effects are, in both men and women, inability to become aroused or to be responsive sexually, and loss of ability to achieve orgasm. In men, orgasmic failure, as a side-effect of the phenothiazine Mellaril, may coincide with ejaculatory failure, although not necessarily with erectile failure (Money and Yankowitz, 1967). Erectile failure (impotence) alone is the most frequent sexological symptom in males occurring as a pharmacologic side-effect.

A curious and apparently extremely rare side-effect of the tricyclic antidepressant drug, clomipramine hydrochloride is the induction of orgasm as a concomitant of yawning (McLean et al., 1983). This side-effect has significance for comparative sexology in that in subhuman primates, for example, baboons, a male's yawn is a signal of solicitation of the female.

The literature on sexological symptoms as pharmacologic side-effects is predominantly, if not exclusively about deficiency or loss of function, not hypertrophy or excess of function. From the experimental animal literature, however, there is a report of compulsive sexual activity pharmacologically induced in rats by treatment with the amino acid p-chlorophenylalanine (Tagliamonte et al, 1969; Gessa et al., 1971). Positioned like links in a chain, one behind the other, the rats, all male, mounted one another reiteratively and engaged in anal intromission. The chemical change brought by administering p-chlorophenylalanine can be obtained also by feeding rats a tryptophan-free diet—in Sardinia, where the experiment was done, a diet exclusively of fresh and uncured mozzarella cheese. Tryptophan is a precursor of serotonin, one of the brain's biogenic amines that functions as a sexuoerotic suppressant and the counterpart of dopamine, which is a sexuoerotic activator.

In human beings, the antiaphrodisic side-effect of some psychiatric drugs, for example, Mellaril, has been construed as a bonus in the treatment of some cases of compulsive sex-offending, but only on a sporadic, not systematic basis, and without clear-cut evidence of a satisfactory outcome.

For paraphilic male sex offenders, a more satisfactory outcome is obtained from a period of treatment with a synthetic steroidal hormone which has antiandrogenic properties, namely, medoxyprogesterone acetate (MPA; trade-named Depo-Provera) or cyproterone acetate (CTA; Androcur), provided the hormonal treatment is combined with sexological counseling (Money, 1970; 1987). For female sex offenders the efficacy of either hormone is open to question insofar as both, in addition to being antiandrogenic in males, mimic the action of progesterone in females. In view of its progestinic properties, MPA subcutaneously implanted in pellet form serves also as a long-term birth-control hormone for women.

As a birth-control hormone, MPA has not been subject to systematic study with respect to its possible side-effects on female sexuoerotical function. Earlier studies on the side-effects of hormonal contraception administered orally as the Pill were confounded by the multiplicity of variables that, in human studies, cannot be manipulated or held constant in view of ethical considerations. The findings of these studies were, therefore, foggy and inconclusive.

In the course of undergoing a sexological workup, informants do not necessarily give a pharmacologic history. Mostly, they give it no thought. Hence it is the obligation of the interviewer to request it. To evaluate whether or not a symptom may be a side-effect of a medication or other pharmacologic substance, one may refer to standard reference sources and also to the compilations of Sitsen (1988, Ch.17) and Buffum et al. (1988).

Peripheral Genitopelvic Pathology

The saying that sex is between the ears as much as between the legs has been repeated so often that it is now a platitude. Nonetheless, the brain and the groin are not so fused that they cannot be deconnected, which is precisely what happens when, in cases of accidental or wartime injury, the spinal cord is completely severed. The outcome is the syndrome of paraplegia, a condition in which, below the break, the body is paralyzed and numb.

Paraplegia has heuristic significance for sexology in demonstrating what the pelvic genitalia can do, sexuoerotically, without input from the pelvic genitalia.

In males and females, pelvic genital function is contingent on the intactness of neural circuits to and from the spinal cord and the genitalia. Recognition of whatever residual function remains is exclusively by watching what happens, or by palpating the genitalia with the fingers. The functions that remain are limited to those of reproduction only.

In the case of the female, insemination is possible, but only with outside help in positioning the numb and paralyzed lower body in a suitable position. Conception is possible, and so also is the carrying of a fetus to term, provided meticulous health care is provided to counteract, for example, paraplegic impairment of urinary function and bowel function. Delivery requires caesarian section

In the case of the male, as of the female, outside help is needed in positioning for impregnation. Erection of the penis is possible in response to tactile stimulation, so that intromission may be achieved, but the maintenance of erection is capricious and does not lead to the inevitability of ejaculation. On the contrary, pregnancy is contingent on collecting semen by placing an electrovibratory device in the rectum and stimulating the prostate gland through the rectal wall until the semen is emitted into a condom, and then transferred to the partner's vagina.

These paraplegic data show that the peripheral organs of generation are, if contrived intervention is provided, to a limited extent independent of the brain as the central coordinating organ of the motor and sensory functions of generation.

There is a corollary to this proposition, namely, that the peripheral organs of generation may manifest pathology independently of the brain as the central coordinating organ. To return to the platitude: pathology between the legs may be independent of pathology between the ears. Embedded in this statement is the dichotomy of organic versus psychogenic, a dichotomy that vexes not only sexology, but all of contemporary medicine.

In both the popular and medical vogue of the present time, it is more respectable, and perhaps more prestigious, to have an organic rather than a psychogenic diagnosis. To the ordinary person, the latter signifies that "there's nothing wrong with you, it's all in your mind," or that "it's in your imagination," and that the cure will require the power of "mind over matter." Among medical insurance carriers, a psychogenic diagnosis is likely to be excluded from reimbursement.

An allegory gives short shrift to this erroneous way of thinking. It is the maritime allegory of the sex organs being like a nautilus or jelly fish, with extremely long tentacles that trail from the brain along the spinal cord and autonomic nervous system to the pelvic organs. At many places along the way something may go wrong. Locating the error is a tricky business, not always successful; so also is figuring out the most effective method of intervention. Failure to locate the error is no justification for dismissing it as psychogenic and, by implication, putting the burden of etiological responsibility on the patient. The correct statement should be: etiology unknown. Ignorance is the enemy, not the patient!

The diagnosis of a peripheral genitopelvic syndrome in many instances precedes attention to its sexuoerotical sequelae and the possibility of their treatment. By contrast, when the sexuoerotical sequelae are the presenting symptoms, and especially if they are prodromal, they present a challenge of differential diagnosis such that, in the absence of extensive sexological training and experience, the correct diagnosis may not be suspected. This is one of the situations in which sexuoerotical symptoms may be wrongly attributed to a psychogenic instead of a peripheral genitopelvic origin.

Symptoms may originate peripherally in response to bacterial, fungal, or viral infections or their long-term sequelae; to vascular dysfunction, as in atherosclerosis; to post-traumatic sequelae of accidental injury or pelvic surgery, including damage to the genital nerve supply as, for example, following prostatectomy; to degenerative neurological disease; and to neoplastic growths of which some are malignant and some, though not malignant, are disabling by reason of their genital location. Examples of the latter are von Recklinghausen's neurofibromatosis, endometriosis in women, and in men Peyronie's disease with its scar-like plaques that bend and distort the penis, induce pain, and sometimes render intromission impossible.

Peripheral genital symptoms may originate in a deficiency or lack of an essential neurotransmitter substance. New findings concerning the role of the body's own nitric oxide (NO) as a chemical messenger apply to penile erection (see above). The sequence of factors responsible for blocking the neuronal release of NO has not yet been identified. It need not always be the same.

Localized genitopelvic pathology does not rule out the likelihood of a secondary overlay of mindbrain-mediated sexuoerotical pathology, in which case the presenting of symptoms present an even more complex problem of differential diagnosis and treatment. Irrespective of their etiology, symptoms of sexuoerotical dysfunction that are genitopelvically manifested belong characteristically to the acceptive phase of a sexuoerotical episode which is preceded by the proceptive and followed, maybe, by the conceptive phase (Chapter 11). Acception is the phase of mutual bodily proximity, typically involving the proximity of genital union.

Albert Moll (1912) referred to the acceptive phase as the curve of voluptuousness and subdivided it into four subphases (p.26): "an ascending limb, the equable voluptuous sensation, the acme, and the rapid decline." Masters and Johnson (1966) renamed Moll's curve of voluptuousness as the sexual response cycle and subdivided it into the excitement phase, the plateau phase, the orgasmic phase, and the resolution phase.

Masters and Johnson (1970) used the over-all term "human sexual inadequacy" for malfunctions affecting the sexual response cycle, and identified them in the male as premature ejaculation, ejaculatory incompetence (failure to ejaculate), and impotence; in both sexes as orgasmic dysfunction and dyspareunia (coital pain), to which should be added genital anesthesia; and in the female as vaginismus to which should be added vaginal dryness or lubricatory deficit. All of these malfunctions may occur without an identifiable locus of etiology in the peripheral genitalia, in which case the locus is presumed to be somewhere else, above the pelvic area ("above the belt") and not within or below it. When the etiological locus is above the belt, the various symptoms of inadequacy are manifested predominantly, though not invariably when two partners are together. Disappearance of the symptom during solo or autoerotic masturbatory activity suggests the possibility of a disruptive relationship between the partners.

Sequelae of Systemic Disease

Among famine victims, and victims of entrapped starvation, as in Hitler's concentration camps, the sequelae of emaciation include progressive depletion of genitopelvic function and atrophy of sexuoerotical function. In the imagery and ideation of their dreams and fantasies, themes of food and eating supplement those of sex and mating. Sexual apathy and inertia are sequelae also of the self-imposed fasting and emaciation of anorexia nervosa (the "virgin Mary syndrome") in women, and in men also. Nutritional deficiency secondary to debilitating systemic disease or illness of any type is accompanied by a parallel deficiency of both peripheral sexual function and hedonic eroticality. Sexuoerotical depletion may be complete in any severely debilitating systematic disease that depletes vital functions overall, such as terminal cancer, kidney failure, respiratory failure, and congestive heart disease.

The treatment of severe debilitating disease may carry its own risk of depleted sexuoerotical function. Such is the case in the treatment of cancer with chemotherapy, and of kidney failure by means of hemodialysis rather than by kidney transplant. The same applies to the treatment of high blood pressure with antihypertensive medication, to which is added the additional complication of coital phobia in either partner, or both, if a heart attack as a sequel to sexual exertion looms as a possible threat. Moderate sexual exertion is, however, usually considered compatible with health, despite a history of heart attack (Wagner, 1977).

Open-heart surgery for coronary artery disease may have untoward after-effects on cortical-cognitional functioning, including sexuoerotical functioning. A possible explanation, still in need of confirmation, implicates the loss of the rhythmicity of the pulse in the brain when, during surgery, the circulation is maintained as a steady, nonpulsatile flow when the patient is put on the heart-lung machine (Chapter 4). Periodicity, as in cycles, rhythms and pulses, is of profound importance in sexological functioning, as in vital functioning over-all.

Some systemic diseases are not wholly debilitating but are characterized by sexological impairments. Diabetes mellitus is one such disease with, in its advanced stage, peripheral vascular and neural pathology that in men is held responsible for impaired erectility of the penis. In women there is corresponding but much less studied impairment of vulvar tumescence and vaginal lubrication (Jaspan, 1989; Slob et al., 1990). In both sexes, diabetic neuropathy may be associated with intense pain attacks affecting limited regions or organs of the body, the genital organs included.

Like diabetes mellitus, hyperprolactinemia (Vance and Thorner, 1989) is a syndrome that, although not wholly debilitating, has a range of symptoms that include menstrual disorder in women and infertility in both sexes. There is also in both sexes an increase of sexuoerotic inertia and apathy, commonly referred to as diminished libido. In men erectile impotence is easily recognized, whereas its counterpart in women is overlooked.

The pituitary hormone prolactin was discovered, purified, and named for its role in lactation in 1928, since which time it has been discovered to have many other roles. An elevated level of prolactin may be induced by pharmacologic substances, notably various of the neuroleptic drugs used in psychiatry. Prolactin may also be secreted in excess from a pituitary gland overstimulated either by a hypothalamic tumor or lesion, or by a prolactin-producing adenomatous growth within the pituitary itself. A prolactinoma may or may not be life-threatening. In some cases surgical intervention is indicated. Otherwise pharmacologic intervention with bromocriptine may reduce the blood level of prolactin, and suppress the symptoms, including erectile impotence, of hyperprolactinemia.

Multiple sclerosis is another systematic disease that may have a history of many years before it becomes completely debilitating. Meantime, it capriciously wreaks havoc all over the body by distributing motor and sensory impairments capriciously, and sporadically recalling some of them into temporary remission.

The symptoms of multiple sclerosis are the outcome of patchy demyelinization of nerve fibers that regulate motor and sensory functions in the spinal cord and in the brain. Though the etiology remains to be ascertained, some evidence suggests that it may involve an auto-immune reaction triggered initially by a virus.

Sexual and erotic genitopelvic functions are adversely affected in multiple sclerosis by localized numbness (anesthesia) and unbearably noxious sensations (paresthesia) of tingling, tickling, pricking, itching, and burning. In addition, there may be neuropathologically induced attacks of weeping, laughing, despair, euphoria, or, among other reactions mediated through the autonomic nervous system, hyposexual apathy or hypersexual urgency. In the male, sporadic or consistent erectile failure also can occur. Its counterpart in the female is obscured by being overinclusively subsumed under loss of libido.

In debilitating systemic illness, sexological impairments are predominantly decreases, not exaggerations of prior function. One exception is priapism or pathological erection, a condition of persistent failure of the penis to detumesce. One of its etiological origins is as a symptom of sickle-cell anemia, a genetically transmitted anomaly in which red blood cells are sickle-shaped. Priapism is one of the symptoms of the disease attributed to thrombosis induced by clumping of misshapen sickle cells in the arterioles and capillaries. With circulation of fresh blood through the penis blocked by thrombosis, the spongy tissue of the corpora cavernosa become fibrotic and their erectility is permanently lost. Early surgical intervention and drainage of stagnant blood from the corpora cavernosa may prevent irreversible impotence. Priapism hurts or aches, is anerotic, and is incompatible with, not relieved by orgasm.

Hyposexual and hypersexual pathology synchronize with the depressive and manic bipolarity of manic-depressive disorder. Erotosexual apathy and inertia may be among the first signs of a swing toward the depressive pole. Conversely, hypersexual exploits, as in so-called nymphomania and satyriasis or Don Juanism, perhaps compulsively and indiscriminately promiscuous, may herald a swing toward the manic pole.

Intracranial Neuropathy

The concept of intracranial locus for human sexual and erotic phenomena has its historical origin in the analogy, known to Hippocrates and Democritus, his contemporary in Greece of the fifth century B.C., between the paroxysmal nature of an epileptic seizure and a sexual orgasm (see Money and Pruce, 1977). In the history of epileptology, sexual intercourse has been cast in the contradictory roles of both precipitating and preventing seizures.

Epileptic foci that affect sexuoerotical function are typically, if not always situated in the right or left temporal lobe of the brain, especially in the region of the amygdala and hippocampus, in what is also called the limbic system or paleocortex. Seizures that originate in the temporal lobe are known as temporal-lobe seizures and also as psychomotor seizures. A seizure that begins in the temporal lobe may spread and become a grandmal seizure with convulsions and loss of consciousness. Alternatively, in a temporal-lobe seizure of the psychomotor type, there is an absence of convulsions, and loss of consciousness is replaced by a trance-like, hallucinatory, or dreaming state with false memories of either familiarity or strangeness, and repetitive movements or actions. Agitated states of anxiety, terror, rage, or sexual arousal may also occur.

In temporal-lobe epilepsy clinics, sexuoerotic symptoms, if any, have been classified, almost without exception, as hyposexual. The terminology used for hyposexuality has been impotence, frigidity, complete lack of libidinal desire or curiosity, and decrease or absence of erotic arousal in dreams, fantasies, or activities, including masturbation. In some cases, though not all, when seizures were successfully controlled by anticonvulsive medication, hyposexuality also underwent improvement. In some severe cases, temporal-lobe surgery was performed to remove the epileptic focus. Post-operatively, some but not all patients manifested relief from seizures and from hyposexuality, either temporarily or long-term.

The neurosurgical literature on epilepsy is almost silent with respect to the coexistence of temporal-lobe epilepsy and paraphilic or quasi-paraphilic sexual behavior. The very few reported cases are of fetishistic behavior. Their importance far exceeds their number, insofar as they draw attention to the structures of the temporal lobe as the region of the brain to which new technologies in sexological neuroscience might be directed in research. Money and Ehrhardt (1972, Chapter 12) wrote as follows.

> There is some evidence, from temporal lobe epilepsy, of a rather close connection in the temporal lobes between visual memory and sexual response. The evidence comes from selected cases of fetishism closely bonded to temporal lobe abnormalities and seizures (Epstein, 1960). Mitchell, Falconer and Hill (1954) reported a case of a bizarre safety-pin fetish, in which a seizure would be induced by gazing at the pin. Left temporal lobectomy relieved the patient of seizures and of the fetish-urge to gaze at the pin.
>
> This same safety-pin fetishist had, prior to surgery, also experienced a confusional state, immediately after a seizure, when sometimes he would dress in his wife's clothing. Transvestism itself, in some instances, represents a form of fetishism, and it may be associated with temporal lobe seizures. Davies and Morgenstern (1960) reported such a case, both symptoms appearing together in middle life. Hunter et al. (1963) reported also a case of fetishism-transvestism and temporal lobe seizures, both of which were eliminated by left anterior temporal lobectomy.
>
> In his followup report, Hunter (1967) also presented a case of long-term, compulsive transvestism which disappeared under the influence of anticonvulsive treatment at the age of thirty-eight. The EEG showed focal disturbance in the left fronto-temporal lobe area. There was no history of actual convulsion, but temporal lobe dysfunction was indicated by reason of déjà vu experiences, vivid dreaming and psychologic-test signs of minimal heterosexual impotence. Treatment was sought prior to marriage. Impotence was ameliorated along with disappearance of transvestite fantasies and practices. Medication was discontinued after six months, and two years later symptoms were still in remission.

A temporal-lobe seizure focus may develop with no known history of its origin. Alternatively, its history may be traceable to brain damage secondary to intracranial infection or neoplastic growth, or to a blow to the head, or penetrating head injury. The grosser the trauma to the brain, the greater the likelihood that any changes in sexuoerotical function will be recognized as sequelae of the trauma. By contrast, a history of lesser trauma or impairment—as for example by toxic substances in prenatal life, or by head injury perinatally—is not very likely to be ascertained if it is not until many years later that epilepsy is a presenting complaint. If the presenting complaint is not epilepsy but some form of sexological pathology, a prior history of brain impairment or trauma is even more likely to be overlooked. The same applies if there has been a history of seizures in which the symptoms of an attack have been quiet and unobtrusive, as is the case in seizures of the psychomotor (temporal-lobe) type. What is in fact a psychomotor seizure may not be recognized as such if it is manifested only as a trance-like, altered state of consciousness, also known as fugue (Latin, *fuga*, flight) state.

In some cases of paraphilia, it is quite visibly and palpably obvious that the paraphilic ritual is carried out in a trance-like state of paraphilic fugue. There are some such cases in which a neurological examination reveals a history of so-called soft neurological signs, or of not so soft signs like squirmy, athetoid movements. In yet other cases, it is only through long term follow-up that definite neurological signs of brain deterioration are revealed. For example, it was only after twenty years of follow-up that Parkinson's disease became overtly manifest and diagnosable in a patient with an earlier history of bizarre pedophilic fugue states in which a boy, after friendly overtures, would without warning be injuriously assailed and left for someone else to rescue.

Even with a well-documented clinical and laboratory history of traumatic brain damage followed by the onset of epileptic seizures, it is possible for sexological pathology of post-traumatic onset to be subject to criminal prosecution without reference to its traumatic etiology. Instead it is attributed to criminal motivation exclusively. In one such case (Lehne, 1984–1986) a man who had been indisputably brain-impaired in an auto crash was arrested and convicted as a sex offender on the basis of a request made on his behalf for a sexological evaluation and treatment. After the accident, he had undergone a bizarre change sexologically. With his eyes in a fixed and staring gaze, he would appear to be dazed as he contrived to spy on his young adult daughter as she undressed or bathed, and to proposition her sexually. She and her mother recognized this behavior to be part of a more extensive post-traumatic behavioral pathology. They had no idea that asking for therapeutic help would make matters worse by bringing about the dissolution and financial ruin of the family. They experienced at first hand what happens when those who serve as professional health-care providers serve also as undercover agents for the sex-abuse police and report their clients or patients as criminals.

A defect or dysfunction within the brain may become criminally evident only after a prolonged period of being subliminal or latent. This possibility is illustrated in the case of the man (see above) who, at age thirty-six, was self-referred with a request for treatment of paraphilic (pedophilic) fugue states, like the one he had within the clinic on one occasion. He was afraid of going out of control and possibly acting violently while in a fugue. He was treated with combined antiandrogen and counseling therapy. Subsequently, from time to time, he gave a follow-up report by telephone. After fifteen years, the report included the information that he had been diagnosed with Parkinson's disease. His case thus raises the suspicion that fugue was the earliest sign of the brain dysfunction that would culminate in fullblown Parkinsonism after an incubation period of fifteen years.

· 11 ·

Sexology: Temporal vs. Causal Explanations, II

Anomalies of Limerence

Infatuation is a term that depreciates the state of being lovesmitten. It implies that the love match meets with disapproval or, in the case of young people, that callow youth is too early to have wisdom in making a good match. Even in a culture where arranged marriages are no longer the universal rule, infatuation like puppy love is discounted as the basis for a union that involves family wealth, status, and power.

Until Tennov (1974) coined the term "limerence," there was in English no nonpejorative word for the lovesmitten state. Limerence means the subjective state or experience of having fallen in love and of being irrationally and fixatedly lovesmitten, irrespective of the degree to which one's love is requited or unrequited (Money, 1988a, p.209).

In the repertory of human experience, the closest analogue of limerence is grief. Both may be of sudden onset, overwhelming, and fixatious. Both bring about big alterations of bodily functions regulated by the autonomic nervous system. Both may be slow to subside and may leave permanent sequelae. Both may occur more than once, and both affect some people more intensely or more frequently than others. Likewise religious ecstasy.

Limerence may begin intensely as the proverbial love at first sight, with exchange of gaze across a crowded room. If both people are equally stricken, then in the vernacular one speaks of the chemistries of love, although the sights and touches of love would be just as accurate. Limerence may also build up gradually and be contingent on the reinforcement of mutual reciprocity.

The body language and other signs of limerent attraction between two people are remarkably constant transculturally according to the filmed evidence of Eibl-Eibesfeldt (1972) whose findings, together with those of Perper (1985), are incorporated into the following analysis. The sequence begins with establishing eye contact and holding the gaze, while at the same time perhaps becoming flushed or blushing. Then one of the pair tests the other by demurely drooping the eyelids and averting the gaze so as to see, upon returning the gaze shyly with a squint, smile, or flutter of the eyelashes, whether the other person has continued to look. This maneuver may be repeated as a prelude to moving closer together. The opening gambit in conversation may be banal, but it is the vocal animation, not the content, that counts. The flow of speech becomes accelerated, more breathy, and louder. Banality is outweighed by the vocal enthusiasm of simply being heard. Laughter, even if the humor is contrived, invites the couple to rotate so that, facing one another, they can share it and bring themselves closer and closer. The tongue emerges, wetting the lips. Clothing is casually adjusted or shed, fortuitously revealing a little more bare skin at least around the wrists, ankles, or neck. Arms and legs change positions, and gesturing brings them, as if inadvertently, in contact with the other person. If there is no recoil, then there is closer touching, patting, or holding, and the two people before they know what they are doing begin mirroring each other's gestures, and synchronizing their bodily movements as if in preliminary rehearsal for copulatory synchrony. Meanwhile, in addition to what is publicly observable, there is the private experience of increased heart rate, rapid breathing, perspiration, and butterflies in the stomach. Over a prolonged period of time changes in eating, sleeping, dreaming, fantasying, distractibility, and concentration may also occur (Money, 1986c). All of the foregoing sequence is applicable to both heterosexual and homosexual limerence.

The very existence of the term "puppy love" is an indication that limerent attraction may occur at an early age. In prepuberty it is sporadic, not universal in occurrence, and probably attenuated in magnitude as compared with postpuberty. In adolescence, the tribulations, doubts, and uncertainties of limerence undeclared or unrequited are manifested as the syndrome of lovesickness, a major source of academic underachievement and failure of boys and girls in high-school and students in college and graduate school.

The natural history of a limerent relationship is that it burns with a bright flame usually for a period of two years or more, long enough for pregnancy to occur. When the baby is born the two-way limerent bond loosens and transforms into a three-way bond, and the baby's survival is guaranteed. When the transition is smooth, the bright flame of limerence burns lower, but with a glow that in its own way is equally satisfactory.

The transition is not invariably smooth. In those cases in which limerence does not loosen, it may persist for years, so that the child grows up as a quasi–intruder. Another unsmooth transition is that in which the baby and only one parent, either the father or the mother, become bonded, with the other parent occupying the role of quasi–intruder. In cases of postpartum depression, mother-infant bonding fails and father-infant bonding increases proportionately in importance.

Among birds, many species remain pairbonded for not only a single nesting season, but a lifetime. Only a few mammalian species, for example the American prairie vole (Carter et al., 1980; 1992), exhibit pairbonded mating for a lifetime.

Among subhuman primates, although troopbondedness is superordinate to pairbondedness, two individuals may become bonded in a favorite, though not exclusive relationship that may be regarded as protolimerent.

Among human primates, limerent bondedness may occur more than once in a lifetime, at any age from youth through maturity into old age. It is possible that more than one limerent relationship may exist concurrently. Serial recurrence is, however, more likely, for limerence at the stage of being in full bloom is all-inclusively possessive.

If when in full-bloom limerence is reciprocal, then it may be considered as a developmental milestone marking the surrender of part of one's own individual uniqueness to that of the partner. The outcome is that the idiosyncracy of each partner increasingly accommodates, hand in glove, to that of the other, in what is subjectively experienced as a positive form of reciprocation.

Other people may judge such accommodation to be not positive but negative. This might be the case in the paraphilic reciprocation of, say, an extreme sadomasochistic relationship of master and slave. Each role may have existed dormantly, one in each partner, even before the two met. Each might have remained dormant for a longer period of time, except that it was awakened by the experience of limerence.

In folk wisdom there is a postlimerent seven-year itch, so-called, that is held responsible for a new limerent affair and the disbanding of a family. Similarly, life begins at forty is, in folk wisdom, a maxim that recognizes a postmenopausal lifting of the constraints of pregnancy when new limerent attractions begin between couples at midlife and beyond.

Perhaps fortuitous chance is a sufficient explanation of the occurrence of limerence once or more after the first time, although the cues that trigger limerence are not themselves fortuitous, but are built into the lovemap (see below).

Repetitious episodes or binges of limerence characterize the lives of some people. They crave the heightened vitality and well-being and, in some cases, the release of stalled creative genius that only a limerent affair with a new partner can bring. They become involved in perilous and self-sabotaging liaisons. They reach the height of limerent ecstasy, but its permanence eludes their grasp. Eventually, the cyclic downswing begins and they crash. Nothing will help except the "fix," to use the addiction vernacular, of a new partner in a new limerent affair.

In binge limerence, each episode lasts for an extended period of time. By contrast, when it is excitement of the chase that counts, limerence does not survive the success of the conquest. Such is the case in the compulsive cruising and sequential seduction of partners named with a touch of envy as Don Juanism in men, and with a tone of disparagement as satyriasis and, in women, as nymphomania.

Erotomania (Greek, *eros*, love + *mania*, madness) is defined generically as a morbid exaggeration of sexual behavior or a preoccupation with sexuality (see Chapter 3). Specifically it is used also as an alternative name for the Clérambault-Kandinsky syndrome. A person with this syndrome has fixated quasi-psychotic conviction of being smitten by the secret and undivulgable limerence of a particular and important personage whose passion dare not be openly proclaimed. The love-smitten victim importunes the important personage for even the smallest disclosure of love. Being ignored or rejected serves only to multiply the victim's maneuvers to be heard and paid attention to. In the well-publicized case of John Hinckley, the ultimate maneuver to gain the attention of the actress Jodie Foster was Hinckley's combined suicidal-homicidal attempt to assassinate President Reagan on March 6, 1981 (Chapter 6).

In many lesser cases of Clérambault-Kandinsky syndrome the importunate suitor, unable to take no for an answer, must be put legally under a restraining order to quit stalking, harassing, abusing, or assaulting the recipient of his/her importunacy. In some cases the outcome is homicide, multiple homicide, or combined homicide-suicide. Not all cases are deadly. There are some in which the personage being pursued surrenders—for example, after a transcontinental pursuit and being held hostage at gunpoint. The subsequent relationship is then one of fiercely jealous possessiveness and abusive restraints on contact with kith and kin.

Possessive jealousy in the Clérambault-Kandinsky syndrome is limerence gone mad. Attenuated in degree, possessive jealousy is a defining characteristic of ordinary limerence; but the line dividing possessive jealousy that is protective from that which is abusive is a thin one, and it is not easily shared equally between both members of a partnership, whether heterosexual or homosexual.

Paradoxical though it may seem, one feature of Clérambault-Kandinsky syndrome is shyness and ineptitude in relating to other people in ordinary social intercourse. Shyness is a manifestation, variable in degree, of introverted ineptitude in troopbonding. It represents a partial impairment of the phylism for becoming a full-fledged, back-slapping, extraverted participant in the primate troop.

In its most pathological degree, as in some individuals with a history of the syndrome of infantile autism since birth, shyness is manifested as autistic aloofness from other people, and near-total or total incapacity to communicate linguistically or gesturally. In these severe cases, the phylism for troopbonding is so completely vestigial as to be nonfunctional. Vestigiation of the phylism for troopbonding does not, however, predicate concomitant vestigiation of the phylism for limerent pairbonding. There is evidence to the contrary among those with a history of infantile autism who are post-pubertal. By ordinary standards, however, the way that limerent attraction manifests itself in association with a lifetime of social ineptitude may seem bizarre.

One example is the case of a young adult woman with a history of both Turner (45,X) syndrome and infantile autism. Misconstruing her thirteen-year-old brother's unstockinged legs or feet as an erotic signal, she accused him of sexual abuse for showing them. She was agitatedly jealous of the courtship of her younger sister who was taller and more elegant than herself, and was permitted by her family to have a boyfriend, a privilege forbidden to her.

Whereas the imbalance between the pairbonding and troopbonding phylisms is extreme in autism, it is mild and attenuated in the syndrome of loveshyness (Gilmartin, 1987). People with this syndrome are introvertedly reticent, retiring, and inept at mixing socially except among familiar friends. They tend to experience autonomic symptoms of panic when thrust in the midst of strangers at a social gathering. Inexperienced in social small talk, their conversation becomes laced with faux pas. Even inviting someone for coffee or for dinner and a movie is a social ordeal, and they are obsessively apprehensive of being turned down. They agonize over being able to make the first move toward a limerently attractive partner, and so stay at home alone, ruminating and fixated on the unattainable one. After having finally found a partner and become initiated into sexual intercourse, if the partnership breaks up, they suffer prolonged and excruciating distress, and possibly become chronically ill with a systemic disease. They may also enter a period of limerent apathy and inertia, which is wrongly construed as lack of sexual desire.

Limerent apathy and inertia has a variety of potential antecedents. The man whose autobiography is recorded in *The Armed Robbery Orgasm* (Keyes and Money, 1993) reported that, for the first year of his prison sentences, he experienced no sexuoerotic dreams or fantasies, no response to formerly arousing stimuli, and no masturbation. Then all suddenly and unexpectedly returned overnight.

Limerent apathy and inertia may have its onset also in one or both of the partners when the initial momentum of limerence in their relationship, especially if it was weak to begin with, has stalled—a far from uncommon occurrence. The limerent history of cross-dressing tranvestophilic men is typical. They marry on a weak wave of limerent attraction, partly on the expectation that marriage will cure the syndrome of transvestophilia. Without the supplemental excitement of cross-dressing, sexual intercourse becomes an increasingly dreary obligation. It progressively declines in frequency and comes to a standstill, whereupon the couple either stay together as noncopulatory friends, or separate.

Cross-dressing is a visible activity. Many other varieties of paraphilia remain secretly hidden behind a facade of limerent apathy and inertia. The facade of limerent apathy and inertia may be long-lasting. Otherwise it may persist until punctuated by an episode of limerence that is reawakened in a new attachment.

A rare, seldom studied, and poorly understood syndrome which does not yet have a name is that of limerent apathy and inertia, apparently idiopathic in origin, beginning at puberty and lasting for several years. While it lasts, sexuoerotic imagery, ideation, and arousal are dormant. So also is sexuoerotic and genital functioning. Men report an absence of nocturnal emissions alone or with dreams, and failure to discover or practice masturbation. Everything awakens rather suddenly with the onset of the first partnership in limerence. In one male case, the awakening was with the first girlfriend at age twenty-one. In another, it was with the first extramarital affair at age forty-six, after years of marriage in which intercourse had been infrequent, desultory, and chiefly for the procreation of three children. The husband had his awakening while away working on assignment. At the same time, at home, his wife had her first extramarital affair and had her awakening too.

The sexuoerotic ecstasy of limerence has a counterpart in the religious ecstasy of piety. The parallel is most evident among those religious whose obedience to the vow of chastity, celibacy, and abstinence render them forever deprived of the possibility of realizing the ecstasy of limerence in a secular partnership. They experience instead the ecstasy of spiritual possession in a divine partnership which, according to Christian doctrine, is a metaphysical equivalent of being a bride of Christ.

Gendermap Transpositions

Human beings are not the equivalent of Ken and Barbie dolls with nothing between the legs. Transculturally, no societies arbitrarily construe masculinity and femininity without reference to what is between the legs—which is precisely what modern-day social constructionist and deconstructionist philosophers are prone to do. Transcultural stereotypes of what constitutes masculinity and femininity are diverse, however, and possibly at variance with one another.

The Sambia tribal culture of New Guinea (Herdt, 1981; 1984), for example, is completely at variance with our own regarding the role of pedophilic homosexuality and serial bisexuality in the rearing of boys to be fiercely masculine head-hunters. According to the principles of Sambia folk medicine, just as an infant needs woman's milk to survive, so also does a boy from age seven or eight onward need men's milk. Otherwise he will fail to become pubertal and will fail also to pass the ordeals of initiation into warriorhood. Therefore, it is the obligation of adolescent bachelors, too young for marriage, to have the semen sucked out of their penises by prepubertal boys until the boys themselves are mature enough to reverse roles and provide men's milk for the age group below them. At around age nineteen, marriage is tribally arranged, after which the now fully initiated warrior becomes a heterosexual husband.

The masculine/feminine difference in sexuoeroticality and procreation is the one that specifically involves the sex organs. It is in reference to the sex organs that the term "sex difference" should properly be used. This specific difference is only one among a larger array of masculine/feminine differences, however. Taken together, the entire array should properly be called gender differences. The nonsexuoerotical, nonprocreational segments of the array are classified as vocational, educational, recreational, sartorial, legal, and semeiological. The latter includes etiquette, grooming, body ornamentation, body language, and vocal intonation.

The rationale for distinguishing the sexual from the nonsexual components of the totality of gender is that the morphology of the sex organs is the criterion by which people world-wide ordinarily define a person as male or female. There is no absolute guarantee, however, of concordance between the morphology and functionality of the sex organs and the other components of gender. Discordance is, for example, a defining characteristic of various syndromes of hermaphroditism and related birth defects of the sex organs.

An illustration is that of a syndrome of male hermaphroditism with congenital micropenis or agenesis of the penis. A person with the syndrome may, when clothed, be indistinguishable from other men; but it would be incorrect to say that he could perform the male sex role in copulation, no matter how praiseworthy his attempt to surmount his handicap. An analogous example is that of a man with accidental amputation of the penis, or of a female-to-male transexual without a penis. In both cases surgical construction of a fully functional penis is not technologically possible. The converse case would be that of a woman with congenital atresia of the vagina prior to surgical vaginoplasty, or of a male-to-female transexual with no vagina, prior to sex-reassignment surgery.

The rarity of such cases as the foregoing adds to rather than detracts from the magnitude of their significance for theoretical sexology and for the principles of gender illustrated in the definitions and exposition that follow.

> **gender:** one's personal, social, and legal status as male or female, or mixed, on the basis of somatic and behavioral criteria more inclusive than the genital criterion and/or erotic criterion alone.

The grammatical and syntactical need of a noun singular with which to circumvent the duality of "gender identity and gender role" is met by telescoping them into the unity of an acronymic noun, G-I/R.

> **G-I/R (gender-identity/role):** gender identity is the private experience of gender role, and gender role is the public manifestation of gender identity. Both are like two sides of the same coin, and constitute the unity of G-I/R. Gender identity is the sameness, unity, and persistence of one's individuality as male, female, or androgynous, in greater or lesser degree, especially as it is experienced in self-awareness and behavior. Gender role is everything that a person says and does to indicate to others or to the self the degree that one is either male or female or androgynous; it includes but is not restricted to sexual and erotic arousal and response (which should not be excluded from the definition). The public manifestations of gender role are, by analogy, on the outside of a revolving globe, whereas the private workings of gender identity are inside.
>
> **gender coding:** combined genetic coding, hormonal coding, and social coding of a person's characteristics of body, mind, and/or behavior as either exclusively male, exclusively female, or nonexclusively androgynous, relative to a given, and in some instances arbitrary criterion standard.

Developmentally, an analogy exists between gender coding and the coding of native language in the brain. Both begin in prenatal life with precoding of the brain in preparation for what will follow. Both continue in postnatal life with their further development and maturation being contingent on brain coding through the senses from social sources.

The coding of language in the brain is bipolar. The positive pole codes for language that is idiomatic, syntactical, and reciprocally shared. The negative pole codes for language forms that do not match the usage of others and so fail to be communicational.

The developmental coding of gender identity (G-I/R) in the brain is also bipolar. The positive pole codes for what I am, boy or girl, respectively, and the other codes for what I am not, girl or boy, respectively. At each pole there is a map or schema of what is coded there. At one pole the map is labeled feminine, and at the other masculine. Everybody, boy and girl, man and woman, has both maps, one depicting "me" and the other depicting "thee." Gender identity disorder is a signal that the "me" and "thee" gendermaps have, in greater or lesser degree, become crisscrossed. One may displace the other, or both may coexist in alternation (a dual personality phenomenon), or one may merge into the other, either transiently or long-term and either partially or, much less likely, completely.

Under ordinary circumstances of development, one expects concordance between the prenatal and the postnatal coding of an individual's gendermap. In addition, one expects that the gendermap will be concordant with the natal sex of the external genitalia. Under circumstances in which the gendermap is discordant with the natal sex of the external genitalia, the source of discordancy may lie in either the prenatal or the postnatal coding of the gendermap, or in both combined. The formal definition of gendermap is as follows.

> **gendermap:** a developmental representation or template synchronously in the mind and brain depicting the detailed coding of one's gender-identity/role as masculine, feminine, or mixed. One of its components is sexuoerotical. Other components are vocational, educational, recreational, sartorial, legal, and, in gender coded etiquette, grooming, body ornamentation, body language, and vocal intonation, semeiological.

What is masculine and what is feminine vary in accordance with changeable societal criteria. In most people, the component parts and subparts of a gendermap typically are concordant with the natal sex and with one another in being predominantly masculine or feminine, respectively. There are exceptions, however, in which one or more parts or subparts of the gendermap becomes discordantly crosscoded or transposed from masculine to feminine, or vice versa. The degree of crossover may be minor or major.

Even a minor crossover may encounter intense societal intolerance, as for example in the 1960s when fathers would become enraged at sons who adopted the new fashion of shoulder-length haircuts, formerly the fashion only for girls. The dichotomy of masculine and feminine is one of society's most sacred antinomies and eternal verities. Even a minor transposition from one to the other is societally misconstrued as the onset of a cascade that will destroy the absoluteness and integrity of both. Historically, over the last century and a half, societal intolerance of transposition has been manifested as resistance against the feminization of voting and civil rights, including the right of access to educational, recreational, and vocational opportunities, and the right of personal sexuoerotical and procreational planning and abortion.

Historically, there has been no more intense intolerance of crossover or transposition within the gendermap than that which pertains to the sexuoerotical component. Allowable masculine and feminine sexuoerotical practices and copulatory positions have been variously dictated by religion, law, and custom, and infringements have been harshly punished.

No infringement has aroused more fanatical vindictiveness than that which pertains to the morphologic sex of the partner in sexuoerotical practices, namely, when the partner of a male is transposed from female to male so that two males are together, and similarly for two females together. This is the transposition for which the modern term "homosexuality" was coined by K. M. Benkert, also known as Kertbeny, in 1869 (Kennedy, 1988; Herzer, 1985), although the phenomenon had been on record since antiquity.

In one type of homosexual coupling, at least one member of the pair of male/male or female/female partners has a gendermap in which all the components, except the one that codes for the body morphology of the partner, are coded in concordance with the natal sex. The person with this kind of gendermap is usually self-defined as gay, if male, or as lesbian, if female. Such a person may be a rugged football hero, or a cover-girl fashion model. They represent the very epitome of stereotyped masculinity and femininity, respectively, except for being sexuoerotically attracted toward, and possibly limerent with a partner of the same body morphology as the self. Not infrequently, such a person is characterized as having a masculine or, respectively, a feminine gender identity, except for a homosexual object choice. More correctly the terminology should be not object choice, but homosexual eroticality.

Homosexual eroticality may have a history of constancy over the course of a lifetime, in which case its defining characteristic will be homosexual limerence, the capacity to be love smitten only by a member of one's own sex. By contrast, homosexual eroticality may have a history of inconstancy either by having been limited to a specific age or period of life, or by having been subject to episodic fluctuations with heterosexual eroticality. Fluctuations may be few or frequent, and they may be spontaneous or contingent on specific circumstances as, for example, under the circumstance of being sex segregated in prison. Even though serving very long sentences, however, some prisoners, male or female, are incapable of responding homosexually, no matter how androgynously alluring a prospective partner may be. Their gendermaps are comprehensively so monosexually coded as heterosexual that they lack a sufficient ratio of crosscoding to allow bisexual fluctuations, irrespective of circumstances.

Conversely, the gendermaps of some people are comprehensively so monosexually crosscoded as homosexual that they too allow no bisexual fluctuations. Such are the gendermaps that fit the popular stereotypes of extreme effeminacy and extreme masculinacy as the hallmarks of, respectively, male and female homosexuality.

In some cases in which the transposition of all the components of the gendermap, nonsexuoerotical as well as sexuoerotical, is permanent as well as comprehensive, the person undergoes hormonal, although not surgical sex reassignment, and lives full time as an impersonating member of the nonnatal sex. The generic name for this permanent and complete transposition is gynemimesis (woman-miming) in natal males, and andromimesis (man-miming) in natal females (Money and Lamacz, 1984). So far as is known, gynemimesis outweighs andromimesis in prevalence as well as degree of completeness. It is transcultural in occurrence, and differently institutionalized from one culture to another.

In India, for example, gynemimetics are hijras. The organization of hijra communities is partly as a caste, and partly as a religious cult (Nanda,

1990). Hijra gurus have for centuries trained their successors in the surgical technique of complete castration, with amputation of both testicles and penis, but they have no surgical technique for vaginoplasty. Their traditional medicine lacks also a feminizing equivalent of the hormone estrogen.

Gynemimesis, instead of being permanent, may be episodic, and manifested as the two names, two wardrobes, and two personalities phenomenon—a gender crosscoded example of the multiple (dual) personality phenomenon, and also of the mental process of dissociation (Chapter 4). In recognition of cross dressing as its most prominent feature, this episodically expressed form of gynemimesis was named transvestism by Magnus Hirschfeld in 1910 (Ellis, 1938). Transvestism, per se, in for example a theatrical or party-going masquerade, is not invariably an adjunct to sexuoerotical arousal. When a male's arousal is contingent on the wearing of women's garments, usually lingerie, then cross dressing merges with fetishism, and simple transvestism becomes paraphilic transvestophilia (see below).

The gynemimetic transvestophile may, while engaged in sexual intercourse, be self-represented in his gendermap not only as cross dressed but also as having a cross gendered, that is, feminine, body image. Reciprocally, the coital partner, if female, is represented in his gendermap as having a male body. The manipulation of this rather complete degree of gender crossing may be episodic for a long period of time, or it may become continuous and permanent. Then transvestophilic gender crossing may either remain constant, or it may mutate into a transexual fixation on sex reassignment. A transexual fixation is not, however, invariably preceded by episodic transvestophilic gender transposition. It may have a long-term history of its own from peripuberty onward, in females as well as males, as a body image disorder (see below).

The principles according to which the gendermap develops with and without one of the different types of gender transposition have not yet yielded their secrets to scientific investigation. In keeping with the official designation of gender transpositions as pathologies, and with medicine's mandate to alleviate pathology, attention has been directed to the presence rather than the absence of transpositions in the gendermap. It has been taken for granted, in keeping with the theological doctrine of natural law, that gender development without transposition needs no explanation. Heterosexuality is set up as a fulfillment of natural law. Hence, in the course of the past century, an inordinate amount of attention has been paid to homosexuality at the expense of heterosexuality. Bisexuality has been all but neglected. It is in bisexuality (popularized as transgenderism), however, that the key concept of bipotentiality is to be found.

As aforesaid (Chapter 10) in the earliest weeks of embryonic and fetal life, the anlagen of the mammalian genitalia are bipotential. Their differentiation as monosexually either male or female is under the direction of a hormonal code. Likewise, the sexual mindbrain is bipotential in its initial development. It too differentiates under the direction of a hormonal code. The timing is from late prenatal to early perinatal life. The resolution of mindbrain bipotentiality into masculine or feminine monosexuality is not exclusively under the jurisdiction of hormonal coding, however. On the contrary, mindbrain differentiation continues to be bipotentially flexible throughout the infantile and juvenile years during which it is dependent on gender dimorphic input via the senses from social sources to resolve bipotentiality into monopotentiality.

In the absence of confirmed hypotheses, it is necessary in the present day and age to postulate a series of working hypotheses regarding the resolution of gender bipotentiality in infancy and childhood, as follows.

First hypothesis: already at birth some infants may have a more tenacious degree of bipotentiality than others and have, therefore, a greater chance than others of differentiating a gender map that incorporates a transposition.

Second hypothesis: there may be a vulnerability or disposition toward a gender transposition that is not congenital but of early infantile, though as yet unascertained environmental origin and that, once in place, remains immutable.

Third hypothesis: the resolution of bipotentiality is, per se, a delicate if not fragile process in all children, and is readily disrupted by various intrusions, for example abusive neglect and cruelty, and by various exclusions, such as not providing opportunities for normal juvenile sexuoerotical learning and rehearsal play with agemates.

Fourth hypothesis: There are some people for whom bipotentiality never closes completely but may remain open and manifested as bisexuality, not necessarily in a 50:50 ratio, but in variable proportions from 99:1 to 1:99.

In the years from later infancy to middle childhood and beyond, the two great principles for the resolution of bipotentiality in the gendermap are identification with persons of the same sex, and complementation to persons of the other sex. For example, a small girl identifies with an older girl or woman, possibly her mother, in learning to dance, but complements or reciprocates the steps of a boy or man, possibly her father, in performing the dance. The identification/complementation ratio may be set askew by social pathogens within a child's living environment, especially the social pathogen of a skewed three-way relationship between the two parents and the child. One such pathogen came to my notice for the first time several years ago (Money, 1984b). It pertained to a morbid sexological relationship between the parents. I made a notation, at the time, as follows.

> I am dictating a note to put on record a new hypothesis or formula regarding the role of the father in the genesis of feminism in a son's G-I/R (gender-identity/role). This is the formula: the father covertly courts his

son's allegiance, in place of what he finds missing in his wife, and casts him in the role of a wife substitute, if not for the present, then for the future. The son, for his part, may solicit his father's allegiance as a formula for keeping him in the household, and for preventing a parental separation. If the father has already gone, or even if he had died, the son's gender transposition may serve to solicit his dad's miraculous return. His life becomes a living fable of the boy who will become daddy's bride, for the evidence is plentiful that a daddy can be counted on to return to the home that his wife keeps ready for him. (Money, 1988a, p.82)

Follow-up outcome studies into adulthood of boys fixated on becoming girls have shown that they have not become transexuals, transvestites, or transvestophiles, but mostly run-of-the-mill gay men with a homosexual gendermap (Money and Russo, 1980, 1981; Green, 1986). Among prepubertal boys with a gendermap transposition, it is not yet known how to differentiate future transvestites, transvestophiles, or transexuals from those whose outcome will be gynemimesis or, more likely, plain homosexuality. The same applies to girls.

Body-Image Fixations

Not all body-image fixations have sexuoerotic significance, and not all sexuoerotic fixations have body-image significance, but there is enough overlap to warrant the new term "sexuoerotic body-image fixation," defined as follows.

> **sexuoerotic body image fixation:** the personal and private recognition of the locations and functions of the sexuoerotic organs or regions of one's own body upon which is superimposed in a highly idiosyncratic and nonconfirmable way a retrospective projection of how they are presumed to have undergone change, or a prospective projection of how they are in the process of undergoing change, or should be changed.

A sexuoerotic body-image fixation may be benign or not benign. To have sexually significant body parts ornamentally tattooed or pierced is benign. To become a eunuch by genital self-amputation, of which the fortuitous outcome may be to bleed to death, is not benign.

A sexuoerotic body-image fixation may or may not be traceable to an intracranial or peripheral neuropathy to which is attributed an alteration of the sexuoerotic body schema. Although the terms "body image" and "body schema" are used somewhat interchangeably, for the most part body image is an endopsychic construct, and body schema a neurological construct.

There are three principles under which sexuoerotic body-image fixations may be subsumed, namely, realignment and enhancement, obliteration and relinquishment, and augmentation and amplification. All three of these principles are exemplified in the procedures of sex reassignment.

The procedures of sex reassignment were originally developed for the rehabilitation of patients whose natal sex was ambiguous or hermaphroditic and whose body image developed to be discordant with that of the sex in which they had been officially named and registered, and in which they were socially assigned and reared.

In the 1960s, sex reassignment (Benjamin 1966; Green and Money, 1969) became recognized as an acceptable procedure for people whose natal sex was not ambiguous or hermaphroditic but whose body image nonetheless developed to be discordant with their natal sex. The same term, "transexualism," names not only the syndrome, but also the method of rehabilitation by changing the body to be concordant with the body image.

In the case of the male-to-female transexual, the body image of the face is feminine and is discordant with that of the actual physiognomy, which in the majority of cases is bearded and has masculine features. The principle of alteration according to which congruence between the femininity of the facial body-image and the actual physiognomy is effected is realignment and enhancement. The method is electrolysis for facial-hair removal, administration of female hormones for feminized skin texture, and plastic surgery for changes of the physiognomy—which are not invariably necessary.

The corresponding alterations for the female-to-male transexual are also of the realignment and enhancement type, but the method is more simple. Treatment with male sex hormone suffices. It produces facial hair, masculine skin texture, and, ultimately, thinning or balding head hair. By enlarging the larynx, it also realigns the voice to conform to the body image—an effortless process unmatched in male-to-female reassignment which requires vocal retraining.

The principle of obliteration and relinquishment is of paramount importance to the male-to-female transexual with respect to the external genitals which are a reproach and an offense to the feminine body image. In a majority of cases, being rid of the offensive male genitals takes precedence over the augmenting and amplifying procedure of vaginoplasty.

In the female-to-male transexual, the offensive organs are those responsible for menstruation. Their extirpation takes precedence over the augmenting and amplifying procedure of phalloplasty, for which, despite its importance to the patient, there is no completely successful surgical technology.

In female-to-male transexuals, the obliteration and relinquishment principle applies also to surgical extirpation of the breasts. By contrast in male-to-female transexuals, it is the principle of augmentation and amplification that applies to the breasts. Hormonally induced breast enlargement (gynecomastia) may fail to match the body image of mammary hyperplasia in some patients, who may then resort to augmentation mammoplasty either by surgery, or by the very dangerous procedure of silicone injections. The latter may also be resorted to for hip enlargement.

The transexual body image is individually variable with respect to the hierarchical position of the three principles of body alteration on the agenda of sex reassignment. Thus, in a case of male-to-female transexualism in which the principle of realignment and enhancement is hierarchically above relinquishment and obliteration, even an appointment with the hairdresser may take precedence over an admissions appointment for genital-reassignment surgery.

In another case, by contrast, in which the obliteration and relinquishment principle is uppermost, the patient may embark on a frantic round of clinic shopping for a surgeon who will extirpate the offending external genital organs on the basis of personal request alone, with no waiting period, and without the delay of a psychologic, psychiatric, or sexologic consultation.

In yet another case, in which the augmentation and amplification principle is uppermost, large breasts may be so high on the agenda that a patient will find a way of meeting the cost of obtaining them, despite failing to meet other medical expenses.

Although the body-image fixation in sex-reassignment cases includes cross-gendered surgical reconstruction of the genitalia, there are some instances in which, post-surgically, the sex life is one of chastity and abstinence. This is what may be expected when a male-to-female transexual continues to live at home as if a sister-in-law of the former wife and an aunt to the children.

Foregoing chastity and abstinence, in other instances the female-to-male will live in a lesbian relationship with another woman. Correspondingly, a female-to-male transexual may live as a gay male. Whereas such cases are the exception and not the rule, they do indicate that a gender-transposed body-image fixation is not simply an artifact of a gender-transposed (homosexual) sexuoerotic attraction. In other words, people do not undergo sex reassignment so as to become socially defined post-surgically as heterosexual. They do so in obedience to a body-image fixation.

Body-image alterations of a change of sex are present from a young age in those children who have a fixation on changing their sex. Thus a boy may insist that his penis is superfluous and will drop off as readily as breasts will grow on a pubertal girl. Conversely, a girl may insist that a penis will grow out and turn her into a boy. In both instances the concepts of a sex change are formulated in advance of knowing about hormonal and surgical sex reassignment.

In cases of sex-reassignment fixation from childhood through adolescence to maturity, the omnipresence of body-image fixation is of such a degree as to warrant reclassifying the syndromes of transexualism, gynemimesis, andromimesis, and transvestophilia as syndromes not of gender-identity disorder, but as syndromes of body-image disorder. Reclassification might open up new avenues of research into the origin of the syndromes, and provide an escape from the dead end of a cul-de-sac in which a hormonal search for their origin is presently entrapped.

Whereas the body-image syndrome of sex reassignment involves the alteration of a plurality of regions and organs of the body, the syndrome of being fixated on becoming a eunuch is restricted to the genitalia. One example is that of a woman with a career in contraceptive services with a fixation on hysterectomy and ovariectomy as a presumed remedy for menstrual cramps and indifference to marital intercourse.

As compared with removal of the ovaries, removal of the testicles of farm animals is surgically simple. The same technique allows a man to become a eunuch by self-castration. A do-it-yourself procedure is, in fact, resorted to by some males with the body-image fixation on being a eunuch, devoid of carnal desire. This condition has been named the Skoptic syndrome (Money, 1988b), after the now extinct eighteenth century Russian religious sect known as the Skoptsy (meaning in Russian castrated rams). To forgo the temptations of the flesh, and to become a full member of the church, male skoptics were castrated and, ideally, had the penis amputated as well; women had the nipples burned off.

In a published case of Skoptic syndrome in a male (Money, 1988b), self-castration failed to obliterate carnality and so was followed by self-attempted denervation of the penis. Although the only definite outcome of both procedures was sterility, not relief from carnality, peace of mind was achieved, ironically enough, with a change of employment, working to promote self-perpetuation by cryogenic freezing of the brain at death in anticipation of future technology of reincarnation.

In another case, partly published (Kalin, 1979) and partly not (Money, unpublished data), a college student of very high IQ manufactured a hypothalamic-inhibiting substance designed to block the release of pituitary gonadotropins. Its impurities when self-injected produced life-threatening ulcerations. Prevented by maternal intervention from undergoing a trial treatment with the antiandrogen Depo-Provera, he returned home and castrated himself. Still not relieved of carnal desire, he studied adrenal surgery alone in the library in preparation for self-adrenalectomy to remove the last vestiges of androgen secreted from the adrenal cortices. After seven hours of self-surgery, the pain of lifting the liver to reveal the adrenals proved so excruciatingly painful that he telephoned for an emergency ambulance and was admitted to the emergency room of the local hospital.

The converse of getting rid of the testicles is their replacement by prosthetic testicles after they have been lost or are congenitally absent. There is no recorded instance of a sexological body-image syndrome characterized by a specific fixation on obtaining testicular prosthesis. By contrast, in cases of testicular agenesis, there are instances of resistance to acceptance of the artificiality of prosthetic testicular implants. In one noteworthy case, the body image incorporated the implanted testicles only after a dream of having swallowed them (Money and Sollod, 1978).

A body-image syndrome may focus on alteration of the penis. There is a multimillion dollar market waiting for the discovery of a fool-proof method of penis enlargement. Among those who would pay for an enlarged penis, however, there are few who qualify as having a body-image syndrome with a fixation on penis size.

One fixation on penis size is known by its Malaysian name, Koro, the shrinking-penis syndrome. Once considered to be culturally limited to southeast Asia, Koro is now known to occur more widely (Money and Annecillo, 1987; Prince, 1992). In the body imagery of this syndrome, the penis shrinks and retracts until, when it has completely disappeared, death may ensue. In actuality, there is no substantiating evidence of penile alteration. The symptoms do not respond to rational appeal, but with supportive understanding the body image returns to its earlier state.

In some penile body-image syndromes, there is a prior history of traumatic injury of the penis, for example, ablatio penis; or of disease of the penis, for example, Peyronie's disease; or of a birth defect of the penis, for example, micropenis (Money, 1984a). The common denominator of such cases is that the penis is unable to effect penetration in either a heterosexual or homosexual relationship. Not all of those so affected, however, develop a full-fledged body-image syndrome. Some find an unpathological means of coping.

Alteration of the penis in a body-image syndrome applies also, in some cases, to its function. Thus there may be a frenetic search, in vain, for restoration of erection from the permanent impotence that is frequently a sequel to priapism (Money and Hirsch, 1965). Impotence as a sexological body-image syndrome is, however, more likely to be manifest as a fixation on failure prior to even trying—in fact it is obsessional fixation on failure that prohibits the attempt to copulate, despite the evidence of full erection in masturbation (Money, unpublished data). In an undetermined proportion of cases of impotence, erectile failure is a body-image syndrome. The same applies to premature ejaculation in which the fixation is on one's penis as an intrusive and offensive organ from which the partner should be protected.

Fixation on the penis as an offensive organ that preordains the absolute impossibility of an erotosexual partnership may pertain to its size or shape. Even though there is no substantiating evidence of penile hypertrophy, a patient may have a penis represented in his body image as being so large that it would tear up any vagina it might penetrate, or as being so crooked that it would wreak similar havoc (Money, unpublished data). In such a case, medical photography poses a threat to exposure of the error of the body image, as does a physical examination. Thus appointments for both are plausibly evaded.

Female counterparts of penile body-image syndromes have not yet been recorded. It is theoretically possible, however, that, in girlhood development, an absence of positive endorsement of achieving orgasm leaves a void in the body image where orgasm should be. Subsequently, the longer this void persists unfilled, the longer does the woman remain unknowing of what an orgasm is.

An analogous situation exists in cases of sex reassignment. Thus there is no guarantee whatever that the female-to-male's body image of a female orgasm corresponds to orgasms as experienced by women. Correspondingly, the same applies to the male-to-female transexual and the male orgasm.

To lose the foreskin after its constancy in the body image has become well established is more traumatic than to have lost it neonatally, or never to have had it. Even so, the body-image syndrome of foreskin restoration occurs not only in men who were circumcised as juveniles, but also in those whose circumcision was neonatal. The morbidity of the syndrome ranges from mild to severe (Money, 1991b). If surgery is resorted to (Greer et al., 1982; Mohl et al., 1981) the outcome may be cosmetically disfiguring. In some cases, self-surgery has been resorted to (Walter and Streimer, 1990; Money, 1991b). As in other body-image syndromes, an appeal to rationality is counter-productive. However, with caring support, even severe cases are likely to go into remission. There is a national network and newsletter for men with a shared interest in foreskin restoration (Berkeley and Tiffenbach, 1983).

Whether or not there is a body-image syndrome as a sequel to female circumcision, so-called, has not yet been ascertained. Variations in tribal custom range from removal of the clitoral hood to removal of the entire vulva, and closure of the wound. As immigrant Africans transplant their custom of female circumcision to Europe and America, it is possible that a sexological body-image syndrome of vulval restoration will become evident in some of their daughters (Lightfoot–Klein, 1989).

Pseudocyesis, or false pregnancy, is a body-image syndrome remarkable for physiological changes that, in conformity with the body image, mimic the early stages of pregnancy. When the absence of a fetus is discovered, grieving ensues as if a miscarriage had occurred. The origin of the physiological changes in pseudocyesis has not been ascertained, but there are animal models that indicate a role for the sense of smell.

A body-image syndrome may merge with a paraphilic syndrome. Such a merger is well exemplified in the case of apotemnophilia (from Greek, *apo*, from + *temnein*, to cut + *philia*, love), the paraphilic fixation on becoming an amputee (Money, Jobaris and Furth, 1977). For the apotemnophile, erotic arousal and the facilitation of orgasm are responsive to and contingent on being an amputee. An apotemnophile becomes fixated on carrying out a self-contrived amputation, or on obtaining one in a hospital. The location of the amputation is highly specific. Though apotemnophilia occurs in women (Money, 1990b), as well as men, it is probably less prevalent in women.

Body-image fixations of a benign type are related to sexuoerotic allure and to conceptions and fashions of being sexuoerotically attractive. Cosmetic plastic surgery as in augmentation mammoplasty and facial reconstruction fall into this category. So also do cosmetic ornamentation of erogenous zones and the genitalia themselves by means of tattoos or piercing for the wearing of gold or stainless steel bars and rings.

Changing the body shape, especially by dieting to lose weight, is related to sexuoerotic allure and body image, but most people who go on a diet do not qualify as having a fixation on body image. By contrast, a fixation on losing weight by fasting, as in anorexia nervosa, does quality as a body-image fixation of which the outcome may be wasting away and dying.

Vandalized Lovemaps

Experimental endocrinology is a twentieth-century phenomenon. Since the inception of reproductive endocrinological research, when experiments have required that female laboratory animals be ready to receive the male, the periodic or seasonal state of estrus or being in heat has been artificially induced by hormonal injections of estrogen and progesterone. The male required no hormonal injection, only the pheromonal odor of the female in estrus, to become sexually responsive. The male's mounting was attributed to the female's receptivity. The gross oversimplification of this equation was brought to attention by Frank Beach, the major animal sexologist of his era, in a 1976 paper under the title of "Sexual attractivity, proceptivity, and receptivity in female mammals."

Among human beings, attractivity is an attribute or quality that anyone, male or female, may or may not possess for anyone else, male or female. Attractivity may be sexual and erotic. It may be parental also, or charismatic. It may be fortuitously possessed, or it may be assiduously cultivated, perhaps in conformity with what is in vogue, or in defiance of it. Attractivity is an asset that lures others and evokes their responses.

As in animals, so also among human beings, proceptivity is the initial phase or manifestation of one's responsiveness to the sexuoerotic attractivity of someone else. The more it is reciprocated, the greater the likelihood that it will merge into the next phase which, especially in human beings, is more accurately termed acceptivity rather than receptivity. Although receptivity may be completely reciprocal, it is attributed in general usage more often to the female than the male. Acceptivity is more readily applicable to both male and female, reciprocally. It is the phase of bodily union and, in particular, genital union. It is followed by the phase of conceptivity of which the outcome may or may not be pregnancy.

Among species as diverse as fish, birds, and mammals, proceptive manifestations are recognized as courtship displays or mating rituals, also referred to as mating dances, songs, and calls. They are species specific and male/female specific. As a general though not invariable rule their origin is phylismic and not augmented by individual learning, and the timing of their occurrence is contingent on seasonal or other fluctuation in the blood level of steroidal hormones, in the male testosterone, and in the female estrogen and progesterone.

In the human species, proceptivity may be manifested as a species-shared stereotypical ritual of courtship (pp. 183–84) that leads onto and merges into copulatory foreplay. As compared with other species, however, human phylogenetic proceptive rituals are highly amenable to ontogenetic and uniquely personalized modification. The modified version can be ascertained not only through observation, but also in verbal report. Human proceptivity exists not only as behavior, but also as the rehearsal of that behavior in the imagery and ideation of dreams, daydreams, fantasies, and thoughts. For each individual, the totality of both the rehearsal and the behavior constitutes the lovemap (Chapter 8). To recapitulate briefly: to the extent that the lovemap is gender coded, it overlaps the gendermap and incorporates its sexuoerotical portion. The two together are analogous with the native language map in requiring the preparatory development in embryonic and fetal life of a brain that is both healthy and human. Then, in postnatal life, the detailed configuration of the lovemap and gendermap is contingent on input through the senses of signals and information from the social environment.

In the absence of any alternative, there is a highly speculative evolutionary hypothesis that one of the prerequisites of the development of a primate with a brain capable of processing syntactical language and of generating hitherto unknown conceptual formulations was the concomitant loosening in the brain of the ancient mammalian heritage of robotic heterosexual proceptivity. Whether or not this hypothesis is science-fictional, the data to which it applies are not. There are an extraordinary range and diversity of lovemaps among human beings some of which justify the maxim that truth is stranger than fiction. In the vernacular, strange lovemaps are known as kinky or bizarre, and as deviations or perversions in the language of the law and medical history. The contemporary medical and scientific term is paraphilia which is defined as follows.

> paraphilia: a condition occurring in men and women of being compulsively responsive to and obligatively dependent on an unusual and personally or socially unacceptable stimulus, perceived or in the ideation and imagery of fantasy, for optimal initiation and maintenance of eroto-

sexual arousal and the facilitation or attainment of orgasm (Greek, *para-*, altered + −*philia*, love). Paraphilic imagery may be replayed in fantasy during solo masturbation or intercourse with a partner. Its antonym is normophilia.

Being possessed of a paraphilia is not itself a criminal offense, whereas performing a paraphilic act may qualify as one. A sex crime may, like sadistic rape, be violent and deadly, or it may, like genital exhibitionism, be noninjurious. In some jurisdictions, consensual oral-genital or anal-genital sex, even between married partners, is a crime. In some jurisdictions the age of consent is eighteen, so that an eighteen-year-old who has intercourse with a seventeen-year-old may be charged with statutory rape. Similarly, a person who has sex with a same-aged adult who is that person's stepfather's child from another marriage may be charged with the crime of incest.

Historically, sex crimes were religious crimes defined in the canon law, from which they were transferred to the common law, and subsequently to the psychiatric nosology. Concordance between the legal classification of criminal sex offending and the biomedical classification of paraphilias is lacking. Not all sex crimes are paraphilic, and only a minority of the forty or more paraphilias come under the jurisdiction of the law. For example, being paraphilically dependent upon the ritual of being administered an enema for sexuoerotical arousal and orgasm (klismaphilia) is not a criminal sex offense.

Like the face or the voice, paraphilias are individually recognizable as well as taxonomically classifiable. Some are thematically simplex or uncompounded, and some are thematically multiplex or compounded with features of two or more simplex ones merged into one complex whole.

There is no evidence that a paraphilia is preformed or ready made in the brain at birth except perhaps as diffusely as a predisposition. Rather their details are the outcome of displacements, deletions, or inclusions in the developmental coding of the lovemap in infancy and prepuberty. This developmental miscoding of the lovemap constitutes a stratagem for rescuing triumph from tragedy, namely, the triumph of saving carnal lust from extinction by cleaving it from affectional love. The historical antinomy between lust and love cuts a deep canyon through our culture and profoundly affects the sexology of all our child rearing. As a society, we are committed to obliterating in childhood the very signs of the lust without which adulthood will be considered defective and deviant.

Although a paraphilic lovemap is a personalized product of ontogenetic development, it is also phylogenetically derived, albeit in an indirect and derivative way. To illustrate: among primates, exhibition of the genitalia is a phylismic proceptive maneuver preparatory to the acceptive maneuver of genital union. In paraphilic exhibitionism, display of the genitals to a stranger is displaced from the proceptive to the acceptive phase. It becomes a substitute for the carnal lust of genital union. If genital union is not completely excluded from an exhibitionistic episode, then it may be postponed to be attempted with an affectional partner later. Successful union is then facilitated by, if not contingent upon a replay of the "mental tape" of the exhibitionistic episode. Eventually, however, the disjunction between carnal lust and affectional love may become completely polarized, with lust and exhibition to a stranger at one pole, and noncarnal affection for the regular partner at the other.

Whereas exhibitionism is a displacement paraphilia of the solicitational type, transvestophilia (also known as transvestic fetishism) is a displacement paraphilia of the allurative type. Like exhibiting, luring is a proceptive maneuver preparatory to the acceptive maneuver of genital union. Proceptively, in the transvestophilic lovemap of a male, the female's garments, especially lingerie, become a fetishistic substitute for the proceptive allure of the female. Allure is displaced from the proceptive to the acceptive phase as the man himself wears female garments as a substitute for the carnal lust of genital union with an affectional partner. Increasingly perfunctory, genital union may eventually become excluded altogether, and supplanted by cross dressing alone. The relationship with the female partner becomes affectional only, and noncarnal. In the male, transvestophilia may metamorphose to transexualism.

In the foregoing two illustrations, solicitation and allure are, respectively, the phylisms that become enlisted in the service of preserving carnal lust in the paraphilic lovemap by disconnecting it from affectional love. The phylism in each instance was displaced from its expected proceptive role to usurp the acceptive role of genital union. Hence the characterization of these paraphilias as displacement paraphilias. The paraphilic counterpart of displacement is inclusion.

In the inclusion paraphilias, carnal lust is deconnected from affectional love by the inclusion in the paraphilic lovemap of a phylism that would not ordinarily belong there. Marauding is such a phylism, and so is predation. Among primates that live in troops, marauding and predation belong more with territoriality and defense against intruders, or with killing for food, than they do with mating rivalry or the abduction of a mate. When in human beings they become enlisted in the service of deconnecting carnal lust from affectional love, they are manifested as paraphilic rape (raptophilia), a clinical syndrome which differs from assertive rape as practiced by, say, a marauding army.

Raptophilic carnal lust, contrary to today's "politically correct" dogma, is very definitely sexual as well as violent. Raptophilic lust is usually directed at unsuspecting strangers, is intensified by the victim's resistance and panic, and is assaultively threatening and cruel. It may include torture and lust murder (erotophonophilia). Like all paraphilias, raptophilia is recurrent. There are multiple victims. The deconnection between carnal lust and affectional love in the lovemap may be so complete that work mates, friends, family members, and even the person in a relationship of affectional love may have no suspicion of the raptophile's paraphilic other life. The recipient of the raptophile's affectional love is not satisfactory as the recipient of carnal lust, and if the combination is attempted, even the replay of raptophilic "mental tapes" does not sustain it for long.

A second example of an inclusion paraphilia is pedophilia. It is one of the eligibilic paraphilias in which the criterion of eligibility for carnal lust is a prepubertal body morphology. Pedophilia is also one of the chronophilias, not to be confused with infantophilia, ephebophilia (teenage-philia) or gerontophilia. The phylism that serves to preserve carnal lust in the pedophilic lovemap is the phylism of parent-child bonding which becomes absorbed into the phylism of sexuoerotic bonding. Initially it may appear that affectional love coexists with carnal lust, at least unilaterally in the lovemap of the older partner. It does not, however, survive the test of time and the onset of puberty in the juvenile partner. Carnal lust and affectional love then become deconnected and the relationship continues, if at all, exclusively as one of noncarnal supportive friendship. A pedophilic lovemap may sustain an affectional relationship with an age-matching partner, but not its integration with carnal lust. Whereas, by statutory criteria, pedophilia is the same as child abuse and molestation, by nonstatutory criteria neither abuse nor molestation may apply. The issue of social tolerance versus intolerance of pedophilia requires other criteria.

The formula of a nonsexuoerotic phylism enlisted in the service of deconnecting carnal lust and affectional love is applicable to the stratagems of all varieties of paraphilic lovemap (Money, 1986a, 1988a). Personalized variations notwithstanding, in the taxonomy of the paraphilias there are seven grand stratagems, named as follows: sacrificial/expiatory; marauding/predatory; mercantile/venal; fetishistic/talismanic; stigmatic/eligibilic; solicitational/allurative; and understudy/subrogational. The ensuing descriptions of these stratagems are taken from Money (1988a).

The **sacrificial/expiatory stratagem** requires reparation or atonement for the sin of lust by way of penance and sacrifice. The extreme sacrifice is lust murder: erotophonophilia when the partner is sacrificed, and autassassinophilia when a person stage-manages the sacrifice of the self. Excluding death, there are varying degrees, from major to minor, of sadomasochistic sacrifice and penance for the sin of lust.

The **marauding/predatory stratagem** requires that, insofar as saintly lovers do not consent to the sin of lust, a partner in lust must be stolen, abducted, or coerced by force. The extreme case of this stratagem is the syndrome of assaultive and violent paraphilic rape (raptophilia or biastophilia). The spectrum of coercion ranges from major to minor. In statutory rape there may be no coercion, but a consensual and pairbonded love affair, one of the partners being below the legal age of consent.

The **mercantile/venal stratagem** requires that sinful lust be traded, bartered, or purchased and paid for, insofar as saintly lovers do not engage consensually in its free exchange. The very existence of this stratagem gets masked by reason of its place in the orgasm trade. Nonetheless, there are some hustlers and prostitutes, as well as their customers, whose paraphilia is chrematistophilia, marketing and purchasing sex. Some chrematistophiles, not in the commercial orgasm trade, pretend with play money, or have the partner impersonate a whore or a hustler with a third person. Some set themselves up to be victims of blackmail or robbery, and some are blackmailers or robbers. The popular military and judicial dogma that homosexuals are more vulnerable to blackmailers, paraphilic or otherwise, applies equally well to heterosexuals caught in clandestine adultery, and to paraphiles of any type whose paraphilia is exercised clandestinely. Homosexuals who have come out of the proverbial closet and have nothing to hide may be subject to prejudice and unfair discrimination, but not to blackmail.

The **fetishistic/talismanic stratagem** spares the saintly lover from the sin of lust by substituting a token, fetish, or talisman instead. Fetishes are predominantly either smelly-tasty (olfactophilic) or touchy-feely (hyphephilic), and both are, in the final analysis, derived from smell and feel of parts of the human body. Devotion to the fetish may be all-consuming or minor.

The **stigmatic/eligibilic stratagem** requires that the partner in hedonic lust be, metaphorically, a pagan infidel, disparate in religion, race, color, nationality, social class, or age, from the saintly madonnas and providers of one's own social group. Morphophilic disparity pertains to disparity in the appearance of the body, and chronophilic disparity to disparity in age. An exceptional example of morphophilia is acrotomophilia, in which the partner must have an amputation stump. The extremes of chronophilia are pedophilia, in which only juveniles (or babies, in infantophilia) are eligible as lust partners, and gerontophilia in which the eligible partners are of parental or grandparental age. Age eligibility limits the duration of a partnership. In pedophilia, for example, the pedophile's own sexuoerotic age remains permanently juvenile and out of synchrony with his or her advancing chronological age. Correspondingly, the partner's eligibility is abolished by the odors and maturational changes of puberty. There is a corresponding limitation on the duration of relationships in ephebophilia (attraction to adolescents) and gerontophilia, and also in what might be called "twentiophilia," "thirtiophilia," and so on. These latter, although seldom recognized as such, underlie the broken relationships, homosexual as well as heterosexual, and the divorces of many couples in the decades of middle adulthood.

The **solicitational/allurative stratagem** protects the saint by displacing lust from the act of copulation in the acceptive phase, to an invitational gesture or overture of the proceptive phase. This might be called in the vernacular the paraphilia of the cockteaser or, in gay argot, of the loving queen. Among primates, exhibiting the genitals and inspecting them are prototypic invitations to copulate. In paraphilic exhibitionism of the penis (peodeiktophilia) and voyeurism (being a Peeping Tom), the preliminary overture displaces the main act in lustful importance. Displacement in this stratagem is the counterpart of the inclusion of something in the other five stratagems. Paraphilic female exhibitionists who expose their genitalia to men, by sitting so as to expose the nude pudendum, for example, almost never get reported to the police, so that their prevalence is unknown. Genital exposure under licit circumstances, as in a nudist resort, is not sexuoerotically arousing to exhibitionists and voyeurs. Their arousal is contingent on the illicitness of their paraphilic actions. Narratives and pictures also may feature as invitational strategies.

The **understudy/subrogational stratagem** is one in which someone who represents saintly love is rescued from the defilement of lust by being replaced by an understudy or subrogate who becomes defiled instead. The understudy is oneself.

The understudy/subrogational stratagem has different manifestations. It applies to some highly specific cases of paraphilic adultery, for example, in which the adulterer saves his or her lust from extinction, but only on the condition of being a stand-in for the adulterous mate's regular partner who would otherwise be lust-defiled instead. There are some highly specific cases of paraphilic incest in an adolescent girl, for example, in which the only condition whereby she is entitled to her own lust is that she become a stand-in for her mother, who would otherwise suffer unwanted defilement by the lust of the man, the girl's father or stepfather, whose lust her mother has renounced. This same girl may eventually run away from home to become a prostitute. She may also become pairbonded as a lesbian, while earning her living by selling sexual services to men.

It may be not a daughter but a son who is the stand-in, saving his mother from the defilement of his father's lust by diverting the latter to himself instead, in a father-son relationship that is both incestuous and homosexual. In that case the understudy/subrogation stratagem entails a degree of gender crosscoding or transposition in the son that may be full-fledged transexualism or gynemimesis at one extreme, or episodic transvestophilia, or at the other extreme entirely noneffeminated male-male bonding. Homosexual incest protects not only one female from the lust of a male, namely, the homosexual son's mother from the lust of his father or stepfather. Insofar as the son becomes himself the recipient of the lust of other males, he diverts their lust away from other women. In addition, he himself does not defile the saintly love of a woman, because his own lust is homosexually male directed instead.

The combination of this understudy/subrogation stratagem with gender crosscoding may occur as a subsidiary or satellite of other paraphilias. Gender crosscoding combined with a sacrificial/expiatory stratagem is exemplified in youths or men who are found wearing women's clothing, maybe the mother's, and dead from paraphilic self-asphyxiation by hanging—one type of autoerotic death.

The taxonomy of the seven grand stratagems takes into account that which may happen generically to human beings as a species so that the outcome is a paraphilic lovemap. It does not, however, take into account the personal ontogeny of paraphilic lovemap formation. Here, as elsewhere, the issue is not one of nature versus nurture, but of nature and nurture converging at a critical period of development and leaving persistent or immutable sequelae.

The personal ontogenesis of lovemaps, paraphilic or otherwise, in the course of childhood development is a black hole in the cosmos of twentieth-century theories of child development. Piaget was both prudish and circumspect in keeping away from childhood conceptions of sex, reproduction, and the erotic, in obedience to the popular maxim of moral pedagogy: "hear no evil, see no evil, do no evil," the accepted duty of adulthood being to guard the sexual innocence of prepubertal childhood against the social dangers and contagions of original sin.

With the publication of his so-called seduction theory in his 1896 paper on "The Etiology of Hysteria," Freud very briefly burned his fingers in the fire of authentic sexological pathology in childhood. Then, by 1897, he was promptly retreating to the phantasmagoric safety of Oedipal theory. Freud's seduction-theory terminology (as quoted in Masson, 1985, Appendix B) was explicit: infantile sexual scenes, sexual intercourse, rape, abuse, seduction, attack, assault, aggression, and trauma. Seduction theory was, however, conceptually too constricting. It failed to account for the development of psychoneurosis in the absence of an explicit history of sexual seduction in childhood. It relied too much on the fortuity of a unique event in the ontogeny of individual development, at the expense of universal regularity in the phylogeny of species development. Nothing short of a universal theory would satisfy Freud. Its attainment required the postulation of a wholly self-contained endopsychic causality which, in turn, required that revelations of traumatic seduction in childhood pertain not to the history of behavioral acts, but to the history of mental imagery and ideation in fantasies and dreams and in the unconscious (Money, 1992, Epilogue).

Freud might have resolved his discontent with seduction theory not by new theorizing but by creating a taxonomy of different species of neuroses of which one species would be hysterical psychoneuroses with its etiology in childhood sexological trauma. This would have rescued the sexology of the long-term sequelae of traumatic experience in childhood from the sexological neglect that became its fate until, in the wake of the rediscovery and renaming of child abuse as the battered-child syndrome (Kempe et al.,

1962), seduction theory was resurrected (Masson, 1985) in the service of the new specialty of victimology.

Recycled under the imprimatur of victimology, seduction theory is over-inclusive, insofar as virtually any disorder in the psychiatric nosology is attributable to a prior history of sexual child abuse. Overinclusiveness not-withstanding, victimology does, despite its basic antisexualism, give incipient recognition to the concept of developmental sexology, and of pediatric sexological health and pathology.

The childhood history of the development of a paraphilic lovemap may be reconstructed retrospectively from personal recall, perhaps with confirmation from the recall of others. Alternatively, although not often, it may be preserved in the pediatrician's record and confirmed in subsequent long-term follow-up (Money, 1991a; Money and Lamacz, 1989). Either way, one is surprised at how often eight years of age, or thereabouts, emerges as a crucial age for the incorporation of a paraphilic intrusion or displacement into the developing lovemap, so as to distort or vandalize it.

Eight is the age when children are ready to grasp the meaning of the double entendre in jokes and puns, and the no-win entrapment of the Catch-22 in which you're damned if you do, and damned if you don't admit to something, or join in something (see Chapter 8). Sex is a veritable mine-field of Catch-22s—either/or propositions, with no compromise in between. For example, eight is the age of sexual rehearsal play between agemates, for which, however, one is threatened with severe sanctions. To quit would bring ostracism and agemate rejection. Not to quit brings the risk of discovery and reprisal. To ask for help brings both.

In the sexological development of childhood, the Catch-22s of sexual information or pursuits generate unspeakable monsters which, being un-speakable, are monstrously traumatizing, in many instances more so than that which must be kept hidden in silence. The more intense the societal sanctions against what a child knows or has pursued sexually, the more intense the power of the unspeakable monster, as in the case of incest, for example.

The penalties and penances that the adult world imposes on children for being entrapped in a sexual Catch-22 constitute, albeit paradoxically, the most prevalent manifestation of child sexual abuse and neglect, and the major source of errancy in lovemap development.

Apart from the dilemma of the Catch-22, the experience of any kind of traumatic suffering, abusive neglect, or injurious violence threatens the healthy development of the lovemap in childhood (Money et al., 1990). Injurious violence includes, but is not restricted to explicitly sexual violence and coercion,which in addition may create yet another Catch-22. Nonvio-lent exposure to sexual or erotic pursuits out of synchrony with one's sexo-logical age, either by being too soon or by being not soon enough, may also have a deleterious effect on lovemap development.

Not enough is known about the concatenation of factors that go into the development of a vandalized lovemap to make predictions about which boy or girl exposed to similar acute or chronic vandalizing experiences will or will not emerge with a paraphilia. An allowance must be made, hypothetically, for a vulnerability factor. One possible vulnerability factor may pertain to a facility or propensity to experience the opponent-process phenomenon whereby negative and aversive is converted to positive and addictive (see Chapter 3).

To illustrate: You recoil at first sight of the world's highest and fastest roller-coaster, and squeal, terrified, when you get up enough nerve to be riding it. Fascinated as well as terrified, you ride it again, and again, until you are hooked. It is terror no more, but ecstasy, and you return not once, but every weekend, an addict. Similarly with the development of a paraphilic lovemap: that which once was horrible and unthinkable flip flops and enthralls you. If you are a masochist, the pain of being paddled and whipped that others would avoid becomes transmogrified into a 10-point earthquake of erotic ecstasy on the Richter orgasm scale.

To be love smitten, one may say, is to be addicted to the love smiter. So also, to be smitten with a paraphilia is to be addicted to the partner and paraphernalia of the paraphilia. For a complete list of the paraphilias, refer to Money (1986a; 1988a).

· 12 ·

Intervention

Three Treatment Options

In distant places and ancient times, a community had three options when it encountered in someone's life a disturbing example of a strategy for coping with an unspeakable monster. One option was to do nothing other than tolerate it. Another option was to get rid of it by banishing, brutalizing, locking away, or destroying its host. The third option was to call in a specialist, pejoratively known today as a witch doctor or shaman, to placate the unspeakable monster with costumed rituals, recitations, exercises, appliances, excisions, materia medica, and sexual and dietary requirements or restrictions.

These three options have survived for millennia. Although modified and changed to suit the high-tech societies of the present-day world, they continue to be the only three options available.

Within the option of tolerance there are, in the course of extended periods of time, changes in which coping strategies are tolerated and not tolerated. That which is persecuted today may have been accepted as inevitable in a former era, and vice versa. Tolerance of gender diversity and stereotypes, for example, has see-sawed over the centuries. Thus homophilia was normalized in ancient Greek society, and criminalized in medieval Christendom. It is presently in the process of becoming, like left-handedness, tolerated, even though not ideologically condoned, as a minority status.

The criminal option, namely, that of banishing, brutalizing, locking away, or destroying the person, has remained remarkably constant over the centuries. Criminal codes, however, have undergone change. Behavior once not criminalized has been criminalized, and behavior once criminalized has been decriminalized. In the eighteenth century, some behavior formerly classified as criminal became reclassified as insane or psychotic. Other behavior, notably of the type herein classified under Pragmatics (Chapter 5), no matter how crazy, insane, or psychotic, has remained criminalized, and those accused and pronounced guilty of it continue to be incarcerated.

There has been some change in the methods of punishment, as in the renunciation of enslavement, and reduction in the use of torture and mayhem. Brutality and abuse, however, have not been abolished, nor has confinement in sensory and social isolation which induces madness, nor has sexual deprivation which is almost universally enforced. The death penalty has not been universally abolished. In the United States it is presently being enthusiastically revived.

Since time immemorial, society has been held in a state of thralldom under the absolutist principle embodied in the criminal justice system whereby the individual is held personally responsible for being possessed of demons, unspeakable monsters, sins, and evil intents, and therefore responsible for saving oneself from them. The principle is embodied not only in the criminal justice system, but also in the membership conformity system that governs small group alliances, families and kindred, and collectives of children, as in the schoolroom. The childrearing traditions of Christendom, as practiced by parents and others with authority over children, include abusive and brutal corporal punishment; sensory deprivation and neglect by being locked in detention; social isolation from friends and agemates, the childhood version of house arrest; and exclusion from activities and conversation, the childhood equivalent of being shunned or excommunicated from religious group membership.

The witch-doctor option has, since antiquity, undergone extraordinary changes of which the outcome is the evolution of medical science and, in the art of healing, the merging of the ancient laying on of hands and holistic medicine with the artifices and measurements of extremely sophisticated modern laboratory medicine.

The most radical innovation of modern laboratory medicine is in its application to epidemiology and public health (Chapter 6). In the extreme case, it is possible to contain the spread of an epidemic by treating not people, but lab results. Thus, if the lab results come back positive for, say, syphilis, treatment with penicillin is administered to the positive carrier who may be identified only by code number, not by name or in person.

Preventively, as formerly in the case of smallpox before it was eradicated in 1979, the person as a code number may be inoculated against the possibility of future contagion, provided a vaccine already exists. Thus arises a situation, virtually unheard of until the twentieth century, in which people who feel well and have no symptoms, are societally mandated to take treatment to keep well. On the basis of religious scruples or other dogmas, some rebel and resist vaccination for either themselves or their children. A parallel situation exists with respect to universal neonatal screening for the detection of chromosomal anomalies for which only remedial palliation is presently possible, or for the detection of metabolic disorders, like phenylketonuria or hypothyroidism for which more effective treatment is available. Dispute arises also over such public health measures as pesticide control of disease-carrying mosquitos; supplementing the water supply with fluoride to reduce dental decay and chlorine to eliminate toxic bacteria; iodizing household salt; distributing sterile injection needles and condoms to prevent AIDS in populations at risk; and administering life-saving blood transfusions.

At the correct time and place, treating the lab results has a bearing on unspeakable monsters in that it may abort them. In the era of smallpox, for example, vaccination in infancy would prevent the stigma of unsightly pockmarks which, in childhood, would be responsible for having to live with the unspeakable monster of social stigmatization.

Prevention of stigmatization is possible also by the application of modern laboratory medicine to the treatment of a single system, as for example in ophthalmology, cardiology, gynecology, or urology, independently of treating the entirety of the patient to whom the organ system belongs. Military surgery has had a long tradition of treating wounded limbs and organs with minimal reference to the wounded person, and this tradition has continued vitality in the practice of emergency medicine. There is no alternative if the patient requiring emergency treatment has already lost consciousness, nor if the patient is a baby too young to communicate. For the patient who can communicate, and under nonemergency conditions, however, being the recipient of treatment to only a limb or organ system is like being an animal in a veterinary clinic.

Time, costs, and avoidance of noxae are three of the considerations in favor of restricting a diagnostic and prognostic workup to a single organ system, but only if such restriction is clearly indicated. In dubious cases, a workup involving all organ systems is indicated. A case is always dubious when the influence of an unspeakable monster is suspected. Conversely, and irrespective of the suspected strength of this influence, an extensive laboratory workup is always in order.

Although a laboratory finding may prove to be noncontributory, the opposite is also possible. For instance, karyotyping of the chromosomes in the genetics laboratory may reveal an anomaly from which is derived a vulnerability to a particular type of unspeakable monster. Thus the missing chromosome in Turner (45,X) syndrome creates a vulnerability to the monster of space-form disability and hence to academic failure in nonverbal subjects. Similarly, brain imaging or a reading of the electroencephalographic (EEG) brainwave pattern may reveal a vulnerability to unspeakable monsterdom.

Positive laboratory findings do not necessarily translate into an effective form of treatment. Even when they do not directly benefit the affected individual today, however, they may be valuable additions to a research data base that will lead to the eventual discovery of new treatments for the benefit of tomorrow's patients.

In addition to a laboratory workup, a complete clinical workup is advisable. There is always the chance that it will reveal a previously undocumented defect or disorder that may have been missed in previous physical examinations. Symptoms involving the genitalia belong in this category if, in deference to a patient's sensitivity, the genital examination has over a period of time been consistently deferred.

There is no shortage of examples of mortifying genital and related anomalies that constitute an unspeakable monster, as when a boy at puberty has a retractile and barely visible penis, together with conspicuous breast development to match that of a girl; or a girl has early appearance of pubic hair, a protruding and enlarged penoclitoris, and no sign of breast enlargement. Another example is that of a boy with the congenital deformity of micropenis, or a girl with congenital absence of the vagina and no menses. There are problems of delayed puberty, of genital imperfections, of genital self-mutilations, and, in girls, the problem of overlooking an early peripubertal onset of pregnancy.

The physical examination provides the opportunity to ascertain the pharmacologic history and possible adverse side effects. The human species is not alone among mammals in self-medication. Other species in the wild are on record as ingesting pharmacoactive herbs and fruits when sick or, possibly, preventively. Alcohol has been in the human self-medicational pharmacopeia for centuries, and so has cannabis, opium from poppy seeds, and cocaine from coca leaves. In contemporary times, hundreds of other synthetic and extracted drugs have become available for self-medication.

Taking pills, potions, and injections, applying ointments, and sniffing fumes and powders becomes for some people an inveterate fixation. It is a fixation so powerful that an ostensibly inert substance may exert a positive placebo effect, at least in some people. The potential of the placebo effect accounts for the widespread prescribing of medications that, although not inert, do not alleviate the symptoms inflicted by an unspeakable monster. A fixation on these drugs, with side-effects that themselves become another monster, may become an addiction. So also may a fixation on self-medicated drugs.

In the explanatory language of childhood, there are cutting doctors, needle doctors, X-ray doctors, and talking doctors. When all have completed their diagnostic and prognostic workup of an individual case, it may become apparent that the unit of treatment, far from being the lab results or organ system, is not even the whole person, but the partnership or family in which that person is a participant. In other words, the unspeakable monsters in each of two or more people exist in a consortium of reciprocative relationships. Each individual within the consortium may be diagnosed and treated separately from one another, but ultimately they must be brought together and treated as an interacting unit.

Six Present-Day Practices

For some diseases and disorders there are methods of intervention that do not eradicate the primordium of an unspeakable monster, but ameliorate its future influence. The residuum of the monster persists. Even in cases in which eradication of the primordium is possible, there may be a persistent residuum of the monster in the form of stigmatization as a formerly afflicted person. The monster persists also, and is unchanged, in those cases which have proved resistant to such forms of intervention as have been attempted.

When unspeakable monsteral symptoms are unresponsive to the interventions of modern laboratory and organ-systems medicine, then there is no other option than to resort to what are essentially the principles of witch-doctor medicine as transformed into present-day practices. The most simple practice, and usually the least expensive, is to provide a supportive convalescent environment, to await the possibility of a spontaneous remission, and, should it occur, to take advantage of it rehabilitatively.

A second practice is to provide treatment with the healing hands, namely, somesthetic or massage therapy which may be extended to include accupuncture for pain relief, relaxation therapy, exercise and fitness therapy, and sensate-focus "homework" in sex therapy.

A third practice is to prescribe a specific dietary regimen that dictates both the intake and the renunciation of various specified foods, fluids, spices, and other alimentary substances. In contemporary American folk medicine, weight-loss dietary regimens of many different varieties are popular and commercially lucrative. They are usually combined with a fitness and exercise regimen. In an earlier era, more than today, the curative powers of food and physical fitness were combined with sexual restrictions, semen conservation, and injunctions against masturbation.

A fourth practice is to provide a patient with the possibility of troopbonding as a member of some sort of therapeutic group defined by a shared interest. Thus there are groups for dance therapy, art therapy, occupational therapy, social-skills therapy, psychodrama, and so on. There are groups formed specifically for, and under the name of group therapy, in which the predominant activity is talking about behavior related to a shared problem, for example, alcoholism in Alcoholics Anonymous (AA) groups. There are also communal living and self-help groups, as in halfway houses that bridge the gap between hospital living and living independently in the community at large.

Self-help groups that follow the example of AA are self-governing support groups formed by like-minded people. Their like-mindedness is that they define themselves as addicts in search of sobriety. Any type of behavior that its practitioners define as an addiction may become the catchword of a sobriety group. Some sobriety groups have closer ties than others to professionally trained organizers and sponsors. Some self-help groups are defined not in terms of sobriety, but rather of likemindedness in defense against oppression and stigmatization.

Little People of America, formed by and for people with statural dwarfism, is the model for self-help groups formed on the basis of a shared diagnosis, or more correctly diagnostic ycleptance (Chapter 2). Membership in such a group is for some people equivalent to self-stigmatization as a freak or pariah, but less so as minority groups define themselves in terms of rights and respect. Membership then becomes an affirmation of the right of the minority to exist.

Some minority self-help groups are in the nature of networks of like-minded people seeking companionship with those of their own minority. Some such networks are private, and membership is only by invitation or sponsorship. Communication may be person to person only, by phone, mail, or visits, or it may be shared in a newsletter or computer bulletin board, and perhaps in an annual rendezvous or meeting. Some self-help networks are comprised of paraphilically like-minded people, for example, those with an amputee fixation, and those with a diaper fixation and infantilism. Transvestophiles and transexuals also have extensive networks.

A fifth practice is to provide training therapy, generically known as behavior-modification therapy. Training therapy is adapted from the method of reward and punishment long known to animal trainers (Chapter 3). Theoretically, it is derived from the principles of conditional reflexology and operant conditioning. When applied in conjunction with electronic instrumentation that displays the degree of the subject's response to a stimulus, it goes under the name of biofeedback.

The sixth practice is to provide talktime therapy sessions modeled after the confessional and the unburdening of personal confidences in dialogues with trusted kith or kin. Psychotherapy is the gentrified name of talking therapy. There are many schools and doctrines of psychotherapy and counseling, all of which trace their ancestry back to the application of hypnosis to psychiatry in the nineteenth century, and its eventual metamorphosis into Freudian psychoanalysis by the end of the century.

In free-associative and nondirective psychotherapy the burden of talk is on the patient. In other varieties, the psychotherapist engages more actively in counseling. Some psychotherapists are oriented predominantly to finding the past history and origins of the present biography, whereas the predominant orientation of others is into finding how the present biography might be changed and developed in the future. Some psychotherapists and counselors use the induction of a hypnotic trance state to facilitate talking, but they are in the minority.

In dialogue with patients, there are five different vectors, by name: proportional, body-image, age-of-onset, partnership, and transcultural, respectively. They need to be recognized in the course of therapy and counseling, recurrently.

The proportional vector pertains to whether a particular function is hypoactive, hyperactive, or contortedly active. In sex therapy and counseling, this vector subdivides into hypophilic, hyperphilic, and paraphilic components.

The body-image vector pertains to the patient's own construct of his/her body and its component parts and its agreement or lack thereof with the construct offered by other people, including the therapist and other health-care professionals. In sex therapy and counseling this vector is subdivisible into masculine, feminine, or androgynous, and into concordancy or discordancy with natal sex.

The age-of-onset vector pertains to the time factor in the history of symptoms, the chronicity as compared with the periodicity or cyclicity of their occurrence, and their short-term versus delayed outcome. This vector is developmentally subdivisible into prenatal, perinatal, juvenile, adolescent, adult and gerontologic phases. Its applicability in sex therapy is the same as in therapy that is not sex specific.

The partnership vector pertains to the degree to which symptoms reciprocally influence and are influenced by the input of other people, especially those to whom a patient is closely bonded or among whom he/she exists in close proximity. Subdivided, this vector applies to family, household, neighborhood, school, workplace, and so on. In sex therapy this vector is specific to symptoms that appear only in the closeness of contact with a specific sexual partner.

To illustrate: a variable history of impotence, premature ejaculation, and erotic anhedonia was defined by a man and his wife as his problem, not hers. Serial consultations and therapy programs, alone and together, had become a virtual way of life. Their marital discontent continued for years until not only his role as a patient, but hers also was, at last, questioned. Then it became evident that she had been handicapped throughout the marriage by a vaginal-penetration phobia secondary to a traumatizing prepubertal upbringing. His symptoms were reciprocating hers in rendering the marriage virtually noncoital, except for procreation.

The transcultural vector pertains to historical, religious, judicial, and ethical relativity regarding the diagnosis and definition of pathology, and its appropriate treatment. Pathology is universally recognized in the case of some syndromes and their symptoms, whereas in other instances its recognition is regionally or culturally specific. In sex therapy there are cultural relativities as to what is defined as sexual crime, sexual illness, and sexual acceptability. All three definitions have been assigned to homosexuality and bisexuality, for example, at different times and in difference cultures.

In all brands of talking therapy, irrespective of how they are named, an irrevocable imperative prevails, namely, that there be an alliance between doctor and patient, or therapist and client, against the syndrome (Chapter 6). The irrevocable corollary of this imperative is that there not be an adversarial relationship between the doctor/therapist and the patient/client. Lip-service to these two principles does not suffice. It is necessary to monitor all the words that exit from the lips so as to guard against the ever present danger of implying that having to get rid of the symptoms or syndrome is the patient/client's own personal responsibility.

It is easy to sermonize about the dignity and freedom of the individual to make personal choices and be responsible for their outcome. Throwing the responsibility of getting sick and getting well onto the patient/client is a cop-out, and an abdication of professional responsibility. Assigning the responsibility of cure to self-cure is, in effect, an admission of one's own therapeutic incompetence and irrelevancy. One's role becomes that of an enforcement officer, disciplining the hapless patient/client for failing to get well. If personal responsibility alone would suffice, then the patient/client would have had no need of professional services, but would have been self-cured voluntarily, by will power, without them.

Being together in an alliance against the syndrome applies irrespective of the origin or etiology of the syndrome. One does not ally with one's patient or client only if the syndrome is attributed to a respectable organic, physical, or medical etiology, and not to a psychogenic or emotional one. In both types of syndrome, symptoms may yield readily to treatment, or be extremely resistant. From the viewpoint of treatment, the key issue is not the etiology of the symptoms, but their fixation or immutability. To harass a patient/client with personal responsibility for being sick with fixated and immutable symptoms, and for failing to show signs of recovery is, in effect, nosocomial abuse and grounds for a charge of malpractice.

The practice of nonadversarial talking therapy and the practice of training, troopbonding, somesthetic, and supportive therapy are all undertaken with the same expectation, namely, that a pathological strategy for coping with whatever constitutes the unspeakable monster in any given case will be, if not corrected, then at least ameliorated.

The logistics entailed in obtaining outcome statistics, either comparatively or as a whole, are too complex to justify credence in any calculations over-all. Nonetheless, case by case, there are some highly successful outcomes, despite the low methodological precision of the only therapies available. They keep alive the flame to be passed on to the twenty-first century when advances in molecular biology of the mindbrain that are completely unthought of today will undoubtedly be made. For these advances, this book may prove to contain a theoretical foundation.

Bibliography

Allen, L. S. and Gorski, R. A. Sexual orientation and the size of the anterior commissure in the human brain. *Proceedings of the National Academy of Sciences USA*, 89:7199–7202, 1992.

American Psychiatric Association. *Diagnostic and Statistical Manual of Mental Disorders*, Third Edition. Washington, D.C., American Psychiatric Association, 1980.

American Psychiatric Association. *Diagnostic and Statistical Manual of Mental Disorders*, Third Edition, Revised. Washington, D.C., American Psychiatric Association, 1987.

Anderson, L. T., Ernst, M. and Davis, S. V. Cognitive abilities of patients with Lesch-Nyhan disease. *Journal of Autism and Developmental Disorders*, 22:189–203, 1992.

Beach, F. A. Sexual attractivity, proceptivity, and receptivity in female mammals. *Hormones and Behavior*, 7:105–138, 1976.

Berkeley, B., and Tiffenbach, J. *Foreskin: Its Past, its Present and . . . its Future?*. San Francisco, Bud Berkeley, 1983.

Benjamin, H. *The Transsexual Phenomenon: A Scientific Report on Transsexualism and Sex Conversion in the Human Male and Female*. New York, Julian Press, 1966.

Berlin, F. S., Bergey, G. K. and Money, J. Periodic psychosis of puberty: A case report. *American Journal of Psychiatry*, 139:119–120, 1982.

Berta, P., Hawkins, J. R., Sinclair, A. H., Taylor, A., Griffiths, B. L., Goodfellow, P. N. and Fellous, M. Genetic evidence equating SRY and the testis-determining factor. *Nature*, 348:448–450, 1990.

Bettelheim, B. Individual and mass behavior in extreme situations. In *Readings in Social Psychology* (T. M. Newcomb and E. L. Hartley, editors). New York, Henry Holt and Company, 1947.

Bick, D., Franco, B., Sherins, R. J., Heye, B., Pike, L., Crawford, J., Maddalena, A., Incerti, G., Pragiola, A., Meitlinger, T. and Ballabio, A. Brief report: Intragenetic deletion of the KALIG-1 gene in Kallmann's syndrome. *New England Journal of Medicine*, 326:1752–1755, 1992.

Bobrow, N., Money, J. and Lewis, V. G. Delayed puberty, eroticism, and sense of smell: A psychological study of hypogonadotropinism, osmatic and anosmatic (Kallmann's syndrome). *Archives of Sexual Behavior*, 1:329–344, 1971.

Breuer, J. and Freud, S. *Studien über Hysterie*. Leipzig and Vienna, Franz Deuticke, 1895. Also in *The Standard Edition of the Complete Psychological Works of*

Sigmund Freud (trans. J. Strachey, with A. Freud) Volume Two. London, Hogarth Press and the Institute of Psycho-analysis, 1955.

Buffum, J., Moser, C. and Smith, D. Street drugs and sexual function. In *Handbook of Sexology, Volume VI: The Pharmacology and Endocrinology of Sexual Function* (J. M. A. Sitsen, J. Money and H. Musaph, editors). Amsterdam, Elsevier, 1988.

Burnett, A. L., Lowenstein, C. J., Bredt, D. S., Chang, T. S. K. and Snyder, S. H. Nitric oxide: A physiologic mediator of penile erection. *Science,* 257:401–403, 1992.

Carter, C. S., Getz. L. L., Gavish, L., McDermott, J. L. and Arnold, P. Male-related pheromones and the activation of female reproduction in the prairie vole (Microtus ochrogaster). *Biology of Reproduction,* 23:1038–1045, 1980.

Carter, C. S., Williams, J. R., Witt, D. M. and Insel, T. R. Oxytocin and social bonding. In *Oxytocin in Maternal, Sexual, and Social Behaviors* (C. A. Pedersen, J. D. Caldwell, G. F. Jirikowski and T. R. Insel, editors). New York, New York Academy of Sciences Press, 1992.

Cesnik, J. A. and Coleman, E. Use of lithium carbonate in the treatment of autoerotic asphyxia. *American Journal of Psychotherapy,* 43:277–285, 1989.

Court Brown, W. M., Price, W. H. and Jacobs, P. A. Further information on the identity of 47,XYY males. *British Medical Journal,* 2:325–328, 1968.

Coxon, A. P. M., Davies, P. M., Hunt, A. J., Weatherburn, P., McManus, T. J. and Rees, C. The structure of sexual behavior. *Journal of Sex Research,* 29:61–83, 1992.

Culotta, E. Red menace in the world's oceans. *Science,* 257:1476–1477, 1992.

Davies, B. M. and Morgenstern, F. S. A case of cysticercosis, temporal lobe epilepsy, and transvestism. *Journal of Neurological and Neurosurgical Psychiatry,* 23:247–249, 1960.

Eibl-Eibesfeldt, I. *Love and Hate: The Natural History of Behavior Patterns.* New York, Holt, Rinehart and Winston, 1971.

Ellis, H. *Studies in the Psychology of Sex. Volume II, Part 2: Eonism and Other Supplementary Studies.* New York, Random House, 1938.

Epstein, A. W. Fetishism: A study of its psychopathology with particular reference to a proposed disorder in brain mechanisms as an etiological factor. *Journal of Nervous and Mental Disease,* 130:107–119, 1960.

Fedoroff, J. P. Buspirone hydrochloride in the treatment of transvestic fetishism. *Journal of Clinical Psychiatry,* 49:408–409, 1988.

Feierman, J. R., editor. *Pedophilia: Biosocial Dimensions.* New York, Springer-Verlag, 1990.

Foulkes, D. *Children's Dreams: Longitudinal Studies.* New York, Wiley-Interscience, 1982.

Foulkes, D., Hollifield, M., Bradley, L., Terry, R. and Sullivan, B. Waking self-understanding, REM-dream self representation, and cognitive ability variables at ages 5–8. *Dreaming,* 1:41–51, 1991.

Gilmartin, B. G. *Shyness and Love: Causes, Consequences, and Treatment.* Lanham, MD, University Press of America, 1987.

Goldberg, R. L. and Buongiorno, P. A. The use of carbamazepine for the treatment of paraphilias in a brain-damaged patient. *International Journal of Psychiatry in Medicine,* 12:275–279, 1982–83.

Graber, B., Hartmann, K., Coffman, J. A., Huey, C. J. and Golden, C. J. Brain damage among mentally disordered sex offenders. *Journal of Forensic Science*, 27:125–134, 1982.

Green, R. *"The Sissy Boy Syndrome" and the Development of Homosexuality*. New Haven, Yale University Press, 1986.

Green, R. and Money, J., editors. *Transsexualism and Sex Reassignment*. Baltimore, Johns Hopkins Press, 1969.

Greer, D. M., Jr., Mohl, P. C. and Sheley, A. A. A technique for foreskin reconstruction and some preliminary results. *Journal of Sex Research*, 18:324–330, 1982.

Grumbach, M. M. and Conte, F. A. Disorders of sexual differentiation. In *Williams Textbook of Endocrinology*, 7th ed. (J. D. Wilson and D. W. Foster, editors). Philadelphia, Saunders, 1985.

Hamer, D. H., Hu, S., Magnuson, V. L., Hu, N., Pattatucci, A. M. L. A linkage between DNA markers on the X chromosome and male sexual orientation. *Science*, 261:321–327, 1993.

Hathaway, S. R., McKinley, J. C. and Butcher, J. N. *Minnesota Multiphasic Personality Inventory-2*. Minneapolis, University of Minnesota Press, 1990.

Hendricks, S. E., Fitzpatrick, D. F., Hartmann, K., Quaife, M. A., Stratbucker, R. A. and Graber, B. Brain structure and function in sexual molesters of children and adolescents. *Journal of Clinical Psychiatry*, 49:108–112, 1988.

Herdt, G. H. *Guardians of the Flutes: Idioms of Masculinity*. New York, McGraw-Hill, 1981.

Herdt, G. H., editor. *Ritualized Homosexuality in Melanesia*. Berkeley, University of California Press, 1984.

Herzer, M. Kertbeny and the nameless love. *Journal of Homosexuality*, 12:1–26, 1985.

Hunter, R. Transvestism, impotence and temporal lobe dysfunction. *Journal of Neurological Sciences*, 4:357–360, 1967.

Hunter, R., Logue, V. and McMenemy, W. H. Temporal lobe epilepsy supervening on longstanding transvestism and fetishism. *Epilepsia*, 4:60–65, 1963.

Ignarro, L. J. Nitric oxide as the physiological mediator of penile erection. *Journal of NIH Research*, 4(5):59–62, 1992.

Insel, T. R. Oxytocin—A neuropeptide for affiliation: Evidence from behavioral, receptor autoradiographic, and comparative studies. *Psychoneuroendocrinology*, 17:3–35, 1992.

Jacobs, P. A., Price, W. H., Court Brown, W. M., Brittain, R. P. and Whatmore, P. B. Chromosome studies on men in a maximum security hospital. *Annals of Human Genetics*, 31:339–358, 1968.

Jaspan, J. B. The neuropathies of diabetes. In *Endocrinology*, 2nd ed. (L. J. De-Groot, editor). Philadelphia, Saunders, 1989.

Kalin, N. H. Genital and abdominal self-surgery: A case report. *Journal of the American Medical Association*, 241:2188–2189, 1979.

Kempe, C. H., Silverman, F. N., Steele, B. F., Droegemueller, W. and Silver, H. K. "The battered child syndrome." *Journal of the American Medical Association*, 181:17–24, 1962.

Kennedy, H. *Ulrichs: The Life and Works of Karl Heinrich Ulrichs Pioneer of the Modern Gay Movement*. Boston, Alyson, 1988.

Keyes, R. W. and Money, J. *The Armed Robbery Orgasm: A Lovemap Autobiography of Masochism*. Buffalo, Prometheus, 1993.

Kluckhohn, C. and Leighton, D. *The Navaho*. Cambridge, Harvard University Press, 1947.

Koopman, P., Gubbay, J., Vivian, N., Goodfellow, P. and Lovell-Badge, R. Male development of chromosomally female mice transgenic for Sry. *Nature*, 351:117–121, 1991.

Lehne, G. K. Brain damage and paraphilia: Treated with medoxyprogesterone acetate. *Sexuality and Disability*, 7:145–158, 1984–1986.

LeVay, S. A difference in hypothalamic structure between heterosexual and homosexual men. *Science*, 253:1034–1037, 1991.

Lightfoot–Klein, H. *Prisoners of Ritual: An Odyssey into Female Circumcision in Africa*. New York, Haworth, 1989.

Maclean, P. D. New findings relevant to the evolution of psychosexual functions of the brain. *Journal of Nervous and Mental Disease*, 135:289–301, 1962.

Masson, J. M. *The Assault on Truth: Freud's Suppression of the Seduction Theory*. New York, Penguin, 1985.

Masters, W. H. and Johnson, V. E. *Human Sexual Response*. Boston, Little, Brown, 1966.

Masters, W. H. and Johnson, V. E. *Human Sexual Inadequacy*. Boston, Little, Brown, 1970.

McLean, J. D., Forsythe, R. G. and Kapkin, I. A. Unusual side effects of clomipramine associated with yawning. *Canadian Journal of Psychiatry*, 28:569–570, 1983.

Mitchell, W., Falconer, M. A. and Hill, D. Epilepsy with fetishism relieved by temporal lobectomy. *Lancet*, 2:626–630, 1954.

Moll, A. *The Sexual Life of the Child* (E. Paul, translator). New York, Macmillan, 1912.

Mohl, P. C., Adams, R., Greer, D. M. and Sheley, K. A. Prepuce restoration seekers: Psychiatric aspects. *Archives of Sexual Behavior*, 10:383–393, 1981.

Money, J. Use of androgen-depleting hormone in the treatment of male sex offenders. *Journal of Sex Research*, 6:165–172, 1970.

Money, J. Human behavior cytogenetics: Review of psychopathology in three syndromes, 47,XXY; 47,XYY; and 45,X. *Journal of Sex Research*, 11:181–200, 1975.

Money, J. Medicoscientific nonjudgmentalism incompatible with legal judgmentalism: A model case report; Kleptomania. *Medicine and Law*, 2:361–375, 1983a.

Money, J. New phylism theory and autism: Pathognomonic impairment of troopbonding. *Medical Hypotheses*, 11:245–250, 1983b. [Reprinted in Money, J. *Venuses Penuses: Sexology, Sexosophy, and Exigency Theory*. Buffalo, Prometheus Books, 1986b].

Money, J. Pairbonding and limerence. In *International Encyclopedia of Psychiatry, Psychology, Psychoanalysis and Neurology, Progress Volume 1* (B. B. Wolman, editor). New York, Macmillan [Aesculapius], 1983c.

Money, J. Family and gender-identity/role. Part II: Transexual versus homosexual coping in micropenis syndrome with male sex assignment. *International Journal of Family Psychiatry*, 5:341–373, 1984a.

Money, J. Gender transposition theory and homosexual genesis. *Journal of Sex and Marital Therapy*, 10:75–82, 1984b.

Money, J. *Lovemaps: Clinical Concepts of Sexual/Erotic Health and Pathology,*

Paraphilia, and Gender Transposition in Childhood, Adolescence, and Maturity. New York, Irvington, 1986a.

Money, J. *Venuses Penuses: Sexology, Sexosophy, and Exigency Theory.* Buffalo, Prometheus Books, 1986b.

Money, J. Universals of sexuality and eroticism in a changing world. In *Proceedings of the Seventh World Congress of Sexology* (P. Kothari, editor). Bombay, Indian Association of Sex Educators, Counsellors and Therapists, 1986c.

Money, J. Treatment guidelines: Antiandrogen and counseling of paraphilic sex offenders. *Journal of Sex and Marital Therapy*, 13:219–223, 1987.

Money, J. *Gay, Straight, and In-Between: The Sexology of Erotic Orientation.* New York, Oxford University Press, 1988a.

Money, J. The Skoptic syndrome: Castration and genital self-mutilation as an example of sexual body-image pathology. *Journal of Psychology and Human Sexuality*, 1(1):113–128, 1988b.

Money, J. Forensic sexology: Paraphilic serial rape (biastophilia) and lust murder (erotophonophilia). *American Journal of Psychotherapy*, 44:26–36, 1990a.

Money, J. Paraphilia in females: Fixation on amputation and lameness; two personal accounts. *Journal of Psychology and Human Sexuality*, 3(2):165–172, 1990b.

Money, J. Pedophilia: A specific instance of new phylism theory as applied to paraphilic lovemaps. In *Pedophilia: Biosocial Dimensions* (J. R. Feierman, editor). New York, Springer-Verlag, 1990c.

Money, J. *Biographies of Gender and Hermaphroditism in Paired Comparisons: Clinical Supplement to the Handbook of Sexology.* Amsterdam, Elsevier, 1991a.

Money, J. Sexology, body image, foreskin restoration, and bisexual status. *Journal of Sex Research*, 28:145–156, 1991b.

Money, J. False accusations of nosocomial abuse: The hand bitten by the dog that it feeds may be your own. *Journal of Offender Rehabilitation* 18(3/4): 225–233, 1992a.

Money, J. *The Kaspar Hauser Syndrome of "Psychosocial Dwarfism:" Deficient Statural, Intellectual, and Social Growth Induced by Child Abuse.* Buffalo, Prometheus Books, 1992b.

Money, J. Hormones, hormonal anomalies and psychologic healthcare. *Wilkins' Treatment and Diagnosis of Endocrine Disorders in Children and Adults* Fourth Edition. (M. S. Kappy, R. M. Blizzard, and C. J. Migeon, editors). Springfield, IL, Charles C. Thomas, 1994.

Money, J. *The Adam Principle: Genes, Genitals, Hormones and Gender: Selected Readings in Sexology.* Buffalo, Prometheus Books, 1993.

Money, J. and Annecillo, C. Body-image pathology: Koro, the shrinking-penis syndrome in transcultural sexology. *Sexual and Marital Therapy*, 2:91–100, 1987.

Money, J. and De Priest, M. Genital self-surgery: Relationship to transexualism in three cases. *Journal of Sex Research*, 12:283–294, 1976.

Money, J. and Ehrhardt, A. A. *Man and Woman, Boy and Girl: The Differentiation and Dimorphism of Gender Identity from Conception to Maturity.* Baltimore, Johns Hopkins University Press, 1972.

Money, J. and Hirsch, S. R. After priapism: Orgasm retained, erection lost. *Journal of Urology*, 94:152–157, 1965.

Money, J. and Hosta, G. M. Laughing seizures with sexual precocity: Report of two cases. *Johns Hopkins Medical Journal*, 120:326–336, 1967.

Money, J. and Lamacz, M. Gynemimesis and gynemimetophilia: Individual and cross-cultural manifestations of a gender coping strategy hitherto unnamed. *Comprehensive Psychiatry,* 25:392–403, 1984.

Money, J. and Lamacz, M. *Vandalized Lovemaps: Paraphilic Outcome of Seven Cases in Pediatric Sexology.* Buffalo, Prometheus Books, 1989.

Money, J. and Norman, B. F. Gender identity and gender transposition: Longitudinal outcome study of 24 male hermaphrodites assigned as boys. *Journal of Sex and Marital Therapy,* 13:75–92, 1987.

Money, J. and Norman, B. F. Pedagogical handicap associated with micropenis and other CHARGE syndrome anomalies of embryogenesis: Four 46,XY cases reared as girls. *American Journal of Psychotherapy,* 42:354–379, 1988.

Money, J. and Pruce, G. Psychomotor epilepsy and sexual function. In *Handbook of Sexology* (J. Money and H. Musaph, editors). Amsterdam, Elsevier/Excerpta Medica, 1977.

Money, J. and Russo, A. J. Homosexual outcome of discordant gender identity/role in childhood: Longitudinal follow-up. In *Annual Progress in Child Psychiatry and Child Development* (S. Chess and A. Thomas, editors). New York, Brunner/Mazel, 1980.

Money, J. and Russo, A. J. Homosexual vs. transvestite or transexual gender-identity/role: Outcome study in boys. *International Journal of Family Psychiatry,* 2:139–145, 1981.

Money, J. and Sollod, R. N. Body image, plastic surgery (prosthetic testes) and Kallmann's syndrome. *British Journal of Medical Psychology,* 51:91–94, 1978.

Money, J. and Yankowitz, R. The sympathetic-inhibiting effects of the drug Ismelin on human male eroticism, with a note on Mellaril. *Journal of Sex Research,* 3:69–82, 1967.

Money, J., Annecillo, C. and Lobato, C. Paraphilic and other sexological anomalies as a sequel to the syndrome of child-abuse (psychosocial) dwarfism. *Journal of Psychology and Human Sexuality,* 3(1):117–150, 1990.

Money, J., Annecillo, C., Van Orman, B. and Borgaonkar, D. S. Cytogenetics, hormones and behavior disability: Comparison of XYY and XXY syndromes. *Clinical Genetics,* 6:370–382, 1974.

Money, J., Jobaris, R., and Furth, G. Apotemnophilia: Two cases of self-demand amputation as a paraphilia. *Journal of Sex Research,* 13:115–125, 1977.

Money, J., Gaskin, R. and Hull, H. Impulse, aggression and sexuality in the XYY syndrome. *St. John's Law Review,* 44:220–235, 1970.

Money, J., Leal, J. and Gonzalez-Heydrich, J. Aphrodisiology: History, folklore, efficacy. In *Handbook of Sexology, Vol. VI: The Pharmacology and Endocrinology of Sexual Function* (J. M. A. Sitsen, J. Money and H. Musaph, editors). Amsterdam, Elsevier, 1988.

Money, J., Schwartz, M. and Lewis, V. G. Adult erotosexual status and fetal hormonal masculinization and demasculinization: 46,XX congenital virilizing adrenal hyperplasia and 46,XY androgen-insensitivity syndrome compared. *Psychoneuroendocrinology,* 9:405–414, 1984.

Money, J., Wainwright, G., and Hingsburger, D. *The Breathless Orgasm: A Lovemap Biography of Asphyxiophilia.* Buffalo, Prometheus Books, 1991.

Nanda, S. *Neither Man Nor Woman: The Hijras of India.* Belmont, CA, Wadsworth, 1990.

Niedemeyer, E. *The Generalized Epilepsies.* Springfield, IL, Charles C Thomas, 1972.

Pedersen, C. A., Caldwell, J. D. Jirikowski, G. F. and Insel, T. R., editors. *Oxytocin in Maternal, Sexual, and Social Behaviors.* New York, New York Academy of Sciences Press, 1992.

Perper, T. *Sex Signals: The Biology of Love.* Philadephia, ISI Press, 1985.

Pomeroy, W. B., Flax, C. C. and Wheeler, C. C. *Taking a Sex History: Interviewing and Recording.* New York, Free Press, 1982.

Pontius, A. A. Specific stimulus evoked violent action in psychotic trigger reaction: A seizure-like imbalance between frontal lobe and limbic systems? *Perceptual and Motor Skills,* 59:299–333, 1984.

Pontius, A. A. Limbic system-frontal lobes' role in subtypes of "atypical rape." *Psychological Reports,* 63:879–888, 1988.

Prince, R. Koro and the fox spirit on Hainan island (China). *Transcultural Psychiatric Research Review,* 29:119–132, 1992.

Rees, H. D., Bonsall, R. W. and Michael, R. P. Preoptic and hypothalamic neurons accumulate ^{3}[H] medoxyprogesterone acetate in male cynomolgus monkeys. *Life Sciences,* 39:1353–1359, 1986.

Sacks, O. *The Man Who Mistook His Wife for a Hat.* New York, Harper and Row, 1985.

Sigal, M., Altmark, D., Alfici, S. and Gelkopf, M. Ganser Syndrome: A review of 15 cases. *Comprehensive Psychiatry,* 33:134–138, 1992.

Sitsen, J. M. A., editor. *Handbook of Sexology, Volume VI: The Pharmacology and Endocrinology of Sexual Function.* (J. Money and H. Musaph, series editors). Amsterdam, Elsevier, 1988.

Slob, A. K., Koster, J., Radder, J. K. and van der Werff ten Bosch, J. J. Sexuality and psychophysiological functioning in women with diabetes mellitus. *Journal of Sex and Marital Therapy,* 16:59–69, 1990.

Solomon, R. L. The opponent-process theory of acquired motivation: The costs of pleasure and the benefits of pain. *American Psychologist,* 35:691–712, 1980.

Swaab, D. F. and Hofman, M. A. An enlarged suprachiasmatic nucleus in homosexual men. *Brain Research,* 537:141–148, 1990.

Tanner, J. M. Growth and endocrinology of the adolescent. In *Endocrine and Genetic Diseases of Childhood,* Second Edition. (L. I. Gardner, editor). Philadelphia, Saunders, 1975.

Tennov, D. *Love and Limerence: The Experience of Being in Love.* New York, Stein and Day, 1974.

Tricomi, V., Serr, D. and Solish, G. The ratio of male to female embryos as determined by the sex chromatin. *American Journal of Obstetrics and Gynecology,* 79:504–509, 1960.

Trimble, M. R. *The Psychoses of Epilepsy.* New York, Raven, 1991.

Ulrichs, K. H. (Numa Numantius) *Forschungen über das Räthsel der mannmännlichen Leibe (Inquiry into the Enigma of Man-to-Man Love),* Vol.2, "*Inclusa*": *Anthropologische Studien über mannmännliche Geschlechtsliebe, Naturwissenschaftlicher Theil; Nachweis das einer Classe von männlich gebauten Individuen Geschlechtsliebe zu Männern geschlechtlich angeboren ist ("Inclusa": Anthropological Studies of Man-to-Man Sexual Love, Natural Science Section; Proof of a Class of Male-Bodied Individuals for Whom Sexual Love for Men Is Sexually Inborn).* Leipzig, Selbsverlag der Verfassers, in Commission bei Heinrich Matthes, 1864.

Vance, M. L. and Thorner, M. O. Prolactin: Hyperprolactinemic syndromes and management. In *Endocrinology*, Second Edition, (L. J. DeGroot, editor). Philadelphia, Saunders, 1989.

Wagner, N. N. Sexual behavior and the cardiac patient. In *Handbook of Sexology* (J. Money and H. Musaph, editors). Amsterdam, Elsevier/Excerpta Medica, 1977.

Walter, G. and Streimer, J. Genital self-mutilation: Attempted foreskin reconstruction. *British Journal of Psychiatry*, 156:125–127, 1990.

Waxman, S. G. and Geschwind, N. The interictal behavior syndrome of temporal lobe epilepsy. *Archives of General Psychiatry*, 32:1580–1586, 1975.

Weider, A., Wolff, H. G., Brodman, K. Mittelmann, B. and Wechsler, D. *Cornell Index*. New York, Psychological Corporation, 1948.

Worth, D. and Beck, A. M. Multiple ownership of animals in New York City. *Transactions and Studies of the College of Physicians of Philadelphia*, 3:280–300, 1981.

Name Index

Subject Index